Ellis Co

"[*The End of Anger*] offers a useful heuristic device for understanding the evolution of race relations. Cose's collection of intergenerational interviews provides tangible evidence of the improvement in racial dynamics over the last fifty years."

—*New York Times Book Review*

"[A] refreshing, readable, and comprehensive look at race in twenty-first-century America." —*Publishers Weekly*

"Cose expertly interweaves his own research into the opinions of others, creating an intriguing dialogue about the future of America as class becomes king." —*Ebony*

"A fascinating read. . . . *The End of Anger* is a worthy look at where we are and where we're headed." —*Philadelphia City Paper*

"Provocative. . . . You never forget the first or second time you read Ellis Cose's *The Rage of a Privileged Class*. . . . Look for even more robust conversation [with] *The End of Anger*." —*Essence*

"Ellis Cose defines what racial equality means to a new generation." —*Uptown Magazine*

"The most important book of 2011, hands down."

—Ian Reifowitz, DailyKos.com

"Ellis Cose has brilliantly chronicled an epochal black Age of Rage and now, with equal originality, the End of Anger. Cose documents the paradigm shift from black rage to a post-angry racial politics in the Age of Obama. In the process, he illuminates the contemporary racial landscape while avoiding the illusion of a post-racial era and the romance of a static racial condition. This is engaged social history and critical analysis at its best!"

—Michael Eric Dyson, author of *Presidential Race*

"Once again Ellis Cose holds up a powerful lens to bring to light the thoughts, dreams, and perspectives of African Americans today. His findings and insights are an important contribution to the national conversation on race, class, and opportunity in America."

—Geoffrey Canada, educator

"*The End of Anger* is a masterpiece in illuminating one of the most significant issues in the history of our republic. But it's more than that—it's a case study of how our values are transmitted and realized through history; of how social conditioning affects perception; and of how a truly gifted journalist can look at even the most painful realities through a filter of compassion and sympathy. It is one of those books every American of conscience should read."

—Robert M. Morgenthau, former district attorney of New York County

"Ellis Cose brilliantly explains why black Americans have become less angry, more hopeful, and more likely to transcend old racial boundaries over the past decade, even as the least educated members of every racial-ethnic group have fallen behind. His eloquent account will inspire hope and pride in black and white Americans alike—but it will also raise disquieting questions about whether we can consolidate and extend the impressive gains he describes."

—Stephanie Coontz, author of *A Strange Stirring: The Feminine Mystique and American Women at the Dawn of the 1960s*

"The most authoritative accounting I've seen of where our country stands in its unending quest to resolve the racial dilemma on which it was founded. With seasoned insight backed by groundbreaking research, Ellis Cose brings us up to date on the transformations that were both wrought by and reflected in the coming of Obama. Cose is among the most rigorous and original observers of the national pageant, and his new book is a moving, sometimes startling, appraisal of this pivotal moment in our history."

—Diane McWhorter, Pulitzer Prize-winning author of *Carry Me Home*

"*The End of Anger* may be the defining work on America's new racial dynamics. Deeply researched, artfully reasoned, and beautifully written, this remarkable and essential book takes you on a revealing journey through recent American history and provides a compelling view of its possible future. Cose deepens our understanding not just of race but of the power of generational transformation."

—Anthony D. Romero, executive director of the American Civil Liberties Union

ALSO BY ELLIS COSE

NONFICTION

Bone to Pick
The Envy of the World
Color-Blind
The Darden Dilemma
A Man's World
The Rage of a Privileged Class
A Nation of Strangers
The Press

FICTION

The Best Defense

The End of Anger

A New Generation's Take on Race and Rage

Ellis Cose

ecco

An Imprint of HarperCollinsPublishers

HarperCollins books may be purchased for educational, business, or sales promotional use. For information please write: Special Markets Department, HarperCollins Publishers, 10 East 53rd Street, New York, NY 10022.

A hardcover edition of this book was published in 2011 by Ecco, an imprint of HarperCollins Publishers.

FIRST ECCO PAPERBACK EDITION PUBLISHED 2012.

Designed by Mary Austin Speaker

Library of Congress Cataloging-in-Publication Data

Cose, Ellis.
The end of anger: a new generation's take on race and rage / by Ellis Cose.—1st ed.
p. cm
Summary: "From a venerated and bestselling voice on American life comes a contemporary look at the decline of black rage; the demise of white guilt; and the intergenerational shifts in how blacks and whites view, and interact with, each other"—Provided by publisher.
ISBN 978-0-06-199855-3
1. United States—Race relations—History. 2. Racism—United States—History. 3. Anger—United States—History. 4. African Americans—Civil rights—History. I. Title.
E184.A1C67 2011
305.800973—dc22

2011009501

ISBN 978-0-06-199856-0 (pbk.)

12 13 14 15 16 OV/RRD 10 9 8 7 6 5 4 3 2 1

For Elisa—

May she see fulfilled the promise of her generation

Contents

Introduction

A New Age and a New Generation

Rage is as American as Old Glory, whose primary hues, red and blue, depict both our patriotism and our polarization. And that anger, which periodically surges through our body politic, seems of late to have reached an ugly crescendo. With the economy barely breathing, political partisanship rising, and the nation changing in ways many find extremely unsettling, anger too often is the natural response. But there is one group whose anger seems unusually tempered, leavened with more optimism than objective circumstances seem to justify. That group is African Americans, who in the last few years have astounded pollsters with their moderation and hopefulness.

The End of Anger is an exploration of why it is that many blacks are feeling optimistic these days. It is also a look at American generations, and at how the increasing maturity of whites, whose attitudes have changed through the years—evolving, most notably, as they moved from parent to child—has freed a rising generation of African Americans and other people of color to aspire to a future their parents could only dream about. Black hope and white growth, in other words, are closely related. This book will explain how.

Finally, *The End of Anger* is a book about success—about a particularly privileged, even indulged, group of African Americans whose experiences in many respects are far from the norm, but who show us, with their collective achievements, what is possible when a people whose history is largely one of dampened, doomed, or shattered expectations are allowed to break free of the limits imposed by unthinking prejudice backed by carelessly wielded power.

But let me begin not with this current generation but with the founding contradiction that for so long prevented America from becoming what it proclaimed itself to be.

From its inception, America stood for equality. When Europe still clung to a moldy aristocracy, America proudly chose democracy—albeit democracy with a twist. For Americans also embraced slavery—"an exception to their social system . . . carefully restricted to one single human race," in the words of Alexis de Tocqueville. That inconsistency—that contradiction at the core of the Union's founding principles—has haunted this nation since its birth. More than a century after slavery ended, African Americans were still struggling for acceptance and affirmation, still uncomfortable in the only land they could call home. Michelle LaVaugh Robinson spoke for many of her race and generation when she acknowledged in her senior thesis in 1985, "I have found that at Princeton no matter how liberal and open-minded some of my White professors and classmates try to be toward me, I sometimes feel like a visitor on campus; as if I really don't belong."

Today, as America's First Lady, Michelle Obama is warmly welcomed virtually wherever she chooses to go. And even African Americans with no White House connection are fully at home in some of the nation's most exclusive establishments. No one present at the nation's founding could have imagined such a thing. Writing in the nineteenth century, even with the abolition movement building steam, de Tocqueville never saw this day coming. "Those who hope that Europeans will one day mingle with Negroes . . . seem to me to be fostering a delusion," he wrote.

Today we are so far beyond mere "mingling." We have a president who happily admits to being the result of an interracial union, who, indeed, presents his life story and his origin as evidence of the vitality of this great nation. Interracial coupling, once grounds for riots, now provokes more yawns than outrage. Blacks, a race of people whose ancestors were dragged to this continent in chains and treated as property, now occupy some of the most privileged positions in the land. For at least some blacks and other so-called people of color, the glass ceiling has simply ceased to exist.

In a now legendary speech, Martin Luther King Jr. challenged America to repay the "promissory note to which every American was to fall heir" and to "make real the promises of democracy." Some believe that happy day has finally arrived. Or so they said in January 2009 on the eve of President Barack Obama's inauguration. A CNN poll found that 69 percent of blacks agreed that Martin Luther King's vision had been "fulfilled." That was double the number who agreed with the statement just twelve months previously. Indeed, in the wake of Obama's election, pollsters discovered an abundance of upbeat news. A *New York Times* poll one hundred days into Obama's tenure found that 70 percent of blacks thought the country was moving in the right direction, and it also found that two-thirds of all Americans believed race relations to be good.

As America prepared for the 2010 midterm elections—which proved devastating for the Obama administration—blacks shared little of the disenchantment that had overtaken many whites, according to a pre-election poll by CBS News. African Americans were more likely than whites to say that the economy was sound. And nearly half (compared to 16 percent of whites) thought that America's next generation would be better off than those living today. Race relations was the one area in which black confidence had faltered. Only 40 percent thought race relations were "generally good" (compared to 63 percent of whites, and down from 59 percent three months after Obama's election)—a reaction, presumably, to what many perceived as a backlash against the Obama administration.

Coming in the midst of an economic crisis that had hit African

Americans particularly hard, the poll results were nothing short of astounding. When I asked David Thomas, a black Harvard Business School professor, about the CNN poll, he laughed. "It's irrational exuberance," he said, invoking the phrase made famous by Alan Greenspan in referring to investors who plowed money into the stock market well past the point where it made much sense. Thomas's point was that the election of Obama was such an astounding and unprecedented event that it drove any number of people to the edge of delirium. Not since Joe Louis defeated Max Schmeling in 1938 had a public event provoked such a display of jubilation in black neighborhoods—or such waves of self-congratulation in liberal white communities. More than two-thirds of Americans rated Obama's election as either the most important advance—or among the two or three most important advances—for blacks in the past one hundred years, reported Gallup.

The reason for the euphoria was obvious: Obama's election made real what had previously been only a dream. Prior to the election season of 2008, it was impossible for many people to believe that a man of color had any chance of being president of the United States. And if a people could not believe that anyone of their race, no matter how gifted, would be allowed a serious shot at the top job, how could they believe that America was really ready for equality?

"I remember when the ex-Attorney General Mr. Robert Kennedy said it was conceivable that in forty years in America we might have a Negro President," wrote James Baldwin in an essay published in the *New York Times Magazine* in 1965.

> That sounded like a very emancipated statement to white people. They were not in Harlem when this statement was first heard. They did not hear the laughter and bitterness and scorn with which this statement was greeted. From the point of view of the man in the Harlem barber shop, Bobby Kennedy only got here yesterday and now he is already on his way to the Presidency. We were here for four hundred years and now he

tells us that maybe in forty years, if you are good, we may let you become President.

Obama was not the first black person to run for president. Numerous others came before him, including Shirley Chisholm, Carol Moseley Braun, Alan Keyes, Al Sharpton, and, most famously, Jesse Jackson. But none of them expected to win. Their campaigns were about something else—about making a point, making a name, or collecting delegates with which to bargain. Obama's run was different—or became so as he progressed through the primaries and the realization took hold that he just might make it.

During a long conversation on a hot Chicago afternoon, Jackson talked of his presidential campaigns of 1984 and 1988. Speaking in the language of biblical allusion, he referred to himself and his contemporaries as "the Joshua generation" and to Obama and his ilk as "the post-Joshua generation." Joshua, of course, was Moses's apprentice and his successor as leader of the Israelites. Though Moses (Martin Luther King, in Jackson's telling) ascended Mount Sinai, it was Joshua who led his tribe into Canaan, the Promised Land. Joshua, said Jackson, took the walls down. "And once the walls are down, bridges can be built from the rocks that came from those walls," said Jackson. "That generation is more acceptable; they are less threatening." The metaphor may not be perfect, but Jackson's point is powerful: Obama represents much more than a victorious candidate, and his rise is proof not just of his political savvy but of progress in a very long and painful journey toward the long-prophesied Promised Land.

Bearing witness to that progress understandably made many people giddy, including, it seems, Michelle Obama, who, in mid-February 2008, just before the Wisconsin primary, committed an unqualified political gaffe.

"For the first time in my adult lifetime, I'm really proud of my country," said the future First Lady. The slip gave Obama's political opponents the opportunity to prattle on about their own patriotism while questioning that of the Obamas—who fell over themselves trying to extricate themselves from Michelle's verbal blunder. She had not really meant what she had said was their defense. "What she meant is that she's really proud at this moment because, for the first time in a long time, thousands of Americans who've never participated in politics before are coming out in record numbers to build a grassroots movement for change," said a spokesman.

Few people seriously grappled with the clear implication of what Michelle Obama almost certainly meant—that prior to her husband's candidacy America had never truly envisioned a black man occupying the Oval Office, and that the country being perhaps on the verge of making such a momentous breakthrough filled her heart with wonder, joy, and pride.

I recall as a very young man realizing—or at least concluding—that president of the United States was one of the many things (and perhaps the most symbolically powerful one) I could not seriously think about becoming. That epiphany convinced me that certain prizes would always be beyond my reach, simply because of my color. I came to that realization reluctantly and painfully, based on my readings, limited experience (which included being fired at the age of sixteen from a part-time job for asking a white manager to hand me a stack of envelopes to stuff), and warnings from my parents; it meant that my life was bound to be circumscribed in ways I would detest, and it meant that fairness for me and those like me was a fantasy.

Over lunch in a Chicago restaurant, Carl Bell, a black psychiatrist on the faculty of the University of Illinois–Chicago and president and CEO of the Community Mental Health Council and Foundation, talked of encountering Barack Obama in an airport shortly before he had formally announced his campaign for the presidency. "Hey, Barack . . . somebody told me you're running for president," Bell called out. Obama replied that he was thinking about it. Bell asked if he was en route to Chicago. "Yes," said the senator. "Good, when you get there, I'm committing you to a state psychiatric facility and I'm giving you a lobotomy, because you've obviously lost your mind," replied Bell.

Obama obviously had not lost his mind. Indeed, in seizing the presidency, he made a fantasy real. He made it possible for people—black, white, and other—to see it as normal for a black person to sit in America's most powerful post. Never again will black parents have to tell our children that some doors will be forever closed. And because of that, there is now the possibility that many of our children will soar in ways we could scarcely have imagined only a few years ago. No wonder so many black respondents are telling pollsters that they see a better future.

When Bell described his response to that realignment of reality, his take didn't really sound that much different from Michelle Obama's. But he, of course, was not involved in a presidential campaign and therefore could be considerably blunter. "Malcolm [X] made a point of saying *the nation* instead of *our* nation," said Bell. "When Barack got elected, I started saying 'our nation,' because it's a huge step closer to actualizing the ideal."

In 1993, I published *The Rage of a Privileged Class,* a book whose central thesis was that even the most gifted African Americans assumed, for the most part, that no matter how talented they were or how hard they worked, they would never be permitted to crash through America's glass ceiling. *Rage* opened with a simple declaration:

> Despite its very evident prosperity, much of America's black middle class is in excruciating pain. And that distress—although most of the country does not see it—illuminates a serious American problem: the problem of the broken covenant, of the pact ensuring that if you work hard, get a good education, and play by the rules, you will be allowed to advance and achieve to the limits of your ability.

Virtually every successful black person I talked to at the time felt America was generations away from achieving anything approaching true equality—even for the most gifted blacks. Almost no one thought blacks would be heading Fortune 500 companies anytime soon. (Although Clifton Wharton, the Harvard-educated former president of Michigan State and former Rockefeller Foundation chairman, invited me to a charming lunch during which he noted that, as the CEO of TIAA-CREF, the world's largest pension fund, he was in fact a black person who had run a Fortune 500 company—even if the firm often did not get credit for being one.)

Few people of any race would claim that full racial equality has arrived in America. Still, so much has changed since *Rage* was published. It's not that discrimination has stopped or that racist assumptions have vanished. But they are not nearly as powerful as they once were. Color is becoming less and less a burden; race is less and less an immovable barrier. Some 44 percent of blacks now claim to believe that blacks and whites have an equal opportunity of getting ahead—compared to 30 percent twelve years ago—according to a survey done by the *New York Times*. And in the lifting of that oppressive weight, many blacks have finally felt free to breathe—and to believe.

"It is not as simple, not as black and white as before. We have seen a real opening up of opportunities . . . for white women, Asian Americans, Latinos," observed Wallace Ford, a black graduate of Dartmouth University and Harvard Law School and president of his own global consulting firm. When I interviewed Ford for *Rage,* he was New York City's commissioner for business services. He also was extremely angry at what he perceived as an immovable ceiling on black aspirations. He sees things differently now, as does an entire generation that has come of age in the post–civil rights era.

That generation has seen a parade of blacks step into high-profile positions: Richard Parsons as CEO of Time Warner, Kenneth Chenault as head of American Express, Ann Fudge as chairman and CEO of Young & Rubicam Brands, and, more recently, Kenneth Frazier as CEO of Merck. The world has become more "rational," says Professor Thomas. Companies have acquired the capacity to see value in blacks that they could not see a generation ago. "If we are Time Warner and we see that we strategically need Richard Parsons to be the new CEO," Parsons will be hired, said Thomas.

This generation has witnessed not only the rise of black corporate hotshots but also the emergence of black movie stars who make tens of millions of dollars a film. They have seen the coronation of Oprah and the ascent of Sean "Diddy" Combs—blacks who are wealthier by far than most whites. They have also seen Stanley O'Neal, former CEO of Merrill Lynch, walk away with a retirement package worth an estimated $161.5 million—after doing, by most accounts, a terrible job, proving that even blacks who are poor performers in the corporate world can at least occasionally do as well as poor-performing whites.

Then there is the phenomenon of Obama, who is both the beneficiary of and the catalyst for a new American vision.

I was in Washington, D.C., on U Street, on inauguration day 2009. Devastated by the angry riots of 1968 sparked by the murder of Martin Luther King, U Street is now a bustling commercial strip with trendy eateries such as the Creme Café and Lounge. There Glory Edim, a twenty-six-year-old marketing coordinator, dabbed away tears as she watched Obama's speech. "I never thought this would happen," said Edim, the daughter of Nigerian immigrants. "It allows me to believe that whatever I want to achieve in this world, I can."

For Oliver Cromwell, a retired government employee, Obama's election was revelatory. "For most of us, something we never thought would happen has happened," he said. "I think it opens the door for blacks. . . . You didn't feel this was possible."

Months after the election, Theodore "Ted" Shaw, a Columbia University law professor who formerly headed the NAACP Legal Defense and Educational Fund, was still in a state of near disbelief: "Like most black Americans, I was hopeful, but still surprised at the election of Barack Obama. I held my breath hoping, but I didn't think I would see this. People like myself have to acknowledge that there were things we may not have thought were possible because we were trapped in our assumptions. I'm happy I was wrong," he told me.

"If an African American can be elected president of the United

States, I don't think there is anything in this country that he or she cannot do. . . . The election of an African American president was a Rubicon to be crossed," said Shaw. No longer are there any excuses for denying blacks anything, or for blacks denying themselves the opportunity to aim as high as they wish.

During a later conversation, he elaborated:

> Does that mean that no African American or no Latino or no women or no member of a group that's been subordinated won't run up against discrimination or a glass ceiling somewhere? No, it doesn't mean that. But it does mean that the rules have changed. . . . For a young black child or brown child to see an African American president of the United States—that, to me, lifts all kinds of mental shackles off of young children.

But even before Obama came on the national scene, optimism was building among blacks—particularly among a new generation of privileged achievers who refused to believe they would be stymied by the soft bigotry that had bedeviled their parents. Manning Marable, professor of history and public affairs at Columbia University, argues that this optimism is very much a response to a new American reality that has rendered racism—and the blatant discrimination that comes with it—déclassé.

"If we went back just to 1964, the total number of black elected officials in the U.S. was about one hundred. The total number of black mayors was zero; blacks in Congress, five. So there was virtually no representation within the political establishment of the country at any level, for blacks," he noted.

> By 1970, there was a Congressional Black Caucus. There were 1,100 elected black officials. By 1983, the year Harold Washington is elected mayor of Chicago, there were about 3,500 black elected officials. By 1990, about 10,000. So the growth in representation by African Americans was exponential during the late decades of the twentieth century. It did not have a parallel within the upper echelon of corporate America. . . . That's

> an event that has occurred really only since the late 1990s. So there's been this remarkable growth of a black middle class.
>
> Black politics and political culture, in the sixties and seventies, was largely defined by the experiences blacks had in struggles to achieve access and opportunity—both within the existing system and to build alternative black-owned, black-controlled institutions outside of it. So there was always a tension, and a debate, between integration and separatism. The space for that debate withered and then largely disappeared by the end of the nineties. Only most blacks didn't realize it. . . . The reason it happened is because of the very successes of the black freedom struggle. We outlawed legal segregation in the country. We achieved the integration of civic life. And one big reason for that was the success of integration of the armed forces. And there was this massive increase of blacks in education, higher education especially. All of those things created a U.S. civil society in which it was very uncool to be a white supremacist.

Obama's election was, in effect, the final revelation—the long-awaited sign that a new American age had dawned. "It blows away the nationalist argument that the system is white and racist and won't ever change," Marable observed.

As part of the research for this book, I conducted surveys of two groups that contain some of the most accomplished people of color in the United States. One is the African American alumni of Harvard Business School. The other is the alumni of A Better Chance.* That program, founded in 1963, sends ambitious and talented youngsters, the vast majority of them people of color, to some of the most selective high schools and prep schools in the country. The hope is that those young people will eventually assume leadership positions in all areas of society.

My surveys are not randomized samples in the classical sense, which is to say that I cannot state with statistical certainty (within a nicely calculated "confidence interval," to use the jargon) that the

* For detailed survey data, visit www.elliscose.com.

views reported precisely mirror those of all black Harvard MBAs or of all ABC alumni. It is better to think of these surveys as mega focus groups—or as huge sounding boards comprised of 193 black Harvard MBAs and 311 ABC alumni who took the time to share their thoughts and feelings regarding some of the most sensitive issues facing this society today. They all filled out lengthy questionnaires and roughly one-third also responded to detailed follow-up questions. The two groups agreed on a stunning array of things. That is not surprising given that they shared an elite educational pedigree. But their agreement is also an indication that their views may be the norm in such privileged circles. And if any group is primed to reap the benefits of this age, it would seem to be these men and women—trained for leadership by some of the most elite institutions in the world and groomed to believe that they are capable of competing against anyone. And certainly, judging by the weight of their pocketbooks, they are doing exceptionally well.

Forty-seven percent of the graduates of ABC schools reported an annual income of $100,000 or more, and 9 percent reported an income in excess of $300,000. The Harvard MBAs were doing even better financially—again, no big surprise given the major corporation and financial industry focus of Harvard Business School. Nearly 90 percent of the Harvard MBAs put their household income at over $100,000, 40 percent put it at more than $300,000, and an astounding 30 percent put it at $400,000 or more—at a time when the typical American household earns under $51,000 and the average black household earns $34,000.

Still, despite their very obvious success, my respondents did not perceive a world where race no longer matters. While their take, in many respects, was decidedly upbeat, it was laced with pain and wariness. They saw a world in which race seriously affects opportunities for blacks and Hispanics, but (and this is a crucial "but") not strongly enough to prevent them from getting where they want to go.

Only 5.2 percent of the Harvard MBAs felt that, in general, "opportunities for blacks in corporate America are equal to those for whites." Ninety-four percent thought they are worse. And 87 percent felt that blacks confront a glass ceiling in corporate America.

But when it came to their own companies and their own fate, the view was markedly brighter. Forty-nine percent saw no glass ceiling for blacks where they worked, and a majority believed that their educational attainments put them on an "equal professional footing (in the eyes of employers or prospective employers) with white peers or competitors with comparable educational credentials." Not just bullish on their own potential to compete, they generally believed that individual effort ultimately prevails. A majority agreed that "everyone has it in their own power to succeed."

The ABC alumni were just as upbeat. While 91 percent of the black alumni (blacks made up 81 percent of those surveyed) believed that blacks face a glass ceiling in corporate America, only 50 percent saw a glass ceiling in their own workplace. And 54 percent believed themselves to be on the same professional footing as their white peers. Interestingly, Latinos, who made up some 20 percent of the ABC alumni sampled (and Latinos, I should note, can be of any race), saw their situation a little differently. Seventy-eight percent believed that Latinos face a glass ceiling in corporate America, and 56 percent saw a ceiling in their own workplace. Some 62 percent saw themselves as on the same footing as their white peers.

As I looked more closely at these results, something jumped out at me: many of the responses are significantly influenced by the age of the respondent. In other words, generations matter—hugely—and not just as a reflection of age. Ever since the civil rights generation shook things up, whites and American society have been undergoing a metamorphosis, and those changes have had different effects on blacks' expectations and aspirations depending on when they were born. Later we explore the implications of this generational divergence in detail.

Columbia University provost Claude Steele was not surprised that my respondents were more likely to see barriers elsewhere than in their own institutions. Similar findings are well known in the survey literature, explained Steele, a world-renowned psychologist who has done groundbreaking work on the impact of perceived stereotypes on performance (a phenomenon known as "stereotype threat"). The responses, he speculated, could be the result of "a self-survival kind of bias."

"One of the most devastating things," he said, "is to think, 'This is a racist situation, and my prospects really will be affected by racism.' . . . It's very devastating to think, 'I'm dealing in a world where the deck is stacked and there's nothing I can do.'" So instead of seeing prejudice as ruling their lives, he surmised, my respondents tended to say, "Yes, there is a glass ceiling . . . but not in my world. In my world, I've got all the options." Steele confided that he had sometimes employed that strategy himself in the past. In confronting situations in his own life where racism might be implicated, he had "almost a private rule. If I could find reason to believe otherwise," he said, "I would believe that . . . and just get through the day, because what else could I do?"

If you believe that a glass ceiling is in place and one is not, you can sabotage your own prospects. You end up "limiting yourself," pointed out Carl Bell, the Chicago psychiatrist. So the smart play is to give the institution the benefit of the doubt. But for an institution to be granted that doubt there has to be, at minimum, the possibility that the doubt is merited. In the days of Jim Crow, it was simply not possible for a sane black person in the South to believe that he or she could ever become a ranking executive in an important white-controlled company, or a partner in a large majority-white law firm, or even a sheriff of a predominantly white town. It was not possible for any people of color to believe, unless they were certifiably crazy, that they could become president of the United States. They might as well have dreamed of becoming king or queen of England. There was no danger of being self-limited by a presumption of discrimination since the reality of discrimination was a certainty. Psychological self-survival—indeed, even physical survival at times—required seeing the world clearly for what it was: as an often capriciously hostile place where a black man or woman would never be allowed to govern whites and where they could in fact be killed for treating whites as equals—instead of deferring to them as superiors.

That was part of the burden the Moses generation bore, and it left scars not only on blacks but on those whites who kept Jim Crow in place. The determination to change that was what enabled people like John Lewis to endure beatings, slurs, and the possibility of violent death as they fought for an end to the age of racial madness.

In his memoir, *Walking with the Wind,* Lewis, now a congressman from Georgia, describes the scene in Selma during Bloody Sunday, March 7, 1965—the day when he and other civil rights marchers who had assembled on Edmund Pettus Bridge in Selma, Alabama, were tear-gassed and nearly beaten to death by police. As Lewis, one of the protest leaders, instructed marchers to kneel in prayer, the troopers and "possemen" advanced. They "swept forward as one, like a human wave, a blur of blue shirts and billy clubs and bullwhips. We had no chance to turn and retreat. There were six hundred people behind us, bridge railings to either side, and the river below," wrote Lewis.

That day of horror provided some much needed impetus for passage of the Voting Rights Act of 1965. Eight days after that violent encounter, President Lyndon Johnson went before a joint session of Congress and declared:

> There is no cause for pride in what has happened in Selma. There is no cause for self-satisfaction in the long denial of equal rights of millions of Americans. But there is cause for hope and for faith in our Democracy in what is happening here tonight. For the cries of pain and the hymns and protests of oppressed people have summoned into convocation all the majesty of this great government—the government of the greatest nation on earth. Our mission is at once the oldest and the most basic of this country—to right wrong, to do justice, to serve man.

Two days later he sent the voting rights bill to Congress, which passed it later that year.

To the post–civil rights generation, children and grandchildren of the Moses generation, that era is ancient history. With every decade since the civil rights revolution, new barriers have fallen. Each new generation has fewer racial neuroses, fewer racial scars, than the generation that came before. A 2009 study of "Millennials" ("the American teens and twenty-somethings who are making the passage into adulthood at the start of a new millennium") by the Pew Research Center noted that more than two decades of Pew surveys showed that the younger generation was more tolerant than the old. "In their views about interracial dating, for example," proclaimed Pew, "Millennials are the most open to change of any generation." That broad-mindedness was shared, to a somewhat lesser extent, by the Gen Xers (born between 1961 and 1981), less so by the Boomers (1943 to 1960), and least of all by the Silents (1925 to 1942).

That generational shifting of the American mind is, as Manning Marable suggested, a direct result of the black struggle for access and opportunity—which has seen every black generation since the Moses generation (the black contemporaries of the Silents) crash through doors slammed shut in the faces of their parents. So it is not surprising that, when it comes to matters of race, a host of surveys, including mine, show that younger people, including blacks, are more optimistic than their elders. Among the ABC alumni age forty and older, 57 percent saw a glass ceiling for blacks at their place of work. Among those younger than forty, the figure dropped to 43 percent. Similarly, among the Harvard MBAs age forty and over, 54 percent saw a glass ceiling at their job, whereas only 46 percent of those under forty thought a ceiling was in place. The younger Harvard professionals were also more likely than their elders (62 percent compared to 48 percent) to believe that they were on essentially equal footing with whites peers or competitors.

Optimism, of course, generally comes easier to the young, who presumably have not yet been slapped down by life and who are often also more able to see and acknowledge change once it arrives. As Claude Steele remarked, "You are formed in an era and it gives you the lenses through which you see things. And things can change before you drop those lenses." Younger people are much less committed to the vision of what used to be, and so today's black professionals, particularly those educated at some of America's most prestigious institutions, see fewer boulders blocking their path.

Linda Anderson, a Columbia University–trained psychologist who teaches at New York's Hostos Community College, has noticed the change among students and among her private clients: "What I'm seeing in the more elite institutions, with young people who come from families whom we would deem successful, is there's a much greater sense of entitlement than we ever experienced growing up in the sixties and seventies." They have a sense, she said, that

> the world will open up, and opportunities will open up if one has worked hard enough to get the credentials—and even if one doesn't necessarily have the credentials. What I see as far as identity issues are concerned is there's a much wider range of ways that people experience their salient identity. There are African American young people for whom being an African American is really not the primary or salient part of their identity as it was back then.

In many respects, Desiree Peterkin Bell is typical of the new breed of young blacks. When we met in mid-2010, the Brooklyn native and ABC alumna was communications director for Newark mayor Cory Booker. Prior to joining the Booker administration in 2006, at the age of twenty-eight, she was senior director of government affairs for New York mayor Michael Bloomberg. Prior to that, she was a special assistant to the mayor of Indianapolis. A standout athlete (she was a triple-jumper, sprinter, and five-time National Collegiate Athletic Association All-American), Peterkin

Bell earned her undergraduate degree from Swarthmore and her master's in public administration from Baruch's School of Public Affairs. Her grades and test scores had been good enough to get her into some of New York's best public high schools. But she chose ABC, which sent her to Strath Haven, an elite regional public school in Wallingford, Pennsylvania.

"It was a hard choice," Peterkin Bell recalled.

> I had gotten accepted into Bronx Science, Brooklyn Tech, and Stuyvesant. And those were the best high schools at the time in New York City. But my mother, to her credit, really saw it as an opportunity for me to get a little farther ahead than anyone else. And that meant stepping outside of the world that I knew and creating a whole new network of relationships, of friends, of people of support.

Although being uprooted was difficult, "I would come back home every so often," Peterkin Bell said, "and see friends who didn't have that luxury, that opportunity." She worried about a childhood friend who became pregnant at the age of fourteen, a bright girl who unfortunately "got caught up in the street." And she wondered whether that girl's life would have turned out differently had she had the chance to go to an ABC school.

In Wallingford, Peterkin Bell discovered a world of relative privilege and also of prejudice. "I didn't know racism until I went away. I didn't know what it was. All my friends were different colors, and we were great. I knew they were different. But I didn't know that people judged you and criticized you and ostracized you because you were different." On balance, however, Peterkin Bell counted the years at Strath Haven as a wonderful broadening experience, and one that gave her the foundation for a high-powered professional career: "I mean, I have folks to this day who serve as part of my network . . . a network of opportunity." The school also literally put her on the path to Swarthmore, which happened to be located across the street from the ABC girls' house in Wallingford.

Peterkin Bell has enjoyed what is, in many ways, a charmed

political career, working at a substantial level for three different big-city mayors before reaching the age of thirty. (She added a fourth mayor to her list in late 2010 when she went to work for Philadelphia mayor Michael Nutter.) She acknowledged the opportunities she had been given, even as she rejected the notion that race no longer matters.

"This whole idea of the postracial, I really don't subscribe to that at all," she said. "I don't believe that things have become so sanitized and homogenized that you can't really tell the difference between certain issues, certain candidates, and certain people."

But she also feels that the opportunities open to her and her peers are essentially limitless.

> We're always testing the boundaries. We don't subscribe to the glass ceiling theory. . . . You no longer think, "I'm not even going to try because I can't reach there." . . . You just say, "What makes sense? Let's try it. If that doesn't work, okay, let's try another angle." . . . We don't subscribe to the [idea that] here's a limit, a box, that . . . because I'm a thirty-two-year-old African American, Panamanian woman, these are the things I can only do.
>
> I'm not an idiot. So I know that there are things that exist out there. Racism exists. Sexism exists. . . . I do believe that. But I'm not going to settle for those isms. I'm not going to let those people and those issues define my trajectory.

Reality was very different for her parents: "I've had conversations with my mother and she . . . had to fight her way to school, fight coming back. I don't have those issues."

Her ex-boss, Cory Booker, has had an even more charmed journey. In 2006, at the age of thirty-seven, he was elected mayor of Newark in a landslide, having lost his first attempt for that office four years previously. That first run was ugly and bruising. It pitted him against a longtime incumbent, Sharpe James, who was a hero to many in Newark's black community at that time. James attacked the suburban-bred, Stanford- and Yale-educated Rhodes Scholar as an interloper, carpetbagger, and race-traitor.

Booker is routinely singled out as one of a handful of promising young politicians of color who will lead America into the postracial age. Shortly after Booker won his second term, we met in his office to discuss his views on a number of issues, including how he differed from those who had preceded him.

"Is there something different about my generation?" he asked, repeating my question.

> Yeah. My father was born extremely poor to a single mother who couldn't take care of him . . . and was raised in a viciously segregated community. [He] did not have the world of opportunities I had. But because he went to North Carolina Central and was involved when the sit-in movement started . . . because of all these efforts . . . they expanded my realm of opportunities. . . . My parents would always tell me, "You have more privilege, more opportunity to do what we couldn't do, but the fight is still the same." . . .
>
> Barack Obama could not have been elected president thirty years ago. It just would not have happened in the United States of America. So obviously I have, again thanks to my parents' generation's work, an expanded set of career options that they didn't have before. . . . I could leave City Hall tomorrow, frankly, and get jobs that my father had to fight to get.

Thanks in part to help from the Urban League, recalled Booker, his father became part of the first wave of black IBM salesmen: "I mean, the stories he told me were outrageous. I don't worry about making a sales call to somebody and having them tell IBM not to send niggers out here to sell me typewriters. So I've got a whole bunch of new options, and that in some ways might be what you call success."

Several weeks before sitting down with Booker, I visited Congressman John Lewis in his Washington office. The day before my visit, Lewis had endorsed Artur Davis, a young Harvard-trained lawyer and fellow congressman who was attempting to become the first black governor of Alabama.

I asked Lewis about the generational difference between himself and some of the young politicians coming up behind him. "I have a great deal of admiration for these young men and young women on the rise," he said.

> They're not tainted so much or scarred by the pain of racism, of segregation, [which is] much of the load and burden that my generation had to bear and had to carry. They're much more educated, and they came in and grew up in a different period. Most of these young men and young women, they never were told, "You cannot do this. You cannot go there." They never saw the [whites only] signs that left scars on the psyche of many of us. . . . So these young politicians, like a Harold Ford or an Artur Davis . . . grew up [in] a different time.

Harold Ford won his first race for Congress in 1996 at the age of twenty-six, while finishing up his last year at the University of Michigan Law School. He took the congressional seat over from his father and namesake and served five terms before barely losing his bid, in 2006, to become the first black senator from Tennessee—and the first from the South since the Reconstruction era. When I met him for lunch in 2010, he was settled in New York, where he had lived for the last three years, serving as vice chairman of Bank of America Merrill Lynch.

"My dad is a little different than John Lewis," he told me, "but there are more generational parallels in their lives than there are to my life versus theirs. . . . People would often say that I inherited my dad's seat, and frankly I wish I could have, because I wouldn't have gone a million dollars in debt."

What his dad did give him, said Ford,

> was an understanding that none of this would be easy and that my challenges would be different than his, [but] that they'd be challenges no less. I ran for Senate in my state, and there's no doubt that some of these issues percolated and rose to the surface, issues of race and so forth played a role. But they played a

role slightly different than when my dad was in politics—but, I think, equally powerful in some ways and less so in others.

He acknowledged that, in many respects, his road was easier than it had been for those of Lewis's generation. "We had a whole different set of tools, or a larger number of tools to confront challenges than they did. . . . My dad and his generation had a hammer in their toolbox. Every challenge they faced they took a hammer to it. . . . We were given screwdrivers, wrenches, saws."

Ford now considered himself a businessman, not a politician, but he admitted that politics always would be "a part of who I am." When I asked about race and the limits it might impose on his future political career, he made it clear that he wasn't particularly concerned: "Race is not going to stop me from saying, 'You know what, I can be senator one day for New York.'"

Ford's confidence—in his own abilities and also in the goodwill of his countrymen—was typical of many people I interviewed. But I also heard several concerns.

Some wondered whether, in these times of economic crisis, they could maintain their privileged positions. And many worried about the huge numbers of young people without sterling academic credentials whose life options seemed worse than ever.

Daysy, a twenty-year-old college student and ABC alumna, said that, for many Latinas of her mother's generation, college simply was not an option. "During her youth, it was very rare for a low-income inner-city Hispanic teen to go to college." Those who did go to college, noted Daysy, were either "geniuses" or people who left high school, took a menial job, and then realized that "they needed to do something more." College "was not the norm. My mother did not go to college. However, throughout my educational career, I have always encountered nonprofit programs seeking talented students of color or from low-income families to assist them for the future." Daysy worried that those programs might not be around much longer.

Marlon Lewis, a fifty-four-year-old Pasadena lawyer and ABC

alum, had much the same concern. Indeed, he felt that Obama's election would make it harder to keep such programs alive: "I think Obama's election is the last stone on the grave of affirmative action. I fear that institutions [that] have stood fast on diversity in education will retreat from their position . . . because a minority has made it to the White House."

Others I heard from were not too concerned about their own futures, which they presumed were bright for the most part, but about the destiny of millions of others stuck in poor neighborhoods and dreadful schools.

"I am much more optimistic about the future of my children than I am about the future of all black children, two-thirds of whom are born in poverty," said a thirty-nine-year-old Harvard MBA. Many of her MBA colleagues echoed her comments. "I think the opportunities are being made [available] to a smaller and smaller population of blacks and that our lower class is growing and becoming more permanent," said one.

Caille Millner, Harvard class of 2001 and a successful journalist and author, wonders whether, in the end, her generation will be as free from the past as its members typically assume they will be. Millner's memoir, *The Golden Road,* garnered admiring reviews, and she has established herself as a talent worth watching. "I definitely feel like we're the first generation who felt like maybe we didn't have to be the doctors and the lawyers; maybe we can try to do something that we actually wanted to do, whether it's go into politics or go into the arts."

But that freedom, she said, is turning out to be less than absolute.

> And it's really only acutely come out now, with the recession and a lot of these other huge economic shifts that we're undergoing as a country. I mean, our white classmates, they have generations of family who can provide safety nets for them and guidance for them and economic help for them if they need it. We don't. So there are still some differences. But I think there is a new sense

> of freedom to be who you want to be and freedom to be who you are. You don't necessarily feel you have to represent the race anymore. But there is that tension because you don't have that long family history of stability, especially economic stability, financial stability. A number of my black classmates are really struggling economically right now.

While I was researching this book, my thoughts often went to my daughter and to the world she will inherit. She is a tall, slender beauty with a smile that radiates warmth and playfulness. As I write this, she has just recently turned eight. She is headstrong yet sometimes shy around those she would most like to impress and precocious enough to challenge parental logic in two languages. She has been watched over by a nanny practically since she was born and has been in school since she was two. Her backyard is New York's Central Park. She sees nothing at all unusual about a black person or a woman aspiring to be president of the United States, and she assumes, with all the confidence of the very young, that she can be whatever it pops into her mind to be.

I wonder, as any parent would, about what the world will do to those assumptions. I know that, at the very least, she will take her place in a world free of the need to pigeonhole her at birth. She will also have many of the benefits of privilege, which, in this world, increasingly trump the previously immutable disadvantages (and advantages) of gender and race.

I doubt that color will disappear as an issue. She has already peppered me with questions about skin color and hair. She wonders why so many of the stars and virtually all the heroines on the children's shows and movies she watches are white—and why, of those white children, so many are blond. She struggled as a preschooler to understand why certain nannies called a friend of hers "fea"—or ugly—because she happened to be very dark. But I am confident that, even if color does not disappear, it will not be a weight around her neck. She certainly will not grow up believing that doors will close on her just because of the color of her skin.

Nevertheless, she is growing up at a time and in a society where the promise of a decent future for those deemed deserving, whatever their race, seems less and less to apply; where well-heeled people of all colors feel anxious; and where—according to research done for the Pew Charitable Trusts—the children of black parents who fought their way into the supposedly charmed circle of the middle class are likely themselves to end up poor.

So where does that leave us? Have we created a society where we have largely overcome the most galling and rigid limitations of racial discrimination only to resign ourselves to even more pernicious forms of inequity? Have we traded in the uncomfortable dynamic of black rage and white guilt for an inchoate, growing, and less racially tinged sense of frustration and impotence? Have we made so much progress in some respects and so little in others that King's dreams provide no clear sense of how to think of today's challenges?

Certainly the answer to the last question is an unqualified yes. King's dream, as he articulated it, was silent on the question of black athletes worth hundreds of millions of dollars or black CEOs of huge corporations. It made no reference to the possibility of a black president or to blacks running for the Senate in Tennessee or for the governor's mansion in Alabama. King's Alabama dream was much more basic than that. It consisted of the hope that "one day, down in Alabama, with its vicious racists, with its governor having his lips dripping with the words of interposition and nullification; one day right there in Alabama, little black boys and black girls will be able to join hands with little white boys and white girls as sisters and brothers."

We are so far from the Alabama that King knew. Yet too often, in the South and elsewhere, little black boys and girls and little white boys and girls still find themselves in separate schools with separate tracks with separate destinations. And even in places where they come together with ease, along with brown boys and girls and Asian boys and girls, their parents, unless they are comfortably wealthy, fret about the fraying of the American Dream.

This is a world that requires a broader vision of equity than the one we inherited from past generations—even as we acknowledge an important victory in the American struggle for equality: the unqualified success of at least a subset of a new generation of African Americans would not have been possible had this nation not essentially vanquished the virulent form of racism that, not so long ago, poisoned relations between blacks and whites.

In later chapters, you will read much about the African American generations I have labeled Gen 1 Fighters, Gen 2 Dreamers, and Gen 3 Believers, as well as their white generational counterparts, Gen 1 Hostiles, Gen 2 Neutrals, and Gen 3 Allies. Generation 1, in this taxonomy, is the civil rights generation—the generation of those who participated in, supported, opposed, or simply bore witness to the defining twentieth-century battle for racial equality. It is the generation of whites who, in large measure, saw blacks as alien beings and the generation of blacks who, for the most part, saw whites as irremediably prejudiced.

Ever since that first generation—made up in large part of blacks who demanded equality and of whites who initially said no—succeeding generations of Americans have readjusted to each other in the ways that characterize their cohorts. We have, in some substantial way, re-created each other—to an extent that our predecessors might find astounding. That in four generations we have gone from cohorts who considered it unnatural for people from different races to socialize at all to cohorts who routinely count people of various hues and ethnicities among their family members and dearest friends is a remarkable societal accomplishment, and one we can justly celebrate.

In the pages that follow, we will meet many accomplished individuals who fully embody the promise of this new American era—and whose stories show both how limiting and how liberating generational lenses can be.

Chapter One

Revising the Racial Contract

For centuries, black Americans lied to white Americans. It was a matter of simple survival. Slaves did not speak in anger to their masters. Yes, America saw slave rebellions—the most famous was led by Nat Turner in Southampton, Virginia, in 1831. But rage was generally held deep within. So most whites, during the years of slavery and for decades thereafter, believed that blacks were content. "They tell us in these eager days that life was joyous to the black slave," wrote W. E. B. DuBois in *The Souls of Black Folk,* published in 1903. But the truth, said DuBois, could be found in the "Sorrow Songs," the Negro spirituals: "They are the music of an unhappy people, of the children of disappointment; they tell of death and suffering and unvoiced longing toward a truer world."

Blacks could not forever hide their anger in spirituals and whispered resentment. In 1940, as the war against fascism in Europe threatened to engulf America, Richard Wright published *Native Son,* the story of a black man, Bigger Thomas, who is filled with rancor and rage. After World War II, as black Americans increasingly equated Jim Crow with Nazism and black soldiers who had fought for whites' freedom abroad were humiliated at home, black anger spilled fully out into the open. Ever since then, whenever African Americans have spoken in public about our experience in this country, anger has been a recurrent and dominant theme.

"There are . . . as many ways of coping . . . as there are black men in the world, but no black man can hope ever to be entirely liberated from this internal warfare—rage, dissembling, and contempt having inevitably accompanied his first realization of the power of white men," wrote James Baldwin in "Stranger in the Village" in 1953. He returned to the theme in 1955 in *Notes of a Native Son.* "There is not a Negro alive who does not have this rage in his blood—one has the choice, merely, of living with it consciously or surrendering to it," he wrote.

Black Americans are no longer fuming—or at least, not anything like we once were. The angry black man—Bigger Thomas and his ilk—has become marginalized, irrelevant, passé. In this era, public anger (fringe kooks notwithstanding) rarely has an explicitly racial edge. We are witnessing, in short, a fundamental shift in the nature of the black-white relationship in America, undergirded by a major evolution in some core American assumptions. As white racism has become unacceptable, unremitting black anger has become inappropriate—a huge change from where things stood only a generation or two ago.

As psychologist Linda Anderson observed,

> Fifteen or twenty years ago, I think our own ambivalence and anger—built-up rage—really was more prominent than it is now. I think we're at a place where those of us who are positioned . . . to make change and acquire wealth, to a certain extent—there's no time for it. We are working so hard to take advantage of the window of opportunity [created by] being in this culture where we have Obama in place.

In *Black Rage* (1968), psychiatrists William H. Grier and Price M. Cobbs argued that anger was a natural and pervasive reaction to the condition of blacks in America. "Aggression leaps from wounds inflicted and ambitions spiked," they wrote in their book, published just four months after Martin Luther King's assassination.

> It grows out of oppression and capricious cruelty. . . . People bear all they can and, if required, bear even more. But if they are black in present-day American society they have been asked to shoulder too much. They have had all they can stand. They will be harried no more. Turning from their tormentors, they are filled with rage. . . . We believe that the black masses will rise with a simple and eloquent demand to which new leaders must give tongue. They will say to America simply: GET OFF OUR BACKS!

In December 1993, Colin Ferguson emptied two clips from a semiautomatic pistol into commuters on a Long Island Railroad train—killing six people and injuring nineteen others. Notes found in his pocket explained his action as a result of the rage he felt as a black man. A month or so later, I returned from an overseas trip to scores of phone calls from reporters seeking my comments on the bloodbath. To my astonishment, they informed me that Ferguson's attorney, William Kunstler, had cited me as an authority on his "black rage defense" and urged them to call me. My credential was having recently published *The Rage of a Privileged Class*. The book had nothing to do with demented gunmen, but it did speak to an anger—rooted in racial slights, lack of respect, and generally shabby treatment—that was rarely voiced but often felt by middle-class black Americans.

Vernon Baker was one such American, though I was not familiar with him when I wrote *Rage*. At a White House ceremony in January 1997, the former second lieutenant received the Medal of Honor from President Bill Clinton. The award was for heroics during World War II. During an epic battle on a hilltop in northern Italy, Baker took out four nests of enemy soldiers. Of the 1.2 million black soldiers who served in the military during World War II, Baker was the only one to receive the medal while still alive. Six others were honored posthumously at the same ceremony during which Baker received his medal.

Shortly before accepting the honor, Baker, who was living in

Idaho, spoke with *Washington Post* columnist Milton Milloy and confided that the white commander of his segregated unit had fled from the battle, saying that he would return with reinforcements. Instead, he abandoned the black battalion on the hill and told his superiors that the men had been "wiped out." That commander, reported Milloy, was recommended for the Medal of Honor, while Baker's unit was written up as "sluggish."

"That was the story of our lives," said Baker. "We used to call ourselves the 'promotion pool' for white officers."

"The main feeling I had during that time was anger. I was an angry, angry young man," said Baker. He repeated the sentiment in numerous interviews, including one with a *New York Times* reporter: "We were all angry. But we had a job to do, and we did it."

In his 1997 memoir, *Lasting Valor,* Baker writes scathingly of the military's disdain for black soldiers, who were considered "too worthless to lead ourselves. The Army decided we needed supervision from white Southerners, as if war was plantation work and fighting Germans was picking cotton."

Elsewhere in the book he observes: "Our commanders made it clear that they considered black soldiers failures, no matter what we did, and that they would ensure history reflected that. It was difficult to tell who the bigger racists were—the commanders behind us or the Germans in front of us."

Baker describes a black sergeant, Napoleon Belk, who reminded him of himself:

> Under that dandy figure was an angry black man ready to raise his fists at the smallest slight. Luther Hall, the company first sergeant, had joined me in pulling him aside soon after his arrival and counseling him not to follow his fists to a dishonorable discharge.
>
> "Maybe you don't get it," Belk had challenged me. "Maybe a Wyoming nigger don't know what a Chicago nigger knows."
>
> I got it. Maybe my introduction [to racism] came later in

life than his. Perhaps the sources were different. But still I was a veteran of anger and outrage, and the Army had baptized me like nothing else.

Because black soldiers were routinely denigrated by white commanders, it took decades for them to receive their due. Only in 1994, after a commission determined that blacks had been systematically denied recognition, did the military initiate a process to set things right. An Army board subsequently recommended Baker and the others for the highest award a soldier can receive.

When Baker died in 2010 at the age of ninety, the *Idaho Statesman* reported, "When he received a call telling him he was to receive a Medal of Honor, at first he was astonished, then angry. 'It was something that I felt should have been done a long time ago. . . . If I was worthy of receiving the Medal of Honor in 1945, I should have received it then.'"

When Baker received the medal and when he died, the stories did not focus much on his anger. Instead, they celebrated the fact that he had finally been given his due and remarked on his grace, dignity, and lack of bitterness. None speculated on the cost, to Davis and his fellow soldiers, of carrying their largely silent anger for so many years. But Davis's quiet secret was the norm for men of his age, color, and accomplishments, as it was for many who followed. And that silent anger stemmed almost totally from coming up at a time in America when black people were routinely subjected to the most humiliating forms of disrespect.

The inspiration for *Rage* came to me during a seminar I had organized for a mixed-race group of newspaper managers. During that session, when the conversation turned to career opportunities, it became clear that the white and black managers had a very different take: without exception, the blacks felt that the deck was stacked against them and as a result they were frustrated and angry. I discovered that what was true for those black managers in the newspaper industry was true for blacks throughout corporate America.

Rage was a revelation to many readers. But its central message should not have been a surprise to readers familiar with the thinking of those who had chronicled the African American experience. Writers from Baldwin to Richard Wright to Grier and Cobbs had already laid the foundation for a work that made the point that material comfort and status did not eliminate rage if one still felt powerless in the face of discrimination and racist assumptions. And until very recently, that sense of powerlessness was palpable—an inevitable consequence of the conviction, rooted in custom and history, that America was a white man's country.

Stephen Douglas, who debated and beat Abraham Lincoln in the Illinois Senate contest of 1858, spelled it out during those debates: "This Government was made by our fathers on the white basis . . . made by white men for the benefit of white men and their posterity forever." The signers meant "white men, men of European birth and European descent and had no reference either to the negro, the savage Indians, the Fejee, the Malay, or any other inferior and degraded race."

In "The American Dream and the American Negro," published in the *New York Times Magazine* in 1965, Baldwin wrote,

> It is a terrible thing for an entire people to surrender to the notion that one-ninth of its population is beneath them. Until the moment comes when we, the Americans, are able to accept the fact that my ancestors are both black and white, that on that continent we are trying to forge a new identity, that we need each other, that I am not a ward of America, I am not an object of missionary charity, I am one of the people who built the country—until this moment comes there is scarcely any hope for the American dream. If the people are denied participation in it, by their very presence they will wreck it. And if that happens it is a very grave moment for the West.

Well, *the people* did not wreck the American Dream. Instead, the civil rights movement picked up steam and forced America to grapple with, and eventually embrace, the notion of real equality.

And now we have arrived at that moment when black hopes, once held in check by the weight of prejudice and discrimination, have begun to soar free and when black rage—corrosive, hidden, yet omnipresent—is ebbing. We have arrived, in short, at a pivotal and defining moment in history, one that has far-ranging implications for virtually every aspect of America's future—and particularly for the dialogue about social mobility and equality.

In his acclaimed 1944 study *The American Dilemma,* Gunnar Myrdal dwelt at length on America's founding contradiction: though the "American Creed" embraced equality, America in reality was a brutally segregated, unequal place. In *Notes on the State of Virginia,* Thomas Jefferson alluded to that damning contradiction and its inevitable (perhaps divine) reckoning:

> And with what execration should the statesman be loaded, who permitting one half the citizens thus to trample on the rights of the other, transforms those into despots, and these into enemies, destroys the morals of the one part, and the amor patriae of the other. For if a slave can have a country in this world, it must be any other in preference to that in which he is born to live and labour for another. . . . Indeed I tremble for my country when I reflect that God is just: that his justice cannot sleep for ever. . . . The Almighty has no attribute which can take side with us in such a contest.

So what happens when those contradictions get resolved? What happens when the nation finally accepts the idea that blacks should be as free as whites and that blacks, Latinos, and other people of color can be as ambitious as whites? What happens when the energy invested in justifying that founding contradiction is instead invested in resolving it? America may well be on the verge of finding out.

I am not saying that America has become a racial paradise, but it has become a country where skin color no longer automatically bars one from even the most exalted positions. And people of color with the proper credentials feel increasingly confident that they will get a shot at those top slots. That confidence, of course, is a direct result of the very visible successes of a handful of highfliers—not just in the minority-friendly environs of sports and entertainment but in the upper echelons of corporate America, which, in some respects, is the last bastion of white privilege. It stems also from a new generational sensibility. As John Lewis pointed out, young blacks coming out of universities and business schools now have simply not had the message pounded into their souls, "You cannot do this. You cannot go there."

In describing his black Harvard Law School students, Professor Charles Ogletree observed, "They're trying not to just work on Wall Street but *run* Wall Street. They're trying not just to work in a law firm, but be a partner or a managing partner . . . or to be a CEO of a corporation. They think it can be done because they've seen others. . . . That was unthinkable when I was in law school in the seventies or when I started teaching in the eighties."

Optimism about the new possibilities of America is not limited to Ogletree's students. A series of polls has picked up a sense of hopefulness and confidence that simply wasn't there a few years ago. In a poll conducted in late 2009, the Pew Research Center found that a majority of blacks believe that life is looking up, and only 10 percent believe that the future will be worse. "Despite the bad economy, blacks' assessments about the state of black progress in America have improved more dramatically during the past two years than at any time in the past quarter century," reported Pew. A Gallup poll released in July 2010 found much the same. Gallup was uncertain about the reason for the hopefulness, but noted that "blacks began to be more optimistic around the same time that Barack Obama was inaugurated as president."

Optimism and rage are not natural mates, so as black optimism has grown, rage has diminished. Columbia University provost Claude Steele tells of a white colleague who was convinced that he could see a difference in how blacks treated whites on the street since Obama's election. During a lunch, this psychologist turned to two other white colleagues and asked whether they had noticed that "black people are being nicer to you." Steele was skeptical about his friend's observation, as am I. But I don't doubt that there is a fresh breeze of hope blowing through much of black America. I do not mean to imply that black people are suddenly dancing deliriously in the streets. For all the new hopefulness the polls are uncovering, they are also documenting high levels of perceived bias. Among black Americans, there still exists a pervasive conviction that life is far from fair. But along with that conviction, rooted in a shared experience of discrimination and the expectation of more of the same, there is a growing sense that things may be turning around.

That sense of hope is not universal. Nor does it make sense for everyone—and certainly not for those barely surviving in this world. A friend who works at a major foundation expressed doubt that there was any shift at all among those in whom he had the strongest professional interest—ex-offenders and young men embroiled in the criminal justice system. I found his point intriguing—so much so that I contacted JoAnne Page, president and CEO of the Fortune Society—a Long Island City–based nonprofit group that works with ex-offenders throughout the New York City area—and asked her to arrange, in effect, a small focus group of her clients.

On a warm day in May 2010, several of us gathered around a small table in the Fortune Society's offices in Queens. Over the roar from a nearby construction site, I asked the men about a range of things, including the impact of Obama's election. The most outspoken was Barry Campbell, a thin man of forty-four with a gentle manner who was born in England of Jamaican parents. His parents brought him to New York as a child. Campbell ended up in foster care and became a hustler and a self-confessed child of the streets. He eventually went to prison for aggravated robbery.

Campbell conceded that Obama's election was significant: "Historically, spiritually, culturally, yeah, it means a lot. There's probably a lot that's changed." But for people in his neighborhood, said Campbell,

> it don't mean a difference one way or the other. . . . Nobody on my block gives a damn what Barack Obama's doing right now

> unless he's going to trickle some of that funding down to our neighborhood. *We really don't care.* We just don't. . . . If you go right now into our local barbershop, no one is having a discussion about Barack Obama. They're talking about 50 Cent and Jay Z, and that's just the truth of the matter.

Heads nodded around the table and a young man mumbled, "I agree." Carl Dukes, who spent thirty-one years behind bars for felony murder and is now in his sixties, took another view. "Opportunity, I think, is there now. I think the possibility is greater." Dukes also pointed out that Obama had not been elected solely by black voters: "White people voted for him too."

The thirty-six other Fortune clients whom I interviewed (via questionnaire) were more inclined to agree with Campbell than with Dukes. Only 43 percent thought that Obama's election had resulted in increased opportunities for blacks. And only one-third thought that workplace opportunities for blacks were equal to those for whites. As for their own life prospects, they seemed realistic. Some 94 percent (and three-fourths of those surveyed were unemployed) thought that their criminal records made it harder for them to find work. But even among those men who had seen an uglier side of America than most and who had abundantly good reason to question America's potential for racial fairness, nearly half said that life for minorities was better now than fifteen years ago.

I am not inclined to make much of a survey of a self-selected group of thirty-six people other than to say that I think their responses give weight to the notion that even among those blacks who have the most reason for despair we are seeing signs of new flickers of hope. It is clear to me that the black rage of the 1960s, which burst upon an unsuspecting nation and engulfed many black neighborhoods in flames, has largely receded. This is not to say that anger at white America has vanished, or that bitterness does not run deep. But the corrosive, omnipresent sense of rage is nothing like the force it once was—except perhaps on the fringe of the black community, where groups such as the New Black

Panther Party wear their anger as a shield as they talk of taking on "crackers" and running cops out of their neighborhoods.

Indeed, the biggest locus of anger these days seems not to be in the nation's black and brown communities but in the white heartland, where numerous people are struggling to make sense of what seems to be a world turned upside down—a world they see as increasingly alien, one from which they are growing ever more estranged and which they desperately want to "take back." Indeed, "Take Back America" has become the unofficial manifesto of the so-called Tea Party, a self-styled grassroots social movement fueled largely by anger and resentment.

That anger exploded in particularly venomous form at an anti–health care bill demonstration convened by Tea Party activists on Capitol Hill in March 2010. In the course of that protest, according to numerous accounts, Georgia congressman John Lewis was greeted with chants of "nigger." Emanuel Cleaver, a black congressman from Missouri, was spat on, and Congressman Barney Frank, who is openly gay, was called "faggot."

In a statement released shortly after the incident, Cleaver said, "I led the first demonstrations in South Carolina. . . . And quite frankly I heard some things today I have not heard since that day . . . when I was marching to try and get off the back of the bus." Cleaver was "disappointed that in the twenty-first century our national discourse has devolved to the point of name-calling and spitting," said his spokesperson.

When I reached Barney Frank several days after the encounter, he said that he had not seen a social movement featuring such angry and ugly speech in years: "I think you have to go back to the sixties, early seventies." The hateful talk then, he observed, was from the radical left, the likes of Students for a Democratic Society. Now, he observed, the divisive, vile rhetoric came from the Tea Party, egged on by, and amplified through, the right-wing media.

For Ben Jealous, the young (then thirty-seven) head of the NAACP, the ugly incident evoked images of the Jim Crow South at its worst. Several months later, at the NACCP's annual convention in Kansas City, Missouri, Jealous spearheaded a move to condemn the noxious behavior. With his blessing, delegates unanimously passed a resolution accusing Tea Party protesters of engaging in "explicitly racist behavior" and of displaying signs and posters "intended to degrade people of color generally and President Barack Obama specifically." The resolution criticized Tea Party leaders for not apologizing and for encouraging "such racist behavior rather than fully repudiating it."

"We need to nip this in the bud," Jealous told me just after the resolution passed. The Tea Party, he argued, was playing a cynical game—the same "hide the ball beneath the sheet" game played by the White Citizens' Council in the 1950s and 1960s. The White Citizens' Council (known as the Citizens' Councils of America), one of the most vicious antiblack organizations of the Old South, served as the white-glove arm of the Ku Klux Klan and sanctioned hatred, even murder, in the name of segregation—even as the lawyers, legislators, and businessmen who were the backbone of the council hid behind a facade of civility and respectability.

"They used to say, 'We're not the Klan. We're respectable citizens who are concerned about states' rights and taxes.' And we're saying we're not going to tolerate that again. It was wrong then, and it's wrong now. If you have racists and bigots in your ranks, denounce them and push them out of your organization," said Jealous.

Jealous was disturbed not only by the behavior at the Capitol Hill rally but by signs that had appeared at various Tea Party protests depicting President Obama as a monkey or suggesting that he be lynched. He was equally outraged at a fund-raising solicitation sent out by the proprietor of TeaParty.org headlined "Obama Pimping Obama-Care, One Last Time!" The fund-raising request featured a mustached Obama in a furry, feathered hat posing as a pimp. Jealous was also troubled by the eagerness with which blatantly racist hate groups—such as Stormfront and the Council of Conservative Citizens—had aligned themselves with the Tea Party. Even David Duke, the former Ku Klux Klan leader, had embraced the Tea Party, noted Jealous.

Sure enough, in a video endorsement of the Tea Party circulated on the Internet, Duke warns of forces trying to "make our people a minority in our own country," accuses Jews of trying to gain control of the Tea Party movement, scoffs at blacks who have appeared onstage at Tea Party events, and defends Tea Partiers as "American people who have watched in silent anger while the nation of our forefathers has been destroyed. The Tea Party movement, as the original Tea Party, is about preserving our heritage and our freedom."

"When David Duke sees the Tea Party go by, he assumes that that's his parade," said Jealous.

Given the menagerie of white supremacists, white nationalists, anti-Semites, and other hate-spewing oddballs who have chosen to place themselves under the Tea Party's umbrella, it's hardly surprising that Jealous was concerned. More interesting, in some respects, was the reaction of various Tea Party spokespeople who, while refusing to repudiate the bigots who carried their banner, fell over themselves denying that theirs was a racist movement.

Even before the formal vote at the NAACP convention, the Tea Party chapter in nearby St. Louis had put out a resolution condemning the NAACP for "lowering itself to the dishonorable position of a partisan political attack dog" and demanding that the organization withdraw its "bigoted, false and inflammatory resolution." After the resolution passed, I called Bill Hennessy, a spokesman for the St. Louis Tea Party, to get a better sense of his reaction and that of his colleagues.

Hennessy acknowledged that racist kooks sometimes show up at Tea Party events, but insisted that the Tea Party didn't put up with them. He described an incident "where there was a guy with some Nazi regalia on his shirt and hat, and we chased him out." He added, "We have a zero tolerance for anybody who's going to act like an idiot and embarrass us." He rejected the notion that anything about the Tea Party's message draws such people: "The fact that there are a whole lot of people with some political purpose gathered on a spot is, I would say, what attracts them." He also dismissed Jealous's White Citizens' Council comparison: "He's absolutely wrong. And you know what, he knows better. He's not just wrong: he's lying."

I asked him why the Tea Party didn't just denounce groups like the Council of Conservative Citizens, which considers itself the reincarnation of the White Citizens' Council. Hennessy responded:

> I'm not going to denounce any specific organization. I will tell you I will have nothing to do with the Council of Conservative Citizens personally, I won't . . . I don't know enough about them to condemn the organizations. I can tell you that I do know enough about them—it bothers me enough—that I won't have anything to do with them. And honestly, I don't sit around and study these organizations. I don't do this stuff for a living. I've got a regular job. . . . I'm a solution engineer for a marketing and motivation company in St. Louis. . . . I will warn people to stay away from those organizations. And if people I know wander into them and stay there, they're not going to be hanging around with me anymore. *I can guarantee you that.* We all have absolutely zero tolerance for that nonsense.

"What frustrates me about this more than anything," said Hennessy at another point in the conversation,

> is the work that needs to be done to fix the problems that we have in the country, especially in the African American community, where you've got 15½ percent unemployment—in many places over 20 percent, especially for males. You have crime problems, drug problems, single-female heads of household. That needs to be fixed. And we think the way to do that is by creating an opportunity society where the economy and the opportunity and the growth and the networking in communities allows people to take risks to achieve and pursue happiness according to their own terms and to achieve their economic destiny. . . . And it just frustrated me that an organization like the NAACP would interrupt the progress toward that goal to mess around with something as stupid as this.

I also called Deneen Borelli, a vocal Tea Party advocate and prominent black face on the conservative talk-show circuit. Borelli described herself as a full-time fellow for Project 21, a Washington-based black conservative public policy group and an offshoot of the National Center for Public Policy Research. The center is a conservative think tank founded in 1982 "to provide the conservative movement with a versatile and energetic organization capable of responding quickly and decisively to fast-breaking issues," according to its website.

Her bio on Project 21's website says that Borelli earned a BA degree from Pace University in New York and previously worked as a manager of media relations for the Congress of Racial Equality and in the information management department of Phillip Morris. She also volunteers at her church, enjoys target shooting, and has worked as a runway fashion model. It was not clear what made her an expert on political movements, but I was nonetheless curious to see how a self-declared black conservative and Tea Party advocate, who was apparently paid for her perspective, would respond to Jealous's demand.

"I am one of the prominent speakers in the Tea Party movement from day one," she declared. "And one thing that is not tolerated is racism or any bigotry whatsoever." She slammed the NAACP for not condemning the New Black Panthers. Virtually every Tea Party defender made the same argument, even though the New Black Panthers have never publicly aligned themselves with the NAACP, as David Duke and Stormfront have tied themselves to the Tea Party.

I told Borelli that I understood that the Tea Party itself may not be racist. So what was stopping the group from simply declaring, "We will not tolerate white supremacists and white racists, and we denounce these various racist groups that have claimed that they are involved in the Tea Party"? She responded with a lecture—the essence of which was that the Tea Party movement has nothing to do with race—before offering up a rationale for why the Tea Party cannot collectively take these groups on: "First of all, there is no one single group that speaks for the entire Tea Party movement. It's a grassroots effort. . . . So you're not going to get one press release from one certain group that's going to say X, Y, Z."

She clinched the argument with a statement I found baffling: "The group is about individuals who do not like big government and have a problem with Obama's policies, and has absolutely nothing to do [with] President Obama's race, because if that was the case, he wouldn't be president of the United States."

I was not sure, I told her, how Tea Party positions had anything to do with President Obama's election.

"Because an overwhelming majority of Americans are part of the Tea Party movement," she shot back.

When I told her that polls put support for the party at about 20 percent (actually 18 percent according to a *New York Times*/CBS poll of April 2010), she replied, "I don't have that data in front of me."

I took the reluctance of Tea Party types to denounce racist supporters as simple political expediency. Most political groups don't want to get into the business of alienating supporters, however obnoxious they might be. But what struck me as interesting, aside from the illogic of some of Borelli's arguments, was the vehemence with which she (and other Tea Party defenders) tried to knock down the accusation of racism.

Indeed, the week after the NAACP made its demand, Tea Party supporters were more determined than ever to rebut the charge of racism—or at least to prove that blacks are just as racist as Tea Party supporters. They did so with a video, gleefully promoted by conservative talk-show hosts, that purported to show a black U.S. Department of Agriculture employee admitting that she had discriminated against white farmers. The story quickly unraveled when it came out that the video was heavily and misleadingly edited. The employee at its center, Shirley Sherrod, had not discriminated against anyone. She had gone out of her way to help a white couple save their farm—and they showed their gratitude by coming to her defense.

Soon Sherrod was swimming in apologies—from the secretary of agriculture, who had fired and reproached her; from the NAACP, which had applauded her firing; and even from President Obama, who told her during a seven-minute call that he regretted she had been put through such an ordeal.

That Tea Party devotees would doctor and distribute a videotape raised obvious questions about honesty and ethics. But sleazy and reckless as it was, the scheme also highlighted a major difference between Tea Partiers and the White Citizens' Council—just as it underscored the big difference between 1960 and 2010.

Though the White Citizens' Council publicly distanced itself from violence and acts of illegality, it fervently embraced segregation—and the racism behind it. Segregation, as the council saw it, was a social good essential to maintaining the blessed southern way of life. In a series on the civil rights movement published in October 2000, the *Jackson* (Tennessee) *Sun* noted that during the 1960s Tennessee's White Citizens' Council ran advertisements in the *Sun* promoting segregation. The *Sun* also reprinted language from an old pamphlet issued by the Association of Citizens titled "Why Does Your Community Need a Citizens' Council?"

> Maybe your community has had no racial problems! This may be true; however, you may not have a fire, yet you maintain a fire department. You can depend on one thing: The NAACP (National Association for the Agitation of Colored People), aided by alien influences, bloc vote seeking politicians and left-wing do-gooders, will see that you have a problem in the near future.
>
> The Citizens' Council is the South's answer to the mongrelizers. We will not be integrated. We are proud of our white blood and our white heritage of sixty centuries. . . .
>
> We are certainly not ashamed of our traditions, our conservative beliefs, nor our segregated way of life.

Whatever sins the Tea Party may be guilty of, publicly promoting segregation is not among them. Indeed, to the amusement of David

Duke, its leadership (however disingenuously) tries to project the image of a multiracial grassroots movement. It's impossible to imagine the White Citizens' Council promoting blacks as members or putting blacks onstage. That the Tea Party needs to do so to maintain credibility as a mainstream organization says volumes about the direction in which America has moved in the last fifty years.

In an article published in the *Wall Street Journal* in May 2006, author Shelby Steele argues that white guilt—over racism and imperialism—has not only ruined race relations at home but undermined American authority and the war effort in Iraq and potentially elsewhere.

> Possibly white guilt's worst effect is that it does not permit whites—and nonwhites—to appreciate something extraordinary: the fact that whites in America, and even elsewhere in the West, have achieved a truly remarkable moral transformation. One is forbidden to speak thus, but it is simply true. There are no serious advocates of white supremacy in America today, because whites see this idea as morally repugnant. If there is still the odd white bigot out there surviving past his time, there are millions of whites who only feel goodwill toward minorities.

I disagree with much of Shelby Steele's analysis. I certainly don't see white guilt as being anywhere near as pervasive as he insists it is, and I think it has nothing at all to do with military readiness. Nor do I see anyone prohibiting anybody—and certainly not Steele himself—from talking about whites' "moral transformation." But he is absolutely right that blatant white supremacy is functionally extinct. For all the Tea Party's fuming and fury, only those on the outer fringes claim white supremacy as their essential cause. So what is all the anger about?

To better understand Tea Party anger, I called Dale Robertson, who operates TeaParty.org, which implores "all patriots" to "Take Back America." Robertson, who claims to have served twenty-two years in the Navy and the Marines, considers himself to be a Tea Party founder. Many other Tea Party activists disagree and have denounced him as a loose cannon, a self-promoter who uses "disgusting language," in the words of a spokesperson for the Houston Tea Party Society. There is indeed a picture, widely circulated on the Internet, that shows Robertson holding a sign that appears to use a racial slur. It is hard to say precisely what the sign means, since the word in question—"Niggar"—seems to be misspelled. Robertson was also the one who sent out the "Obama Pimping Obama-Care, One Last Time!" e-mail solicitation.

Nonetheless, I thought he might be able to provide some insight into the source of Tea Party rage. So I called him and asked who it was exactly that he wanted to take America back from. His answer: "These people in Washington who are entrenched." When our conversation turned to the question of illegal immigration, I asked whether he was concerned at all about alienating Latinos or blacks. "I'm in Texas, I grew up with a lot of Hispanics and blacks, and there's plenty of Hispanics who are born and raised and came to this country legally, and they're just as upset about illegal immigration as anybody now," he replied. When I asked about his personal motivations for getting involved in the movement, he responded with a short anecdote:

> I started a coffee shop after I got out of the military here in Houston, and I kept getting broken into. And I realized the political forces have destroyed our country to the point that a guy like me who just put a hundred thousand dollars out wasn't going to have a chance, because we have basically become so desperate as a society that we're willing to rob each other. And we're not going to be able to give the little guy a chance.

As an angry, middle-aged, middle-class, college-educated, white male, Robertson is somewhat typical of Tea Party supporters. According to the *New York Times*/CBS poll, 75 percent are age forty-five or older, 70 percent have at least some college education, and 59 percent are male. Only 1 percent of Tea Party supporters are black, 1 percent are Asian, and 3 percent are of Hispanic origin. Six percent classify themselves as "other," and 89 percent say they are white. Some 53 percent describe themselves as angry, compared to 19 percent of all Americans.

Tea Parties are more than twice as likely as all other Americans (25 percent versus 11 percent) to say that Obama's policies favor blacks over whites. They are also more likely (52 percent to 28 percent) to agree that in recent years "too much has been made of the problems facing black people." Eighty-four percent hold an unfavorable opinion of Barack Obama. Seventy-three percent think that he doesn't "understand the needs and problems of people like [myself]." And 75 percent think that he does not share "the values most Americans try to live by." What is most stunning is that only a minority of Tea Partiers—41 percent—are willing to concede that Obama was born in the United States. The majority either say that they think he was born abroad (30 percent) or that they do not know (29 percent)—despite the fact that pollsters told respondents that the U.S. Constitution requires the nation's president to be a "natural-born" citizen.

In an article titled "Tea Party Supporters Doing Fine, but Angry Nonetheless," *New York Times* reporter Kate Zernike noted that Tea Party supporters "are better educated and wealthier than the general public. They are just as likely to be employed, and more likely to describe their economic situation as very or fairly good."

So where does all that gloom and anger come from? Clearly, a lot of the anger among certain whites stems from the same things that have fueled a new sense of optimism among blacks. Obama's election, widely seen among blacks as a harbinger of brighter days, has been seen by many conservative whites as a tragic event. The ongoing economic crisis has compounded that sense of unease, even among many who are not seriously affected personally. And to top it all off, many Americans feel a growing sense of dread over what America is becoming in an ethnic and racial sense—as Latinos pour in from the south and blacks rise to increasingly visible positions.

"It's not really driven by antiblack animus," said Professor Manning Marable. "It's a hatred of the state. And there's a desire to go back in time." But he conceded that race plays a role in the Tea Party movement. "What they're talking about is a time when racial minorities weren't in charge, a time when Negroes knew their place. That's really the heart of what nativist populism has historically been. They're trying to recapture the past that constantly recedes from view."

Many Americans are "very uncomfortable with this large number of Latinos, particularly darker-skinned Latinos, coming into the country," Cesar Perales, president of Latino Justice PRLDEF (formerly the Puerto Rican Legal Defense and Education Fund), told me.

> And what I hear . . . is things like, "I'm sick and tired of having to dial 2 for English. . . . Why are all of these signs up in Spanish?" And I think what is really bothering these people is a sense that their position in the society is threatened, that they are going to be worse off tomorrow then they are today. And they are angry. And, frankly . . . having a black president makes it worse because that is evidence to this large number of Americans that their world has changed.

One sign of the depth of that unease—and not only among self-declared Tea Partiers—was the introduction of a bill in Arizona to deny citizenship to children born to illegal immigrants—despite the constitutional guarantee of citizenship to all born within this nation's borders. In the town of Prescott, Arizona, some residents were so disturbed by the dark face of a Latino boy on a school mural that officials demanded that the artist lighten his face—"in order to make it a more comfortable situation," according to the artist.

What better way to mobilize around all those fears than with a campaign to "take the country back"—even if it is less than clear exactly whom it is to be taken back from, or how that process is supposed to work?

But what makes this moment fundamentally different from backlash moments of the past is that while the growing visibility and impact of people of color is implicated as part of the problem, it cannot be the explicit focus of rage, at least not in any way that appears blatantly racist. So, with the Tea Party, we get a ragtag band of angry activists raging against, well, the political establishment and the status quo—which, ironically, is precisely what Barack Obama campaigned against.

So what does that say about America's ability to move forward as one nation? It says, for one, that agreeing that racism is evil and even electing a black president have not exactly put the racial genie in the bottle. In her spirited Facebook defense of the Tea Party from the NAACP's attack, Sarah Palin declared, "It seemed that with the election of our first black president, our country had become a new 'post-racial' society."

In posting the note, Palin was, in effect, conceding that we are not yet there, but she was also doing something else. She was underscoring, even as she denounced the NAACP, the point made by Shelby Steele in his *Wall Street Journal* article that racism no longer has a serious constituency. The challenge facing those on the left as well as those on the right is how to turn that relatively new consensus against racism into a meaningful commitment to equality.

"Our country is in an incredibly fluid moment, and a new racial contract is being negotiated," observed john powell, head of the Kirwan Institute for the Study of Race and Ethnicity at Ohio State University, during a discussion of this current age.

That contract will not be drawn up along the lines that most Tea Partiers want for the simple reason that the old America is gone. And for all their anger and noise, the Tea Party cannot bring it back—no more than it can bring back the unsettled prairie, the kerosene lamp, or teenagers blissfully unaware of sex. At some level all but its most irrational members realize this, which is why Tea Party leaders fight against accusations of racism and struggle to adapt to the new America even as they refuse to let go of the old.

The Tea Party, in other words, is not America's future—though, as the 2010 midterm elections made clear, it is very much a part of

America's present. And it will continue to complicate any attempt at postpartisan governance. As Marable put it:

> They refuse to play by the rules of the political game that even conservatives do. [John] Kennedy once said, to govern is to choose. You can't govern without compromise. They don't intend to govern. They intend to disrupt and destroy. . . . They're so desperate for finding ways to recapture the past, and so quick to demonize their opponents. That movement will express itself in different types of ways over the next twenty years. It's not going to go away. It may morph into something else.

Nonetheless, in time—and sooner than Tea Partiers believe—that particular brand of rage will wither away. It is too rooted in old ideas and in old people to survive much beyond this generation. The challenge for thinking people of conscience will be seeing our way beyond the fog of this current anger to the construction of a society, anchored in the future instead of the past, that is strong enough to embrace us all.

Chapter Two

Children of the Dream

If the future doesn't belong to those looking to "take back America," to whom does it belong? In a demographic sense, it will increasingly belong, we are told, to ethnic groups considered to be minorities today. But in a more general sense, it clearly belongs to those unafraid to look forward, to those ready to construct something new instead of those yearning for the old. Since 1963, a New York–based organization called A Better Chance has been striving to mold such people by preparing young Americans—mostly racial and ethnic minorities—from around the country to take their place among the nation's elite. It sends them to top-ranked secondary schools and, at its best, fosters a sense of limitless potential.

Many of the young participants hail from schools that essentially function as forts—walled off from communities hostile to young dreams, these schools typically feature a police car out front, a metal detector at the door, and a hint of violence in the air. "By the time you get in, you're stressed out," said ABC president Sandra Timmons. She contrasted these schools with the ones where her ABC students end up. "You pull up to one of these places with rolling green hills and somebody lying on the bench reading a book." You enter a French class "set up like a French café with . . . little tablecloths and the Eiffel Tower in the background. And it's next to the library with thirty thousand volumes." There is a world of difference between schools "where stairwells [have] been made into a makeshift classroom" and those "built to promote love of learning." ABC seeks out such schools, and it aspires to give kids a shot not just at a good education but at those life-expanding experiences and high-powered expectations that wealthy Americans enjoy as a perquisite of class.

Some years ago, over lunch, New York mayor Ed Koch told me his solution to the educational crisis in America's poor black communities. He suggested shipping the kids off to something roughly resembling an Israeli kibbutz. I found the suggestion off-putting: Koch seemed to be saying that these youngsters had to be removed from the only culture they had known in order to thrive. On later reflection, however, I realized that Koch might have been on to something—that there are in fact many harmful influences in poor communities that prevent most kids born into such circumstances from realizing their potential.

I e-mailed Koch and reminded him of our conversation. "Your memory is excellent," he replied.

> I believed then and currently do that we should create a dozen regional public prep schools where children below the poverty line should in competition be given access to sleepaway schools similar to the schools now available for the upper-middle class. All expenses would be paid by the federal government, which would set the curriculum and run the schools. We should see where such an experiment takes us.

In many respects, that is what ABC already does (though its schools are not primarily funded by the federal government and most of them are not public). Every year it invites students to participate in a yearlong selection process that ends with about five hundred of them attending some of America's most celebrated boarding, day, and public schools. And since the program has been going on for nearly fifty years now, we know that this experiment works quite well.

In the early 1990s, I wrote *The Rage of a Privileged Class* because I thought that the successful African Americans who had struggled so hard to make it and had crashed through barriers impenetrable to previous generations had something valuable to say. They could describe, in the most personal terms, what the journey had cost them, what had compelled them to make it, and what, because of it, they had won.

I saw ABC—whose alumni hail from selective academies and prep schools—as a natural starting point for bringing the perspective of the "privileged class" up to date. I am indebted to the 311 ABC alumni who filled out the lengthy survey instrument—and especially to the 80 who also participated in an extensive follow-up interview process.

Most ABC students start out poor. They have not grown up confident that a top-tier secondary school is in their future. Many come from neighborhoods where public schools are temples of mediocrity. And they often face substantial adjustments. For the most part, friends and family are delighted to send the young stars off to their fancy new schools, although one recent ABC grad was probably not alone in worrying that she would "let many people down" because expectations around her had been raised so high. Roughly one-third of survey respondents said that their acceptance by ABC—welcome as it was—had created problems. Many found the new environment alienating. Others were accused by old neighborhood friends of abandoning them.

A woman who graduated from boarding school in 1983 lamented that even her own family "didn't understand the changes in me when I came home." One man, class of 1973,* remembered being "accused of thinking I was better than others because I did not go to public school." A black woman from the class of 2007 was labeled a "white girl" because of her diction. A Latino male, class of 2001, was beaten up when he returned home during winter break: "I attribute it to not fitting in."

---

* All graduation years cited in this chapter are for secondary school graduation unless otherwise noted.

Janice,* class of 1999, ended up "isolating myself from the neighborhood kids and some friends. I entered ABC at age thirteen. At that age, most kids are dealing with various identity issues. Being called a white girl angered me and was stressful. . . . Transitioning to a different school situation was somewhat of an added stress."

"Just the concept of going someplace different was new. So people didn't know about it. It was hard to describe something for which people had no frame of reference," said Francene Young, an oil industry executive working in Houston, class of 1971.

Alan Blackwell's friends in his native South Bronx refused to believe him when he told them his good news. "Most people thought boarding school was a cover story for being in jail." Back then, said Blackwell, who graduated from Choate Rosemary Hall in 1973, "no one in my community was aware of boarding school opportunities. When your peers disappeared for long periods of time, it was assumed that you'd been incarcerated."

For many, the issue was not renegotiating neighborhood ties but trying to feel at home in a foreign place. "I went from a poverty-stricken . . . neighborhood to an environment of jets, yachts, horses. . . . It was a difficult transition, but I learned some important lessons about how to integrate myself among different classes of people," said Yvette Walker, class of 1979.

Dorothy,* class of 1994, had virtually nothing in common with her prep school colleagues. She coped by reminding herself that she did not have to fit in. "I was focused on being a student, being an athlete, and being a role model. I didn't necessarily have a lot of fun, but I was doing what I went there to do."

Vanessa Ortiz, class of 2003, went from a largely Latino community in Los Angeles to the heart of the Midwest. "When I arrived in Minnesota, I was in a state of total culture shock. I had always been ridiculed growing up for being a mixed breed of half-Caucasian and half-Mexican, but to see what a true Norwegian-Scandinavian looked like was mind blowing." Despite her initial astonishment, Ortiz quickly adapted and made her differentness into a virtue: "When I

* This is a pseudonym, as are all named marked with an asterisk.

spoke in my heavy South Central Los Angeles accent, which always caused people to question my background, I never felt annoyed. . . . I simply enjoyed educating others, as I was being educated by them."

Jamie,[*] class of 1995, went from a working-class area of Oakland, California, to Foundation Valley School in Colorado Springs, Colorado: "These kids, for the most part, came from money." What made things easier for Jamie was his friendship with a fellow Oaklander who was a year ahead of him and whose presence made him feel "a wee bit more comfortable."

Erika, class of 1994, credits her prep school experience with helping her to navigate the "extreme segregation" at the University of Pennsylvania. "The experience was hard on the psyche and would have been harder if I hadn't experienced a taste of this already in high school."

ABC president Timmons acknowledged the difficulty of navigating two worlds: "We had one little guy who played the violin, and when he practiced, instead of taking his violin home, he used to leave it at school. He lived in Brooklyn somewhere, and somebody from his family would have to meet him because . . . the kids in the neighborhood would beat him up when he came home with his violin. . . . I don't get as many of those stories now." She speculated that people might be getting more tolerant, or perhaps the existence of charter schools in many inner-city communities is taking the stigma out of intellectual pursuits.

Even those ABC scholars who suffered in pursuit of a good education were overwhelmingly glad to have it. Asked to rate their satisfaction with their secondary school education, 98 percent pronounced themselves satisfied (including 89 percent who said they were "very satisfied").

"I believe that my opportunity to be an ABC scholar saved my life," said Yvette Walker. In leaving Lumberton, North Carolina ("a small, southern, racist town") for Stuart Hall boarding school in Staunton, Virginia, she learned that her life did not have to be "bound by racism." The all-girls school also gave her "confidence as a female."

Reflecting on what had happened to those who remained in her old neighborhood made Vanessa Ortiz feel fortunate: "Half of my graduating class had . . . dropped out, been incarcerated, or died . . . because they had not received the same challenges that I had."

James Forward, raised in South Central Los Angeles, was sent to Lowell Whiteman School in Steamboat Springs, Colorado, and graduated in 1976. Always considered a gifted student, he found that an array of options opened up for him at Whiteman. He went to Europe and Mexico as part of the school's foreign study curriculum, which planted the notion of attending college abroad. "Instead of going into a music program in an American university, I spent my first two years . . . at Schiller College in Strasbourg, France, studying music and theater and speaking French." That experience led to the San Francisco Conservatory of Music and later to the equally prestigious Aspen Music School. He got his master's degree from the University of California at Santa Barbara, which resulted in his meeting Heiichiro Ohyama, then assistant conductor of the Los Angeles Philharmonic and conductor of the Crossroads School Chamber Orchestra, for which he was hired as Ohyama's assistant. "I'm very sure things would have turned out quite differently if I had not had ABC in my life."

Bradford Hobbs left Brooklyn for Lawrence Academy in Groton, Massachusetts, from which he graduated in 1982. Hobbs, founder and principal of BizBrand Foundry, a brand strategy and marketing consultancy, is now a trustee at Lawrence. Like Timmons, he believed that life is getting easier for those who go to prep school from a rough neighborhood. Students are more determined than ever to escape violent communities, he believed, and boarding schools have become more committed to helping these young people succeed. Also, all Americans, including the privileged kids in prep school, have grown more accustomed to cultural and ethnic diversity; when Hobbs was in prep school, he encountered kids who had never interacted with an African American before. Hobbs noted as well that kids from underrepresented groups now often "have parents and alumni . . . who can help them navigate." He had no such network.

Nathan Prince, class of 2002, believed that social media make it easier for those now coming up: "I had about six ABC students from the Amherst program come to my wedding, and we all keep in touch with Facebook. . . . It changes the way that you can keep in contact with people."

By any reasonable standard, ABC alumni are doing well—much better than most Americans, regardless of race. Roughly half (48 percent) report an annual household income of $100,000 or more—at a time when the median household income in America is just over $50,000, under $34,000 for blacks, and less than $39,000 for Latinos.*

But far more impressive than their paychecks is the length of their journey. Many have raced, at breathtaking speed, from near the bottom of the American status heap to somewhere near the top. They embody the dream that you can start out with nothing and pretty much end up with it all. Over 90 percent now live in neighborhoods that are middle class, upper-middle class, or wealthy, though 55 percent grew up poor. Eighty-seven percent reported higher household incomes than their parents at a comparable point in life, and they are also significantly better educated.

Only one-fourth (27percent) of their fathers had completed four years of college or gone further. Another one-fourth of fathers (27 percent) had not even graduated from high school. Their mothers had done a bit better: one-third (34 percent) had earned at least a bachelor's degree, and only 18 percent had not graduated from high school. Nonetheless, 99 percent of the ABC respondents had earned a baccalaureate degree, and 59 percent had graduate training. One-third had ended their education with a master's degree, another 13 percent had a law or medical degree, and 5 percent had earned a PhD. The vast majority—70 percent—lived in communities that were either predominantly white or very integrated.

This stunning story of upward mobility was unfolding at a time

* For detailed survey data, visit www.elliscose.com.

when, even before the Great Recession, moving up was becoming more difficult in America, particularly for people of color. Even black children born into the middle class have a difficult time staying there. A majority "fall below their parents in income and economic status," reported a 2008 study by the Economic Mobility Project of Pew Charitable Trusts, which looked at intergenerational mobility from 1984 to 2004. For those who started out poor, the outlook was particularly bleak: only 4 percent of African American families in the lowest quintile managed to leap into the highest quintile—which is where a majority of ABC alumni comfortably reside.

It seemed likely that the members of this very privileged group—this living testament to the power of faith, hard work, and hope—would be practically overcome with joy as they reflect on America's progress and in particular as they digest the implications of an African American becoming president. And certainly there was elation over Obama's victory, which has shown "black men that anything is possible," proclaimed Jamie,* voicing a common refrain.

But while jubilation is part of the reaction, it is not the total reaction. Many believed that Obama's victory has made America an unhappier, more volatile place. Only 27 percent of those I surveyed believed that his election has led to better race relations. And only 27 percent thought that his election has led to increased opportunities for blacks in the workplace. What they did believe, overwhelmingly, was that Obama's election has caused whites to leap to a false conclusion. His "election and presidency has led to a perception *among whites* of increased opportunities for blacks that exceeds the reality of the present situation," said 80 percent of respondents.

My ABC mega focus group didn't necessarily agree with Gallup's respondents who said that Martin Luther King's dream has been fulfilled. Nor did it echo Pew, which reported in January 2010 that, despite the bad economy, "blacks' assessments about the state of black progress in America have improved more dramatically during the past two years than at any time in the past quarter century." A majority of African Americans also told Pew that Obama's election has made race relations better.

So why are the ABC folks so much more pessimistic than Pew's respondents? For one thing, David Thomas, the black Harvard Business School professor, is right. In the aftermath of Obama's victory, "irrational exuberance" reigned. During that moment, Obama could have been proclaimed the new messiah and a substantial number would have said, "Amen."

Even Pew, in its survey one year after Obama's election, registered what could be interpreted as a dip in black optimism—at least as regards interracial relations. When asked in 2008, some 74 percent of black voters had predicted that race relations would improve during Obama's presidency, but two years later only 54 percent said that race relations had in fact improved. Something similar happened with Gallup's numbers. The June before Obama took office, 65 percent of blacks thought that race relations would improve if he won. When asked the same question one year after his election, 53 percent said that race relations had improved. Interestingly, when the wording of the question was changed and blacks were asked whether "in the years ahead" Obama's presidency would improve race relations, 79 percent of blacks (and 58 percent of non-Hispanic whites) said yes.

What can we make of all this? Clearly, whatever their initial expectation may have been, many blacks have concluded that Obama did not exactly usher in an era of racial harmony. Their excitement has been tempered, at least in the short term. But when asked about "the years ahead"—phrasing that puts any reckoning into a faraway future—most blacks (indeed, most Americans) were willing to have faith.

Also, the ABC alumni responses came in at a time when hate speech directed at the president was growing ever more virulent, when nativism was raging, and when Arizona was passing undocumented immigrant legislation that was essentially an invitation to racial profiling. It was a time, in short, when white resentments were in clear view and on people's minds.

Obama's presidency "has really brought out the hatred in a lot of people toward people of color, especially black people," commented Veda McClain, an educational consultant in Kentucky, class of 1975. His presidency "has emboldened an element in white America that questions the very value of majority-minority civility, tolerance and acceptance," said attorney Marlon Lewis. Jacqueline,* a self-employed architect in Stone Mountain, Georgia, class of 1999, noticed that white coworkers who had not formerly considered politics a fit subject for workplace chatter were eager to criticize Obama: "There are times when the environment is very intense."

"I guess my opinions have changed, especially after hearing all the Tea Party stuff and things that people have been saying and images of him on posters and things like that," said Deborah,* class of 2005. "I don't think things have improved."

The upsurge in hateful rhetoric has reminded many people that America's contorted race relationships are not about to be rearranged overnight. And for many ABC alumni, who are better educated and more sophisticated than most Americans, the idea that things would turn around just because a black man is in office seemed silly. As Sharon,* a longtime finance professional, class of 1985, put it, "Anyone who thought that electing the first African American president of the United States would improve race relations in our country was naively optimistic."

On the other hand, she added,

> I believe that having an African American president has caused all people, black and white, to confront values that were put on the shelf. It seemed that everything was going along smoothly. Young black and white folks were going to school and hanging out together, working together, worshiping together, even dating and marrying one another. Racism wasn't discussed. It seemed to be organically taking care of itself. With President Obama's election . . . deep-seated and perhaps forgotten . . . beliefs and opinions have resurfaced. This is particularly

apparent in older Americans. . . . Therefore, in my opinion, his election has hurt race relations. However, I think that's a good thing. It's much easier to confront and address an issue if people are willing to admit that there is a problem.

Even though ABC alumni generally rejected the notion that Obama's presidency has suddenly improved race relations, they remained extraordinarily upbeat. Ninety-three percent said that they are satisfied with their life; nearly half thought that blacks are better off now than fifteen years ago; and nearly 60 percent judged things to be better for Latinos. There is a sense, particularly among younger respondents, that racial prejudice is fading.

Amalia,* a UCLA graduate student, ABC class of 2006, grew up in Oakland, California, surrounded by people of all ethnicities: "Both of my parents grew up in the Philippines and immigrated here as adults, so they viewed other races a lot differently than I did." They hated seeing their children date outside of their race or Catholic religion. "For my sister especially this was hard, as she went from a serious Punjabi Indian boyfriend to a Baptist black boyfriend in high school and college. It has been six years, and I see that my parents have changed some of their views about race. My sister is now engaged to her Baptist black boyfriend, and my parents are fully supportive of the couple."

Jamal Releford of Decatur, Georgia, class of 2009, noted that his parents "grew up during a time when they were facing racism" while the civil right movement was in bloom. "I feel like now that we're recovering from that . . . I feel like it can only get better."

When asked whether the standard of living would be better for their children, more than half of ABC respondents said yes, and two-thirds thought it would be easier for them to "achieve the American Dream." Some of that sentiment no doubt stems from the natural optimism that any loving parent has for his or her own child. But it is also something else: a solid vote of confidence in the America of the future and in America's ability and inclination to open up more than it ever has for young people of color—or at least for those whose parents have degrees from fancy prep schools along with the contacts, cachet, and other advantages that come with that.

This faith coexists with a reality, according to Pew, in which discrimination is seen as a huge fact of life. "Big majorities of the public," reported Pew, believed that Hispanics, blacks, and women face discrimination. And nearly half said that Asian Americans and whites are victims of prejudice.

Indeed, while all groups that Pew studied saw themselves as subject to discrimination to some degree, there were stark differences in how serious that discrimination was deemed to be. Some 43 percent of blacks said they suffered "a lot" of discrimination, whereas only 13 percent of whites thought blacks were so afflicted. And 10 percent of whites thought whites also suffered "a lot" of discrimination.

ABC alumni also perceived a high degree of discrimination: 70 percent of black respondents thought blacks faced a lot, and 64 percent of Latino respondents believed the same to be true of Latinos.

Audrey,* class of 1970, complained that at work "I always have to be the sharpest around. I have to be the quickest, the most creative, and pretty much ahead of my white counterparts in order to at least be abreast of them." Things had gotten somewhat better over the years, "but it's still not where it should be. I see young white people getting promotions or getting jobs, and they're mediocre at best."

While a majority reported occasional discrimination, only 9 percent said that they often face discrimination at work. And among those reporting discrimination, two-thirds said that it had not significantly affected their career. Workplace discrimination was something they faced, they were saying, but in the end it had not defeated them.

By contrast, an overwhelming majority reported discrimination outside the workplace—from shopkeepers, cops, taxi drivers, and teachers. Their stories were often detailed and filled with outrage and pain. Frank,* class of 1979, told one of them.

Currently working as a university dean, Frank had his first serious brush with bigotry while attending college in Oklahoma, shortly after graduating from an ABC school. He called up and secured an interview with a hotel that he had heard was hiring, but when he showed up, "They didn't even talk to me." The manager waved him away. He called again and was told to come in, but when he showed up, they again turned him away. "I figured maybe that's just the way the area was back in the seventies."

After moving with his fiancée to New York City in the early 1980s, he went looking for an apartment. Over and over, people told him over the phone that he and his fiancée sounded perfect: "a young couple, about to get married, both with good jobs." But when he showed up, there was nothing available. After about ten such incidents, "I started keeping track of each building and address," said Frank. Finally, in despair, he turned to his minister, a white man, who called up a friend who was a landlord but neglected to tell him the couple's race. "So we showed up, and the landlord's assistant showed us the apartment." But the apartment didn't come through. After the couple had been quietly rejected in several neighborhoods over a period of months, "it got down to the last few weeks before our wedding. So we went ahead and settled into [predominantly black] Stuyvesant Heights, [where] we fit right in."

Asked to reflect on those experiences, Frank said, "I think it's a closed society for minorities who want to live outside of an area that is supposed to be where they are. [And] I think that for most minorities, they're not going to complain . . . because they're uncomfortable."

Stories like Frank's were a large part of *The Rage of a Privileged Class*. And it was not just complaints about blatant and random racism—being hassled in stores, disrespected by cops, scorned by educational and social inferiors—that made the stories interesting; it was also a sense, pervasive among the highly educated people I interviewed, that there was simply no way for them to get what they felt they deserved from American society.

Psychologist Linda Anderson doesn't believe that things have changed very much in terms of the racial slights blacks are likely to experience in random encounters: "Within a work context, within the context of professional success, we may be lauded, we may be experiencing the level of respect and affirmation that we deserve; however, that doesn't necessarily translate into other domains of our lives at all." Where she does see change, however, is in the faith that blacks are showing in their ability to achieve the American Dream—at least in terms of opportunities in the workplace. As she put it, "There's an increasing motivation among those who feel that they are in close proximity to actually becoming, or living, some of that dream."

What strikes me is how much the sense of futility—so evident when I wrote *Rage*—has faded, and how much faith there is now, particularly among well-educated, younger people, that they will be allowed to shine, at least at work.

Yes, the vast majority of ABC respondents said that blacks and Latinos "confront a glass ceiling in corporate America," but only half believed that such a ceiling was in place where *they* worked. And among those under forty, the number drops dramatically: 43 percent of younger respondents saw a glass ceiling for blacks at their present workplace, and only 37 percent saw one for Latinos.

Those under forty were also more likely to believe that employers will treat them fairly, and some (19 percent of all respondents and 21 percent of those under forty) actually saw their race as an advantage "when competing, professionally, against white peers with comparable educational credentials."

"I've personally never had a negative experience as far as discrimination is concerned, but I am aware of the fact that being considered someone [of] Hispanic origin . . . has played into my favor," said Raymond Ramos, who graduated in 1987 from Deerfield Academy in Massachusetts. "By the spring of my junior year, I was receiving a great deal of interest from colleges. And almost every letter . . . stated that they were interested in me because I was a minority student."

But even many of those who *didn't* see their race as an advantage, who instead struggled against what they perceived as prejudice, nonetheless refused to let racial slights discourage them.

"I do expect to encounter some glass ceilings, both because of my race and my gender," said Lydia Williams of Riverdale, Georgia, class of 2000. "I plan on going into medicine, and historically African Americans have never been well represented in the medical systems. And older physicians aren't accustomed to the influx of younger African Americans." But though she expected some resistance, that was not going to affect what she decided to do.

Asia Hoe, a recent graduate of Bryn Mawr College, ABC class of 2005, works for a website strategy marketing firm. She has wrestled with the issue of racial limits and how they will affect her: "I believe race often plays out in much more of a covert fashion than it did for my parents' generation, but to declare that it is a non-issue is a . . . mistake," she said. Even Barack Obama, she argued, has not escaped racism: "A black man can become president, but there are still those who will fight to strip him of the respect that role deserves." As to whether she herself would face limits dictated by race or gender, she was uncertain. "I could definitely face it one day. Women remain outnumbered in my industry, but there are signs that the tide is turning. . . . At times I think my race and gender can be viewed as an advantage."

Daysy, a college student from California, thought it was unlikely that she would encounter a glass ceiling simply because of her choice of profession. "I want to do social work in the future, especially focusing on foster care agencies in New York City." Those agencies, she suspected, were not likely to discriminate.

What is striking about ABC respondents, particularly those under forty, is their sense that race is simply not the huge barrier it once was. The mind-set—and indeed the creed—of this generation can be summed up as: "Yes, there may be prejudice out there, but I am talented enough and tough enough to overcome it."

Jacqueline,* the architect in Georgia, born in 1981, typifies that attitude. She has encountered a great deal of harsh treatment just for being a black female. "In school, someone took the time to tie a noose and hang it over my desk. Initially it made me livid. But after a while I just laughed, because I knew that there was nothing anyone could do or say to deter me from my dream of becoming an architect."

Today, she said, engineers and contractors often leap to the conclusion that she is not qualified, and her white coworkers, who don't have Jacqueline's credentials, have to make the case for her. "Perhaps I have become a bit numb. Every time that happens, I just smile." She now shares her stories with young people as a way of telling them, "Someone else's thoughts about you will never determine your successes." I have named Jacqueline's generation of black achievers "Gen 3 Believers." And the attitude she personifies is a defining attribute.

The idea that generations matter—that when you were born has much to do with how you view the world—is not new. In *Generations*, William Strauss and Neil Howe endeavor to analyze the whole American experience, beginning in 1584, through the "collective mind-set" of different generations.

I am an agnostic when it comes to Strauss and Howe's idea that history is largely a story of recurring generational phenotypes. But I do believe that how blacks and whites view each other has a lot to do with the era that spawned them. I believe, to be more precise, that the civil rights revolution fundamentally transformed black-white relations and that every generation since then has seen a further shift in that relationship. I will elaborate on this at length in the chapters that follow. For now I will leave it at this: Gen 1s (those born prior to 1945), Gen 2s (born between 1945 and 1969), and Gen 3s (born between 1970 and 1995) all have their distinct ways of looking at race and place. And black Gen 3s are particularly inclined to believe they can evade the racial traps that ensnared many of their parents.

"I am the only African American in my graduate program," said Fatimah Rashad, class of 2001. "It has made the journey to getting my degree a more challenging one." Nonetheless, she added, "I have been able to navigate and find some support. . . . I totally expect this to be the pattern—that is to say, being a pioneer of sorts, experiencing difficulties and learning the best way to overcome them. This was a skill that I obtained during my time at Exeter Academy."

What one ultimately gets from sifting through the ABC surveys is a sense of people struggling with how to navigate a world where opportunities for accomplished people of color abound but cannot be taken for granted.

Yolanda Wade, of Peachtree City, Georgia, class of 1986, was raised in Newark and went to Atlanta for college. She returned to the New Jersey area for medical school and residency. But after her youngest child was born, she returned to Georgia to make sure her children were surrounded by black role models who were "in positions of power and influence" and who supported academic and professional achievement. Not that such people "didn't exist in Jersey, but percentages were so much less." And she didn't want her children to suffer because of that. She wanted them to have every opportunity, as she had had with ABC, to embrace a world of unlimited possibilities: "I don't think enough children . . . have that."

Black women like Wade are dealing not only with the complexities of race—for themselves and for their children—but also with issues of gender.

Vonetta,* a corporate manager, class of 1985, formerly worked as a lawyer. Black males had a difficult time getting hired by firms, she said, but once hired they did better than black women; they "could socialize around golf and so on, and they didn't have the same challenges around parenting."

Christina,* a New York dermatologist, class of 1984, recalled a consistent bias in favor of white males when she was in training. She persevered because she was determined "not to let them defeat me." Along the way, she concluded that "gender discrimination [is] often a more palatable way for people to mask their racism." Once, a male colleague defended a supervisor she thought was racist by saying, "He's not racist. He's just sexist." That comment struck her as ridiculous: "As if that were okay . . . as if that were cute."

As the ABC alumni declared their faith in America—and even

more so in themselves—they also embraced the reality that life will sometimes be difficult simply because of race, that they might have to work both harder and smarter. Many also acknowledged another reality rooted in America's racially troubled past: the Great Recession, which officially began in December 2007, has not been an equal opportunity adversary—it has hit minorities much harder than whites, and one reason it has been so difficult is that even many successful people of color do not have the cushion of resources, handed down through generations, that insulate and protect many whites.

Nevertheless, in its 2010 survey, conducted in late 2009, Pew found that blacks are amazingly optimistic—much more so than in a previous poll conducted in September and early October 2007.

> In the teeth of what may be the deepest recession since the Great Depression, nearly twice as many blacks now (39%) as in 2007 (20%) say that the "situation of black people in this country" is better than it was five years earlier, and this more positive view is apparent among blacks of all age groups and income levels. Looking ahead, blacks are even more upbeat. More than half (53%) say that life for blacks in the future will be better than it is now, while just 10% say it will be worse. In 2007, 44% said things would be better for blacks in the future, while 21% said they would be worse.

My ABC focus group was not quite so upbeat. One reason, it seems, is that they took greater note of the impact of the recession, which has made many people, not just blacks, significantly worse off than they were five years ago. Only 25 percent thought that black folks are in a better situation now, compared to 56 percent who thought it is now the same as five years ago; 40 percent judged the situation of Latinos to be better, and 44 percent thought it is the same. When the time frame was longer, however, the ABC group's responses were markedly more upbeat. When asked about whether things are better now than fifteen years ago, 49 percent said yes for blacks, and 59 percent for Hispanics.

What the ABC respondents were saying seems clear. The outlook for people of color has substantially improved in the nearly two decades since *Rage of a Privileged Class* was published. Certain barriers have fallen, and new opportunities have opened up—at least for those who are well educated. Nonetheless, the recession has taken a toll.

Erika, class of 1994, formerly worked in finance. "When I was growing up, I always heard from older blacks that blacks are 'last hired, first fired.' Somehow I thought that with excellent educations and stellar résumés, my generation would not be victim to that same old story," she confided. "And then I watched all of the blacks in my circle . . . who went into investment banks between 2006 and 2007." They were refused resources, assigned to "apathetic mentors," and then eased out the door. Of the ten blacks she knew in investment banking in New York and Chicago, "only one remains." All those let go had similar stories: they were encouraged "to do recruiting and be the face of the organization, and then penalized for spending time recruiting and not working for clients." They were ambushed during performance reviews with complaints that had never previously surfaced. "The layoffs disproportionately impacted people of color and women, especially considering there weren't many of them to begin with." One firm, she said, "single-handedly wiped out their female and black bankers at the associate level or above in one sweep of layoffs in 2008. . . . It seems as if [that] should be illegal."

"What is still withheld from us is the equal opportunity to create multigenerational wealth," said one alumna, class of 1982. "I wish I could wrap that up in a box and hand it to my son in the same way as the Euro-dynasty families have done for their legacies in the form of trusts and endowments." Instead, having lost her job, "I sit, between résumé-sending marathons, in my close-to-foreclosure home in a recently gentrified neighborhood with no room for me or my young son."

Many were also concerned about the growing gap—in values and in options—between people like themselves and those left behind. When they were asked whether, in the last ten years, "values held by middle-class people in your ethnic or racial group and the values held by poor people in your ethnic or racial group" had become more or less similar, 60 percent said they had become "more different." They were essentially in agreement with Professor Manning Marable, who sees a breaking down of what he calls the "linked fate" of blacks across the socioeconomic spectrum. "This is the paradox of integration," Marable told me. "As we integrated into the mainstream institutions of society, as a product of the victories of the civil rights movement, we lost the space for racial solidarity and common ground linking the poor with the elite." And partly because of that dynamic, Marable fears, the poor are being increasingly marooned in neighborhoods without much of a future.

Jason Thomas, class of 1990, is a PhD economist who manages billions for wealthy individuals but worries about those who can only dream of the life he has. "For upwardly mobile blacks, this is a world of opportunity," he said. Their skills are "in high demand," and racism has less and less power "to undermine our professional skills, educational credentials, and global opportunities. . . . Upwardly mobile blacks have the same opportunities and concerns as their white peers: achieving career success, giving their children every opportunity, finding some measure of satisfaction in life." But for "poor blacks, the walls of the world are closing in. Most don't have a clearly defined set of skills, or [they] have skills which are not in demand." There have always been poor and upwardly mobile blacks, he acknowledged, but they are now in competition with immigrants and cheap labor from around the world. Moreover, the gap is increasing over time. "This divergence seems to clearly undermine racial unity," he noted, "but whether it affects racial progress is unclear."

For upwardly mobile blacks, he continued, "I believe that time and globalization will diminish the importance of race." But for those "stuck in an environment where belonging—to a race, a gang, a religion—[is] increasingly important and can determine job prospects and, sometimes, life and death . . . I have yet to encounter an idea which will turn the tide."

William Dorsey, class of 1970, lives in Philadelphia and works as a consultant for community development financial institutions. He also believes that the divide between blacks "based on skin color, education, and profession" is worsening, in part because

> middle-class blacks fail to lead or challenge notions of injustice or racism or economic disempowerment even when they sit in positions of power. . . . They choose private academies for their kids rather than advocate for higher-quality education for all. Yet it was these very loud, assertive poor blacks that formed the backbone of the civil rights movement or took part in the urban insurrections that created paths of opportunity for middle-class blacks.

"I spent thirty-two years in the information technology industry and am currently pursuing a teaching degree in math," said a business executive, class of 1973. "I see over the past fifteen or twenty years a decrease in the number of minorities, especially black men, in industries like technology." He had returned to school in order to get training "to teach math to students so they can be better prepared for jobs in the future." He hoped to impress upon young people of color "that they're just as good and can compete for these jobs. . . . I want to be able to encourage them that they can be successful," despite the "challenges and hurdles they will have to overcome."

In talking of the hurdles that blacks have yet to surmount, numerous ABC respondents worried that relatively few blacks have access to the kind of high-quality education that had been such a force in their own lives. "The only reason I'm middle class or upper-middle class is because of education. . . . There are a lot of talented people who don't get the same exposure and aren't in the environment to be encouraged," said Dillon,* class of 1974.

In poor black neighborhoods, "I see very little knowledge being passed on to children [about] how to achieve through education," observed Marlon Lewis, the Pasadena lawyer. "The parents, neighbors, peers don't seem to understand how to attain in America, and the teachers don't perceive themselves as a vehicle to convey this information." His kids, said Lewis, are very aware of his own beginnings in an impoverished area of Washington, D.C. "And they look at me and say, 'Dad, how did you make it out of that world?' I tell them, 'I could see beyond the false messages that were prevalent in the black community.'"

He recalled a conversation he had when he was about twelve with a friend of his older brother. Lewis said something in jest to the man, who sharply admonished him. "Don't play with me," he said. "I just got out of prison and am someone to be respected." Lewis did not respond, "But I said to myself, 'Does he really believe being in prison is something I should respect him for?'" Even at that age, Lewis realized that the man's take on life—and on what demands admiration and respect—was tragically self-destructive. Today he worries that young people in poor minority communities are in greater danger than ever of falling for such nonsense. They "must traverse through a lot more peer pressure that sends the wrong messages," he said.

Chapter Three

From the Hallowed Halls of Harvard

After Hal King graduated from Harvard Business School in 1975, he quickly realized that his education had not prepared him for the world as it was. "Harvard Business School focused me on large enterprises. As an African American coming out of business school in 1975, the obstacles I encountered made me see that there wasn't any meaningful future that was going to be sustainable and sooner or later I was going to have to go out on my own to be successful."

King did well enough in the corporate world: within several years of graduating, he was running the San Francisco office of a major advertising agency. But when he looked around, he didn't see much evidence that he had a future: "There wasn't a black face in the joint." And he was not aware of any blacks at the senior level in advertising.

In 1985 he struck out on his own, founding a market research company and also, initially, making himself available as a manager for hire. His company now employs twenty people, has $6 million in annual revenue, and is one of the leading sources of market research for software companies in the country.

Now in his midsixties, King acknowledged that he has been very successful. But when he reflected on the black Harvard MBAs of his generation, he became gloomy. One of his classmates spent time as a cabdriver, another became a minister. Two, he believed, ended up in jail. Of those in his graduating class, he could think of only two who successfully pursued major corporate careers. Not that he regretted getting a Harvard MBA. Harvard taught him a lot, and the degree had made it easier for him to get work as a consultant. But in the corporate world, he had found a wall of frustration: "I often came up against people whose goal was to subjugate me."

In many ways, King is typical of those I interviewed for *The Rage of a Privileged Class*. For black professionals of his generation, even the best credentials often were not good enough. But that story is changing—especially for those with fancy degrees, such as a Harvard MBA.

An MBA from Harvard doesn't guarantee success. No degree can do that, regardless of color. But it does tilt the odds heavily in the graduate's favor—and these days that seems just as true for black graduates of Harvard Business School as for others.

The median starting salary (plus bonus) for 2009 graduates was $134,000, according to Harvard's career placement office. Median cash compensation for HBS graduates who had been in the workforce for an average of twenty years was $230,000, according to a 2009 analysis by *Businessweek*. (This figure is for individuals, not households.)

For me, the decision to survey the black alumni of Harvard Business School was a no-brainer. They were a unique cohort of accomplished African Americans who could shed a great deal of light on what one spectacularly successful group of blacks thinks about a range of subjects. Happily, the Harvard Business School African-American Alumni Association agreed. This chapter owes everything to the 193 HBS alumni who filled out my survey (distributed by the HBS AAA), and above all to the 45 who participated in the (at times demanding) follow-up interview process.*

For statistical sticklers, allow me to state again that I am not representing this as a random sample of the views of all black Har-

* For detailed survey data, visit www.elliscose.com.

vard MBAs. Virtually any survey (including those purporting to be unbiased and free of so-called nonsampling errors) reflects some element of self-selection, and clearly those who responded to my survey were more interested in this topic than those who did not. That said, I would not be discussing these results if I did not believe they have something important to tell us. The responses (again, think of them as a large focus group) say a great deal about the worldview of 193 black Harvard MBAs, whose perceptions, I suspect, go far beyond this particular group of 193.

In many ways, the Harvard MBAs are very different from the folks at ABC. Most are males (61 percent), compared to 38 percent of ABC respondents. That reflects the male skew at Harvard Business School, which reports that 64 percent of its class of 2012 is male. (The male percentage among all alumni of this once all-male school is much higher.) The MBAs are also more corporate: 54 percent work for a corporation or other for-profit enterprise, compared to 35 percent of those from ABC. Only 9 percent work for nonprofits, compared to 21 percent of those from ABC. With an average age of forty-six, the MBAs are a little older (the ABC alumni average thirty-eight), they are more likely to be married (56 percent compared to 48 percent), and they are considerably richer. Twenty-nine percent reported a household income of $400,000 or more, and 60 percent claimed an income of $200,000 or more. Among ABC respondents, only 15 percent reported a household income in excess of $200,000.

The MBAs hail from more privileged backgrounds. The overwhelming majority (72 percent) were raised in middle-class or upper-middle-class neighborhoods, whereas most of the ABC alumni (55 percent) described their childhood neighborhood as poor. The MBAs also had better-educated parents. Over half of their fathers (51 percent) had completed a baccalaureate degree, 13 percent had a master's, 11 percent had a medical or law degree, and 6 percent had a PhD. Their mothers were equally well educated: half (51 percent) had earned at least a bachelor's degree, 23 percent held a master's, 4 percent had a law or medical degree, and 7 percent were PhDs.

Despite coming from relatively well-off circumstances, a stunning 97 percent of the Harvard MBAs claimed to have a household income that exceeded that of their parents at a comparable point of life. In short, they had started well ahead of not just blacks but most other Americans, and they had ended up even further ahead.

Intriguing as their demographics are, I find it even more intriguing that the vast majority asked to remain anonymous. They did not want to comment publicly on anything related to race. Sara Scott,* a utility executive in the South, explained why.

Early in her career, recalled Scott, she once tried to explain to a focus group the difficulties that blacks and females were experiencing within her company. An apparently stunned white colleague announced that he had "never realized that I was so pessimistic and jaded." She tried to explain that she was only reporting the facts, which included bias, often covert, that he, as a white male, had never experienced. "Fast-forward an additional ten years. He was a vice president, and I had not advanced beyond where I was, despite my having more education." Scott also had a more impressive work record. She blamed her tongue for holding her back. The encounter taught her the painful lesson that speaking about experiences of discrimination was not only unappreciated but punished. One risked being labeled a malcontent and becoming estranged from the corporate culture, someone who should be tossed aside or relegated to the sidelines. She concluded that she would thrive only by hiding such opinions, by engaging in "a masquerade. . . . The corporation for me is a theater, and I try to remember to stay in character."

An accountant from California made much the same point. For blacks to be successful in corporate settings, he said, "they must give up some blackness, or at least appear to have given up 'being black.' You cannot create bonds of trust if you dare to discuss social inequalities in business or social settings with whites in the power structure. The implicit deal seems to be, 'If we let you in the club, you need to show your appreciation by keeping your mouth shut.'"

These comments took me back to the publication of *The Rage of a Privileged Class* in the early 1990s. At the time, I was doing quite a bit of public speaking, much of it in corporate settings. Often, at some point during such engagements, I would be pulled aside by minority workers who thanked me for telling their story and then asked, discreetly, if I could explain to their white bosses what they could not and make their bosses understand why so many of them felt undervalued, unhappy, and excluded.

The good news, from this survey, is that Harvard MBAs are extremely content. But what is also clear is that black executives—even those with a Harvard MBA—inhabit workplaces that are far from color-blind. Still, these particular professionals felt that they had an edge, one granted by the Harvard degree, and we would be hard-pressed to prove them wrong. Ninety-five percent were either satisfied or very satisfied with their Harvard education, and 73 percent guessed that they would not have been so successful were it not for their Harvard MBA.

As one woman, class of 2002, put it, "HBS legitimizes me. As a black woman in finance, I need as much 'gunpowder' as possible to compete and have peers and managers view me as capable. . . . HBS brings an automatic stamp of approval and allows me to clear early hurdles. The subsequent hurdles are up to me to maneuver past."

Jasmine Washington,* class of 1998, who earned her undergraduate degree at a historically black university, discovered that her "black" degree was not particularly respected: "I don't have that issue when it comes to HBS. They find other ways to question me, but academics is no longer one of them." Ethan Bruce,* class of 1974, also discovered the almost magical power of the degree: "Having a Harvard MBA made it more difficult for fair-minded white people to overlook me."

Some valued the credential because it made the workplace easier to navigate. "Having attended HBS has allowed me to step out of the workforce—[owing to] early widowhood—soul-search, and step back into the workforce in a way that might not have been possible without the HBS MBA," said a member of the class of 1993.

Even those who thought their Harvard education wasn't particularly relevant to what they ended up doing deemed the degree well worth having. It enhanced their prestige with clients, plugged them into invaluable networks, both in the United States and abroad, or otherwise provided them with a competitive advantage.

Some, however, cited drawbacks.

"Sometimes I feel as though it has been a curse, that people think I feel I am better than them," said Nancy Malcolm,* class of 2001. Others experienced the degree as a magnet for others' insecurity and spite. "Outside of Ivy-controlled industries, the Harvard MBA is a useless credential, which has actually led to me losing opportunities because non-Ivy supervisors feel threatened," said Paula Jefferson,* class of 1978. "I have had white people who were openly jealous and vindictive," said Craig Triplett, managing director of the LeRoi Group, an Atlanta-based executive search firm. And one man, class of 1999, said that he had found the degree to be a liability in looking for certain types of work: "After Harvard, when I lost my last MBA-level job in 2001, I found that I routinely had to hide my Harvard MBA because I otherwise would be overqualified. No employer would hire me even when I informed them I did not mind working for less money at a lower-level position."

Because the degree often comes with a huge amount of student loan debt, it can severely limit career choices. "There is a lot of pressure to go into consulting or investment banking," said Carlton Madison,* class of 1995, but because most blacks lack connections to rich friends and powerful family members, who often are the initial clients in these high-paying fields, they typically don't rise very far.

Nevertheless, any disadvantage that may come with the degree is generally far outweighed by the benefits. "It provides instant credibility," observed Triplett. And for blacks, who often have to struggle to be seen at all, that credibility and legitimization—that "gunpowder"—is their best hope of blasting their way past any barriers to a glorious career. And when considering the prospects for blacks in business generally, the Harvard MBAs saw barriers aplenty.

Eighty-seven percent believed that blacks confront a glass ceiling in corporate America—the identical figure posted by ABC alumni—but like their ABC counterparts, half also said that no such ceiling was in place where they currently worked. And again like their ABC counterparts, the younger HBS alumni were the most upbeat.

Some said that the glass ceiling is as impenetrable as ever: "Despite doing all the right things, [people] get tired of beating their heads against the wall. Or they push ahead aggressively and are derailed. . . . This affects blacks more than white women, as white women are still white and can more easily adjust and assimilate," argued Sara Scott, the utility executive.

Some argued that prejudice, though virtually ubiquitous, can be maneuvered around. "I think when you're a minority, you have to know that there are certain biases, [but you have to] be able to deal with them. I don't think anyone has said anything nasty to my face. . . . But I think that there's a little bit of a question mark . . . when . . . looking at a minority candidate. So I make sure that my credentials speak for themselves," said marketing executive Joahne Carter, class of 2002.

Others believed that while bosses are more open-minded than ever, they are also more indifferent. Dwayne Brock,* a retired corporate executive, class of 1975, recounted his own experience:

> When I started, it was just at the age of affirmative action. So getting in was easier, but getting up wasn't as easy. For people starting out now, more functions are open. You used to only be able to do public relations and human resources. Marketing was tough, and other areas were difficult or impossible to get into. That seems to be gone. But being black is not necessarily an asset anymore. . . . With the election of Barack Obama, people feel like everyone's made it and [they] don't have to do anything special anymore.

Many searched for a new vocabulary to describe a workplace that is very different for people of color—more welcoming and yet still difficult—from anything of the past. "We need to drop the idea of a color barrier and transition to the concept of a color filter, which is permeable," said Kimberly Franklin,* class of 1991. A filter, she explained, blocks some people of all races, but allows minorities with the right attributes to get through. "The ceiling clearly has holes in it," said Stephen Walters,* a former military officer, class of 2005. Those with determination, skills, a track record, and the ability to "negotiate the terrain" can push through, he maintained. Amara Baillie, a business consultant, class of 2009, used a vivid analogy to describe her workplace:

> [It's like] your colleagues are swimming in water and you're swimming in oil. It's more a diffuse series of challenges you face. . . . As a black woman, if I get upset about something, they perceive me as being angrier and more belligerent than someone who is not a black female. My emotional responses have to be much more controlled, but I don't think this adds up to a glass ceiling. . . . But it still takes three times as much work.

Simone Jenkins,* an executive with a major hotel firm and member of the class of 2005, was fed up with talk of a glass ceiling. "I'm getting really tired of this blasted term. . . . It just conjures up images of being shackled and held back. How can we excel if we perceive ourselves as trapped? I'm beginning to wonder if we are the caged birds who don't realize the cage door is open."

Many people of Jenkins's generation—at thirty, she is a Gen 3 Believer in my scheme—have taken to heart Michelangelo's words: "The greatest danger for most of us is not that we aim too high and we miss it, but we aim too low and reach it." They worry more about limiting themselves by fixating on corporate bias than about bumping into a glass ceiling. They are also certain that whatever burden their parents' generation (Gen 2 Dreamers) shouldered, theirs is not the same.

"I think as generations go on it's becoming a lot easier to break through," said Garry Thaniel, a twenty-eight-year-old alum from the class of 2009. "I feel like I've been blessed. . . . Going to Bucknell, Harvard, I've had some amazing educational experiences." Those experiences "[have] put me in a position to hopefully break through the glass ceiling one day." He saw no reason why, as an African American male, he should settle for anything less than his white buddies who aspire to be CEO. "My thing is, if on paper we measure up, then it'll just come down to performance."

Jerome James,* an executive in a U.S. technology company in Japan, was also uncomfortable with the notion of an impermeable ceiling. What matters is "being plugged into the right networks and using them to develop personal bonds with people," said James, class of 1995. "I don't think this is easy, but I also don't see this as some sort of explicit barrier."

"You've gotta crank things out, and you've gotta perform," said Ryan Terry,* class of 1999. "People still have their own insecurities and their own racial biases, but at least in this current situation I don't feel a big concern about that."

To talk to many of these young Harvard MBAs—and also to some of those who are not so young—is like listening to voices from a different, rosier universe than that inhabited by those interviewed for *Rage*. They see a world with prejudice but ultimately no limits—a place where race has costs and benefits, but what ultimately happens is up to them. This view is particularly common among Gen 3 Believers.

Occasionally during the research for *Rage* I would come across a die-hard optimist, a person who argued that the time was ripe for blacks to rise to the top and that only their fears and caution prevented them from doing so. But overwhelmingly the message then was this: "I would like to believe in the dream, but I can't. Every time I have tried to climb, I have been slapped down." Some of those I talked to anguished over the inability of African Americans to figure out the mysterious secret that would allow them to advance. A black phone company executive I interviewed wondered whether blacks are partly responsible for their own misfortune. "I don't think it is all corporate America's making," she said. "I think we have had opportunities to perhaps build stepping-stones to that [glass] ceiling to break through and we've choked . . . by not learning what it is that we have to do in order to break through and not being willing to do it because of some fear, real or imagined, that we will compromise our blackness or our femininity or whatever else it is." But this attitude, common among the younger Harvard MBAs and the ABC folks, was rare a generation ago. As Charles Ogletree observed, talking about his Harvard law students who are no longer content to be workers but dream of becoming the ultimate boss: "They think it can be done because they've seen others [do it]."

Those students were not under any illusion that racism had vanished. Indeed, said Ogletree, they dealt with it regularly. "And they will let me know when they encounter some issue that they are troubled by—police profiling, [white] students who think [blacks are only there because of] affirmative action, [going] to a department store and being followed." Black women complained about

> going to a party or an event to relax on the weekend and being unable to get a cab back at one o'clock in the morning because the cabdriver thinks they're a woman from Dorchester, Roxbury, Mattapan, [or some other largely black area] and not from Harvard. And you don't want to show an ID and say, "I'm from Harvard." . . . It's a major issue for them when they are outside the bubble, when they are outside Harvard . . . and in some sense, even when they're inside Harvard.

But Ogletree's students now have the examples of people like Obama and Massachusetts governor (and ABC alumnus) Deval Patrick: "And now they're saying, I don't just have to be a partner in a law firm, I can be the mayor, I can be the governor, I can be a senator."

The generation of black professionals now coming along is the first for whom it is possible to believe that corporate America will treat them remotely fairly. And many of them—particularly those with an Ivy League or prestigious prep school pedigree—who have watched their white buddies soar are eager to test their wings in this new environment. What further emboldens them is that they are also the first generation of black professionals with bosses who not only encourage such dreams but actually seem to mean what they say. Mansur Silvers,* age twenty-nine and class of 2008, explained why he felt that his potential was unlimited:

> I see the company CEO publicly stating that we are not presently where we would like to be from a diversity standpoint and that he is going to hold leaders accountable through the performance review process for meeting diversity objectives. I also have access to high-level leaders who are willing to mentor me and foster my own personal development to help me achieve my own career goals.

Said Ashley Allen, class of 2007, who is twenty-nine years old and works in the health care industry in Indiana,

> My life experiences to date have instilled in me the mind-set that nothing is impossible and that the only barrier that will prevent me from realizing my full potential is myself. I have not had any experiences in corporate America yet that have made me feel that being a female or African American is a limiting factor. . . . Actually, I have had quite the opposite experience of being fortunate enough to have many opportunities for growth and development. . . . I am always aware of the fact that in most situations I will be in the minority, and I do feel a slight pressure, whether real or self-imposed, to always be "on top of my game" and continuously demonstrate my competence and abilities, [to show] that I am deserving of these opportunities. . . .
>
> One thing that is interesting to consider as we discuss the role gender and race play in corporate America is whether they can have a positive impact on one's career. In other words, are people given opportunities strictly based on the fact that they are minorities? With all of the scrutiny corporations face from the public, government, shareholders, and employees about the

need to have diversity initiatives in place, it may beg the question, particularly in the minds of minority talent who [have] excelled in their career, whether they have achieved based on their own merits. I will not lie and say that this has never crossed my mind . . . but I prefer to stand firm on the opinion that I have simply benefited from working hard and demonstrating high performance.

Indeed, some Gen 3 Believers show signs of what could be called affirmative action guilt. Ruby Nelson,* class of 2004, confided:

> With every job I have had, including attending Harvard Business School, I've always had in the back of my mind that affirmative action probably played some role in my successes. For B-school, I knew that I need only break 600 on the GMATs [Graduate Management Admission Test] to be considered a viable candidate since I was black and female. And of course, I had an impressive résumé that included an Ivy League undergrad degree. For my jobs post-HBS, I was well aware that these corporations were very mindful of their diversity pool, which essentially made me a shoo-in or meant that I was competing against other blacks for the "token" award.

One of the most thoughtful discussions of what makes this new age so liberating—at least for those with certain credentials—and how to think about navigating it came not from an idealistic twenty-something but from a man of almost fifty, a certified public accountant who earned his Harvard MBA in 1995.

"I don't think any black Harvard Business School MBA would admit to a glass ceiling. If that is how you see the world, you have defeated yourself," said Carlton Madison.* "Is race a factor? Yes. But less because of the blackness itself [than because] being black may make it more difficult to form the trusting bonds that are required for people in positions of power to take personal risk and place a bet on a 'black horse.' The ability to assimilate comfortably into the power structure is a key factor for success."

Earlier in his career, said Madison, he made the mistake of thinking he had assimilated into the white corporate structure, but he later realized that he was wrong: "I now understand that you are not truly comfortable until you no longer feel like you have to demonstrate how smart you are. That's when you are no longer a threat and it becomes safe for you to be welcomed into the inner circles of the power structure."

Madison grew up in a tough neighborhood—Compton, California—and was accustomed to fighting to survive. So even as he traveled far beyond Compton, he kept fighting. But finally he had an epiphany: "The trick to being accepted among the 'privileged class' is to not *look* like you are fighting for success—the trick is to look like you have already achieved success, and therefore you do not represent a threat to those around you. . . . When I lived in London, the Brits called this 'being like a duck'—calm and unruffled on the surface, but paddling like hell underwater."

In his world, said Madison, there is no "impenetrable glass ceiling." There is "a lock on the glass, and you have to know how to pick the lock." That is done, he argued, through building "trusting bonds."

Madison was excited to learn that his daughter had been admitted to a nice prep school:

> [It's] a private school with lots of rich white girls. I want her to grow up feeling socially comfortable around rich white people. Once you get past the social comfort barrier, the performance barrier is much easier to break. Unfortunately, I tried it the other way around—performance first. Why? *Because that is what I was taught at home.* I was taught that all you have to do is perform and success will follow. This may be true for middle management, but to get to the exclusive [top] level requires as much relationship-building as performance. Our white counterparts simply do not have to navigate this additional level through the lens of cultural differences. It's easier for them—harder for us.

Just as racial assumptions are being tested in this new age, so are those about gender, especially for those (black females, in particular) who must deal with both race and gender. What many are discovering is that there are few absolutes these days. Joahne Carter observed that

> women are thought of as being more collaborative and [as listeners]. People tend to be more open with you because of that. And that just helps you make better decisions. . . . On the other hand, there are negative stereotypes that women aren't as decisive or aren't as good [with] quantitative information. . . . [Success is] about embracing those things that are positive biases and making sure that I nullify those negative assumptions.

For Martha Newton,* class of 1988, gender was never easy to get a fix on. Its impact

> was either positive or negative—never neutral—depending on the year or situation. I was definitely subjected to sexual harassment and inappropriate comments twenty years ago, many of which would be legally actionable today. Frequently, I have been the front-runner for positions or promotions because I was the sole or one of the few women amongst a sea of primarily male candidates. In this regard, being a woman has been a positive. It has been a negative when I have been unable to bond with my male peers or superiors because of our lack of commonality or our perceived lack of commonality.

"As a black person, I tend to think about race relations much more [than gender]," said Amara Baillie.

> But it's always hard to disaggregate what people are responding to. . . . I see [being a woman] as a behavioral thing. I think women learn different behaviors than men. Women tend to have a much more nurturing leadership style, but that's perceived as being less bold, less decisive; but on the other hand, I wouldn't change any of those things. . . . I think there are certain behaviors that woman do at work that are taken nega-

> tively that are probably easier to manage around than issues of race. . . . I don't see being a woman as being as much of a handicap, though being a black woman does become one.

"I think in some ways my gender has been really beneficial in that I have all of the qualifications for a job, and a company gets to check two boxes, race and gender, on their diversity scorecard. [On the other hand,] I have a general sense that I am underpaid and that a man may be more aggressive when negotiating total compensation," said Rita Goodwin,* a corporate strategist in a health care company, class of 2006. Goodwin suspected that her gender has also made it easier for her to find mentors: "I [have] found older white men to be my best mentors and sponsors. I am not sure if it is genuine interest, curiosity, desire to leave a legacy, or guilt that makes them take me under their wing, but regardless of the reason, I have benefited from their interest."

"Gender has always had a huge impact on the progression of my career," said thirty-one-year-old Ebony S. Morczinek, class of 2007, a self-described Afro-Trinidadian working in the food services industry in Germany.

> As a young professional it allowed me to fly under the radar of office politics and male displays of power, while allowing me to let my star shine. My generation was the first one where women were not afraid to use femininity to their advantage in the workplace—for example, through alternative methods of resolving conflict. However, as I took on more senior roles, my gender began to be more of an issue. I realized that many of the ways in which I was socialized to be feminine also got in the way of me taking my place as a leader in the organization. I kept coming face to face with my need to be a "nice girl." With time, I became comfortable with letting go of that notion and taking up the "strong woman" mantle. Now that I am seven months pregnant with my first child, I have hit another seeming roadblock, which I have no doubt I will navigate as I have others. In Germany most people do not expect that I will have a fam-

ily and continue to work. The child care, education, and social benefits systems are set up as such. As a result, most women find themselves between the devil and the deep blue sea—work without having a family or become a stay-at-home mother.

"Early in my post–business school career," said Simone Jenkins, "I worked for a consulting firm where, of the twenty new people, I was the only black person and one of three women. I was the second black female the company had ever hired for a client-facing role, despite the fact that it employed over a hundred people in the middle of Atlanta."

I tried hard to hide my gender—wearing the "consultant uniform" of button-down shirts and slacks—and carefully avoided any conversations regarding race. In retrospect, part of my reluctance to embrace my race and gender at work was related to insecurities about my ability to perform, because quite frankly, it wasn't the right role or company for me but the salary was too hard to resist. I was trying to hide out, and that strategy is emotionally taxing and ultimately unsuccessful.

Now, said Jenkins, she embraces her femininity.

I wear dresses all the time. Why? 'Cause I'm a confident woman who knows what she's doing in her job and happens to have great legs. This past spring my coworkers and I had a movie date to watch *Good Hair* together because they are fascinated about why every Thursday night I run out of the office at 6:00 P.M. to make my hairdresser appointment. These thirty-somethings have been dying to ask these questions but never felt comfortable enough with a black female to do it. When I was the only black girl in my private school days, I found it incredibly irritating when people asked questions about my culture, particularly my hair. Now, I realize, there's no need to get defensive. People just want to learn. When I share who I am outside of work, it helps build a rapport at work that allows me to feel comfortable fully being me, even when I'm the only black person or woman in the room. I have found that having that confidence enables me to excel in my career.

My survey did not ask specifically about gender discrimination, but it is clear that the men and women perceived the workplace in different ways. Fewer women than men (47 percent to 54 percent) felt that their educational attainments put them on an equal professional footing with white peers. And though women were somewhat less likely to believe they had been discriminated against at work (75 percent to 81 percent), those who had been discriminated against were much more likely to think that discrimination had seriously affected their careers (58 percent to 42 percent). Women also were not doing as well financially. Fifty percent of women reported a household income of $200,000 or more, whereas 66 percent of men did. Only 16 percent of women reported incomes of $400,000 or more, compared to 38 percent of men.

One likely reason for the disparity in household income is that the women were considerably less likely to be married: 43 percent compared to 73 percent. Also, they were a bit less likely to be in the highest-paying fields. Fifty-eight percent of the males were in one of three relatively high-paying "occupational categories" (finance and insurance; professional, scientific, and technical services; and management of companies and enterprises) compared to 48 percent of females.

For me, the most fascinating numbers in the survey were not about gender but about entrepreneurship. A majority of respondents of both genders (63 percent of women and 54 percent of men) agreed that "generally speaking . . . blacks are better off becoming entrepreneurs than working in predominantly white corporations." One-fourth of all respondents (25 percent of females and 24 percent of males) had actually turned their backs on the corporate world and were self-employed (compared to only 12 percent of ABC respondents who were self-employed).

Those numbers leapt out at me for the simple reason that people, for the most part, don't go to a prestigious business school in order to become self-employed; they go to get the credentials that will allow them to climb to the top of big corporate structures—to become captains and czarinas of the universe. So why were so many working for themselves? And why did even more—in fact, most—believe that blacks should ditch corporate life for entrepreneurship?

I contacted Harvard to get comparison stats for all business school graduates, and was told that they were not available. But I did find an article by Professors Richard DeMartino and Robert Barbato of RIT in the *Journal of Business Venturing,* based on survey data from alumni of an unnamed top-ten business school. In their study, 11.5 percent of men and 16.2 percent of women expressed a preference for entrepreneurship. These numbers, which presumably are in the ballpark for Harvard, are far below those in my survey.

High as the numbers were for my black alumni respondents, I was not totally surprised. One of the more poignant interviews I conducted for *Rage* was with a Harvard MBA who had speculated about why so many of his black peers seemed to be going the entrepreneurial route.

> The evening had been long and the dinner pleasant, with hosts who were a portrait of success. Their suburban home was spacious and tastefully furnished. Their children—three away in college and two in elementary school—were academically accomplished, popular, and athletic. Both parents held advanced degrees from Harvard and were well respected in their fields. For two whose beginnings had been fairly modest, they had more than ample grounds for contentment, even conceit.
>
> As the husband and I sat nursing after-dinner drinks, his cheery mood progressively turned more pensive, and he began to ruminate on his achievements since earning his MBA. By any normal standard, he had done exceedingly well. Within years after graduation, he had risen to a senior position in a national supermarket chain. Shortly thereafter he had taken a job as manager of a huge independent supermarket and had used that as a base from which to launch his own business. He had thought the business would

make him wealthy. Instead, he had gone bankrupt, but in the end had landed on his feet with yet another corporate job.

Still, he was not at all pleased with the way his career was turning out. At Harvard, he had always assumed that he would end up somewhere near the top of the corporate pyramid, as had most of his white peers. Yet shortly after graduation he had begun to sense that they were passing him by, so he had opted for the entrepreneurial route. Now that his business had failed and he was again mired in the upper layers of middle-management, he found it galling that so many of his white classmates had prospered with such seeming ease. A considerable number had become corporate royalty, with seven-figure compensation packages, access to private planes, and other accoutrements of status and power about which he could only dream. Despite the good life he had, he felt he deserved—and had been denied—so much more.

I remember that evening well, in part because much of what my friend said came as a revelation. He had noticed that among his fellow black Harvard MBAs, many had dropped out of corporate life to start their own businesses. Most of them had left, he said, because they had given up any illusion that they would ever be allowed to rise to the level of their aspirations and skills. The only way they would ever be fulfilled, they had concluded, was to strike out on their own.

It was because of that long-ago conversation that I had included the questions about entrepreneurship on my survey. So I was prepared to hear respondents sing the praises of entrepreneurship and bitterly complain about their corporate fate, but what I was hearing was more complicated than that. While many said that corporations still were sucking the life out of black talent, others proclaimed the arrival of a new day—the dawn of an era in which talented blacks can do as well as comparably credentialed and talented whites.

For Alisa Knox,* that day still seems far away, and until it arrives she feels she is better off trying to make it on her own. She spent nearly twenty years trying to climb the corporate ladder. "Most executives above me were white males. Most had little interest in 'connecting' with me." She spent eighteen months working for her last corporation boss but only saw him if she scheduled a meeting: "I never had a single meal with him—lunch or dinner. Yet it was very clear he was spending a great deal of informal time with the white men on the team. The African American man on the team had the same experience that I did," said Knox, class of 1989.

Some respondents surmised that it is not explicit discrimination that drives blacks away from corporations, but cultural discomfort. Diron Sims,* class of 2006, noted that

> the culture of many of the premier corporations in the U.S. is very difficult to overcome if you come from a certain background and were not trained in the nuances of white culture. . . . If you are white and come from an economically depressed environment and make it to one of those institutions, you have more chances to succeed than your ethnic counterpart. Conversely, there is a level of acculturation or assimilation needed for African Americans or Hispanics to succeed. For some, it's hard to commit the level of assimilation necessary to break through the glass ceiling.

Charles Chisholm,* class of 1972, started his own firm in the 1970s with the specific intention of employing other blacks. "I wanted to start a company that was world class. I was very clear that I wanted to train as many talented blacks as I could. I felt a moral and ethical responsibility to help other black people." His task would have been easier had he hired more whites and fewer blacks. "I would have gotten more contracts. But that wasn't my purpose. My purpose was to hire people who were black like me. . . . I could have paid the price and probably done well in corporate America, but that wasn't my drive. That wasn't part of my DNA—being part of the civil rights movement, being part of the first wave of black successful people."

Hedge fund manager Damon Aiken,* a self-described driven

person, had resolved to start his firm even before entering Harvard Business School. "Business ownership is the only route to full participation in a capitalist society," said Aiken, class of 1984. His main objective in starting his business was to get very, very wealthy. Escaping prejudice in a big corporation was just "the brown sugar on top."

For Connie Jackson, managing partner of Strategic Change Associates, a consulting firm based in London, the decision to start her own firm had more to do with gender than race.

> As a woman, divorced, no children, it's very easy to work endlessly because there's nothing pulling you home. And that high-achieving tendency to work all the time as you get older can be a problem. . . . Having worked twelve-, fourteen-hour days for the past twenty-plus years, I just really needed to rebalance. Initially it was supposed to be a break, but the project work just kept coming.

Jackson, class of 1986, has found that being her own boss frees her to follow her instincts. "While everyone [in a corporation] has to make a case for pursuing new projects, the hurdle to get buy-in from superiors is often higher for blacks. . . . This can be valuable time that is lost that wouldn't have been for an entrepreneur," said Jackson.

Sean Williams, owner of Williams Accounting Services in Boynton Beach, Florida, class of 1995, found "too often" that what governs promotional decisions in the corporate world are "factors, such as keeping quiet when you have a dissenting opinion or getting to know the right people." He also had the bad luck of working for corporations that were downsizing: "So I was a member of a sinking ship." But he discounted race as a reason for striking out on his own: "It is a small possibility that if I were white, I may have progressed better at corporations and thus would be making too much money to quit and work on my own. That is the only way I think race could have played a role in my career." Certainly now, race plays no discernible role in his operation: "I firmly believe I can earn the business of any client seeking high-level accounting services despite my race. . . . I currently have clients who are black, white, Hispanic, Jewish, senior citizens, under twenty-one, Haitian, eastern European. . . . Several of my biggest referrers of new clients are white or European immigrants."

For some, going their own way meant being able to pursue contracts that specifically target minorities. Others who are not specifically focused on minority contracting still believe that their race is a plus.

"I think certainly it makes you more memorable," said Connie Jackson. "There aren't that many people that look like you. I up-end a lot of people's perceptions, particularly of black women." That she stands out because of her race is a "double-edged sword," but "I think for most of my career it's been an advantage for me in most situations. I think gender has been probably more of an issue, particularly because I started out in investment banking, where there are so few women."

Even for those who are successful, the entrepreneurial route can be difficult. As bad as the corporate world could be, at least it "had rules," said Ethan Bruce. "You can't do anything about unfair treatment from clients." Bruce left a career in finance after a series of disappointments. The final insult was when a man with fewer credentials and much less experience was promoted above him. Bruce loves being free of corporate restraints. Still, he acknowledged a downside. "The bad news for black entrepreneurs is, you don't have the corporate logo to lend credibility."

That lack of corporate credibility can make life hard. Said Ella Bingham,* class of 1990:

> We regularly experience the "Black Tax" of having to jump through more hoops and face more closed doors as we pursue new business opportunities and try to raise growth capital. We have to work harder, be smarter and more persistent than our majority-owned competition, or else we would be crushed. This adds a level of stress to our work environment that majority-owned firms do not have to manage.

Those MBA respondents who opted to become entrepreneurs were, in most respects, very much like the rest. There were, nonetheless, some interesting differences. They were more likely than those still working for others (94 to 84 percent) to believe that blacks in corporate America labor under a glass ceiling. But they were much less likely (38 to 56 percent) to see a glass ceiling at their current workplace. (Since they are entrepreneurs, any ceiling presumably would be imposed from outside by others, such as clients.) Not surprisingly, they thought (73 to 53 percent) that blacks are better off becoming entrepreneurs than working in corporate America. They were more likely (82 to 77 percent) to believe that they had been discriminated against at work and much more likely to believe that discrimination had seriously affected their careers (60 to 44 percent). To the extent that these findings reflect a broader reality, they strongly supported the suspicion that my friend voiced in that melancholy conversation more than a decade and a half ago.

For black Harvard MBAs, as for members of any other group, the decision to start a business has multiple origins. Sometimes, particularly for women (as Professors DeMartino and Barbato concluded), it is driven by family considerations. Often it is motivated by a simple craving for more autonomy, for the opportunity to make one's own mistakes, create one's own opportunities, and garner the rewards that come with that. But for many blacks—certainly for many who responded to my survey—race plays an explicit role. As one business owner (class of 1988) put it, "In corporate America, you don't know whether your success or lack thereof is a function of ability or race, or something else. As an entrepreneur, those questions are clearer. So you have more peace of mind."

Nevertheless, most of my respondents, like almost all MBAs, were not starting their own businesses, whatever they might have believed about the desirability of doing so. They continued to function in a society and in work environments that virtually all of them perceived as more difficult for blacks than for comparably credentialed whites. (While 60 percent thought that blacks face a lot of discrimination in American society, essentially none—fewer than 1 percent—believed that whites are often discriminated against, and 94 percent believed that there are fewer opportunities for blacks in corporate America than for whites.)

For those who find the corporate environment somewhat alienating, black networks can be an important source of support. Fifty-seven percent of my respondents said that "racial or ethnic minority social-professional networks have been an important part of [my] life."

Such networks "give me perspective," said marketing executive Joahne Carter, class of 2002. "I've used my minority network to help my husband get a job." Her generation, she acknowledged, had made a lot of progress in the business world, and she saw the use of minority networks as a way of making sure that progress continued: "Affirmative action, quota programs, all those things are no longer going to exist, so we have to leverage our network."

Justine Bland,* class of 1989, said that her involvement in the National Black MBA Association yielded a range of benefits. "I gained mentors through networking and experience that I wasn't getting initially at work. It even gave me access to the president of my own company, which I never had at work."

"Having successfully spent sixteen years on Wall Street, I can attribute a large part of my success to the mainly informal racial social-professional networks I have been a part of," said Charles Stovall,* class of 1994.

"I would say, and I'm probably fairly representative in the HBS group, I wouldn't have gotten as far as I have gotten if I wasn't comfortable being the only minority frequently in a work team," said Amara Baillie. "The average friend that I have feels much less comfortable being the only black person in the room than I do." She attributed some of her comfort level to having worked on a trading floor "where I was the only black person who was not support staff. I'm used to being the only woman in a conversation." Almost all the top people in her field are white, so "I obviously have to cultivate mentors who are outside of my group. And to be honest, some of the people who have most gone out of their way to help have been white men. I'm fairly conscious about that." But it is very important to her to have a black professional network: "Very often I plug in for informal support. I'm not typically coming to them with tactical professional questions." If she is having a hard time emotionally or thinking about quitting, "or I'm really depressed, or the vibe of this team doesn't fit . . . I guess you could call it psychological support is very much what I turn to my fellow black colleagues for."

"I network with other black professionals to keep me sane," said Simone Jenkins. When she feels like she's "going crazy at work . . . I use my network of black professionals as a sounding board and source of honest advice and peer mentorship."

The importance that so many high-achieving blacks place on such networks is just one of many signs that, even in this age of opportunity, being a black professional navigating the upper echelons of corporate life comes with a special set of pressures. Psychologist Linda Anderson said that she has seen such pressures drive some black professionals to extreme measures:

> Because the dream is realizable and because there are so many barriers to actually accessing that dream, there's an extraordinary amount of work and personal sacrifice that's involved. . . . I see a tendency to work beyond what one really is capable of, whether it's sleeping in your office at night in order to make an early-morning meeting or [taking] a loan to go on business trips because they may not have access to the cash that's required.

The workplace is not the only source of pressures. Like other African Americans, Harvard MBAs exist in a society where blackness is often equated with poverty and crime; they are stereotyped by those who don't know them despite their dazzling Harvard degree. That was the point Professor Ogletree was making when he mentioned black students being unable to get a taxi home at night.

I thought about the conversation with Ogletree late one evening as I was trying to hail a cab near my Upper West Side home in Manhattan. Several taxi drivers glanced my way and kept going. One slowed but sped off after taking a closer look. Another switched on his NOT FOR HIRE light. One finally stopped and waited for me to get in. There are so many taxis on that stretch of Amsterdam Avenue that this all took place in only a minute or so. I was sure that my driver, who appeared to be Pakistani, had seen some of the others shun me, but I nonetheless described what had just transpired and asked what he made of it. "Some drivers don't like to pick up the bad people," he responded. "But I pick up everybody."

His comment struck me as so hilarious that I had to stifle a chuckle, but it occurred to me that had there been fewer taxis available, or had I been in a different mood, I might have ended up enraged instead of amused. For what he was saying was that until evidence was presented to the contrary, he presumed that a black man waiting for a taxi belonged to the class of "bad people."

Interviews detailing the anger and frustration engendered by such encounters make up a large part of *Rage*. One of those interviews was with New York mayor David Dinkins, who declared with a rueful smile, "A white man with a million dollars is a millionaire. And a black man with a million dollars is a nigger with a million dollars." Dinkins's point, I wrote,

> is that many whites have great difficulty differentiating a black go-getter from a black bum, that at night on a lonely stretch of highway a malicious cop is as likely to bash one black head as another. And even if Dinkins doesn't believe his own words, plenty of other blacks do—or at least believe that countless cops see color first and class later, if at all. . . .
>
> When the senior partner in the big law firm goes to a store and is treated "like I make two cents and am uneducated," he is in exactly the same boat as Dinkins's "nigger with a million dollars." When an accomplished jurist complains of white counterparts who "want you to do well, but not that well" and wonders

what he might have achieved had he really "been given a fair shot," he is making the same point: that the benefits of material success do not include exemption from being treated as a "nigger."

As much as certain things have improved in the last decade and a half, I had no real expectation that the dynamic of the random encounter had fundamentally changed. But I included a question in my survey to gauge that. "Have you personally experienced discrimination outside the workplace?" I asked, and I offered several possible options for sources of discrimination: police, shopkeepers or servers, taxi drivers, landlords, fellow students, teachers, banks or lenders, and other. When I administered the survey to the ABC alumni, 86 percent said that they had experienced such discrimination. But several complained in the comments section of the survey that I should not have limited them to one choice. So in the Harvard survey, which I administered several weeks later, I allowed respondents to choose as many sources of discrimination as they wished. The number reporting discrimination was essentially equivalent to the number reported by the ABC alumni: 89 percent. The interesting result, however, was how many chose multiple sources. On average, respondents chose 3.4 sources of discrimination, with the most common being "shopkeepers or servers" (78 percent), "taxi drivers" (57 percent), and "police" and "teachers" (each 43 percent). No category garnered fewer than 25 percent of responses.

This probably comes as no surprise to any reader who regularly listens to blacks complain about such things, but it is nonetheless a stunningly high number in a nation that has made such an effort over the last several decades to turn itself into a discrimination-free zone. And unlike many of the questions having to do with discrimination, responses did not vary as a function of age. Ninety percent of respondents under forty said that they had faced such discrimination, as did 88 percent of those forty and older. Nor did responses vary by gender. Ninety percent of males and 88 percent of females reported discrimination outside of work. What did diverge were the sources of discrimination reported. Some 57 percent of males said that the police had discriminated against them, as did only 22 percent of females. And 65 percent of males reported discrimination from taxi drivers, compared to 44 percent of females. There was also a gender difference in the number of sources, with males averaging 3.7 and women 2.9 sources of discrimination.

The numbers paint a picture that is stunningly clear: blacks, no matter how well educated and well positioned professionally, are overwhelmingly likely at some point, during random encounters on the streets and in shops, to be treated with gross disrespect, to be objects of contempt, fear, or both—and this is particularly true for black males.

"[When] we walk down the street, and our wives go to the department store, [we're] at a much higher risk of being mistreated," NAACP president Ben Jealous observed during a lengthy conversation over wine. In the past, he said, mistreatment was based on "presumed inferiority," but now it is largely based on "presumed criminality," although class and status matter.

> Once you're vetted, once you're known, they don't clutch their purse, instinctively. They don't presume you're a criminal. You're the vice president of operations, or you're a fellow Columbia man. . . . You're in the club, and everybody knows you. When you are not known, then you're just a random black man. And that space is a very dangerous space to be in—that space of anonymity where the mask of a criminal is involuntarily cast across your face.

Jealous recalled that a retired federal judge had been pulled over with his speakers blaring rap music. Once the judge produced his credentials, the attitude of the police officer abruptly changed, and he asked if he could escort the judge home: "But that moment when a black man is pulled over as a presumed intruder, even if it's into his own neighborhood . . . One false move and you're dead . . . it makes you angry," said Jealous.

For Harvard MBAs, no less than for other blacks, that reality is a source of anxiety, not only for themselves but for their children—and particularly for their male children. "When the African American male walks onto the street, they're African American males, number one, and they're a threat. And this is in every aspect," said real estate executive Ruby Nelson. "When my sons walk out of my door, the world assumes they're bad. It's different for African American males than any other group. It has been a challenge at every step of the way as a parent."

One of her sons is twenty-two. He attended a private school in Los Angeles that had only three black students in kindergarten. He was humiliated his first day when the teacher insisted that he recite the Pledge of Allegiance, which he did not know. From that point on, teachers expected little of him. One told the administration that he shouldn't be in the school. "There was no real reason. They thought he wasn't smart just because he was quiet." The headmaster, who knew their family background, intervened. But "every step of the way it was a challenge." Her younger son was more outgoing, but the school was no less a challenge for him. Instead of talking to his parents if the kid was goofing off, "they just wrote him up." Teachers told her that he didn't have what it took to go to college. Nonetheless, he ended up graduating first in his class. "It's tiring," she said. "You work so hard to improve life for your kids, and it's still a fight. It saddens me that they've had to go through this."

Jacinda Branham,* class of 1984, was similarly concerned:

> We have two young adult sons, one headed to law school in the fall, the other in college. Raising two African American males in today's society with all the negativity focused on them has been difficult. Even in upper-middle-class communities with excellent schools . . . there is an assumption that they will not succeed, and we have had to actively manage their schools in order to ensure that they are given educational opportunities.

As worried as the respondents were for their children, most assumed that they would be okay in the end and that the advantages they could provide their kids, as privileged and successful parents, would ultimately ensure their success and enable them to prevail over the "negativity" in the environment. They were not so confident, however, about the fate of the children of the poor.

"I feel like my son and my daughter, who have been exquisitely educated, are [among the] few who have escaped the fate of African Americans of our country," said Hal King. "I am chairman of court-appointed special advocates and chairman of the child abuse prevention council. When I look at the state of African American children, it makes me want to cry. . . . We are condemning a generation of African Americans to lives of misery, and it makes me angry."

"I believe that the opportunity for high achievement amongst blacks absolutely exists today more so than before," said Jasmine Washington. "However, I think the opportunities are being made [available] to a smaller and smaller population of blacks. . . . Our lower class is growing and becoming more permanent. It seems to be harder for collective advancement these days."

"I think that particularly if you think about midcentury, the civil rights struggle, it was really a galvanizing time, and the poor and middle class were very much aligned," said Connie Jackson. The catalyzing force of the civil rights movement is now gone, so "people go back to their ethnic and class squabbles. It's causing a really two-tier system of everything, which doesn't bode well for the future."

In their 2007 survey, Pew researchers asked respondents whether the values of the black poor and the black middle class have become more different or more similar. Sixty-one percent of blacks said that they have diverged. Among my Harvard respondents, 67 percent said the same thing—as did 62 percent of my black ABC respondents. When Pew asked whether the two groups have values in common, only one-quarter (23 percent) said that they have a lot in common, but a majority (65 percent) said that they share at least some values. Again, my ABC respondents agreed—with 25 percent saying that the two groups have a lot of values in common and a majority saying that they have some. I thought it would be interesting to ask the question a bit differently of the Harvard group. Instead of asking about values, I simply asked how much the two groups have in common. Only 16 percent of the Harvard respondents said that they have a lot in common, though a majority still agreed that they have at least some things in common.

As I noted previously, the black poor and the black privileged class are in fact becoming more and more different. The Harvard MBAs who pull down high-six-figure salaries and dream of becoming chairman of the board are in an altogether different universe from the youths who drop out of high school as a prelude to a life of poverty and unfulfilled hope. On the one hand—the hand holding the Harvard degree—this difference is an achievement worth celebrating, evidence that the nation is increasingly willing to acknowledge and reward talent, whatever package it happens to come in. On the other hand, it is an indictment of a country that has abandoned so many whose biggest and original sin was being born in the wrong community. But this is not just the story of blacks in America; it is more and more the story of America itself—a place where the gap between the poor and the privileged is growing by the day. There is an interesting irony in the fact that just as the barriers of race are coming down, those of class are rising higher than ever—putting the concept of one America more at risk even as we finally embrace the full ethnic and racial spectrum of the American rainbow.

Chapter Four

Fighters, Dreamers, and Believers

As I conducted interviews for this book, one thing became very clear. Though many of my interviewees superficially shared a certain profile—in that they were accomplished and black—they differed, often subtly, sometimes radically, on how they viewed issues of race and opportunity. And at least part of that difference, I realized, had to do with their generation—with when they were born relative to America's modern civil rights struggle.

I did not set out to do a book on generations or to come up with a new scheme to describe them. But as I studied the five-hundred-plus questionnaires that people filled out at my request and reviewed the transcripts of the more than two hundred interviews I oversaw or conducted, generational themes emerged that were too strong to ignore.

I am not the first to recognize that African Americans can be divided into different cohorts depending on their closeness to, or distance from, the defining civil rights battles of the twentieth century. As noted previously, preachers such as the Reverend Jesse Jackson routinely speak of the Moses and Joshua generations. Barack Obama adopted that language for a 2007 speech in Selma, Alabama, commemorating the famous "bloody Sunday" march in 1965.

Obama began his oration by paying tribute to John Lewis, Jesse

Jackson, and other notables who were present, but then turned to the subject of his presidential campaign. When he had announced his candidacy some weeks earlier, said Obama, certain commentators "questioned the audacity of a young man" reaching for such a prize. But the Reverend Otis Moss Jr. had written him with words of encouragement: "And he said, if there's some folks out there who are questioning whether or not you should run, just tell them to look at the story of Joshua, because you're part of the Joshua generation."

> So I just want to talk a little about Moses and Aaron and Joshua, because we are in the presence today of a lot of Moseses. We're in the presence today of giants whose shoulders we stand on, people who battled, not just on behalf of African Americans but on behalf of all of America; that battled for America's soul, that shed blood, that endured taunts and . . . torment and in some cases gave the full measure of their devotion.
>
> Like Moses, they challenged Pharaoh, the princes, powers who said that some are atop and others are at the bottom, and that's how it's always going to be. . . .
>
> I'm here because you all sacrificed for me. I stand on the shoulders of giants. I thank the Moses generation, but we've got to remember, now, that Joshua still had a job to do. As great as Moses was . . . he didn't cross over the river to see the Promised Land. God told him, your job is done. . . .
>
> We're going to leave it to the Joshua generation to make sure it happens.

Jackson agrees with the terminology but disagrees with where Obama should be placed, since Jackson believes *himself* to be a member of the Joshua generation. During our conversation, he spoke eloquently of his view:

> Moses is scarred. Dr. King led demonstrations, went to jail, and got his house bombed. . . . And those of us who came out of that army . . . our mission was to tear down walls. So Jesse Jackson's up

> here marching into Cicero, boycotting the A&P and Jewel and Red Rooster and making all these demands on [Mayor Richard J.] Daley and unseating the Daley machine [at the Democratic National Convention] in Miami in 1972. . . . So Joshua was seen as threatening as Moses was. He extends that tradition. Once the walls are down, bridges can be built from the rocks that came from those walls. [The generation that walks across those bridges] is more acceptable. They are less threatening. . . . The doors we had to have the National Guard to get us in [are now open]. They can go to Harvard . . . Columbia, or the University of Texas. So that's the third generation, not Joshua, but the third generation. They have been socialized differently and accepted in different circles.

"I feel honored I went to jail in Greenville," declared Jackson.

> I feel honored I went to jail in Greensboro. I feel honored I went to jail in Chicago fighting for schools. I feel honored I went to jail to free Mandela, got [former Haitian president Jean-Bertrand] Aristide back. To me those are badges of honor. . . . And as a ballplayer, I know so well that while the halfback gets the credit, halfbacks don't run through walls. They run through holes made by blockers, and the blocker on a team feels as gratified to look up and see the guy made it through the hole as the guy who scores. I mean . . . you're knocked out, but the guy you block for is in the end zone. We win. You hear my point? *We* win.

His presidential candidacy in 1984, Jackson pointed out, changed the Democratic Party rules to allow for more proportional allocation of delegates:

> So following the rules of proportionality, even when Barack was losing he was winning. . . . So the difference is that twenty years later, President Barack is able to go across a bridge. He has no scars from knocking down walls. . . . He ran the last lap of a sixty-year race. But [there were] fierce battles to make the bridge possible. And those who knocked down those walls got scars.

To talk with Jackson about such subjects is to feel a sense of history but also of loss. As he reflected on the scars that made it impossible for him to be embraced by the mainstream, I found myself wondering what he could have become had he been born into an America that was ready to fully recognize and reward his gifts, that had provided another path to prominence that didn't necessarily go through the church and into the movement or require that he become a voice for his race. As impressive as Jesse Jackson is as a civil rights icon, he could have been equally impressive in any number of other fields. Yet he had little choice but to devote the full measure of his talents to fighting a battle that should not even have been necessary—to the struggle to get himself, and his people, respect; to playing the faithful disciple to a fallen Moses.

I understand why preachers—and at least one politician—are drawn to the religious analogy, but I am not convinced that it fits. Joshua, after all, was Moses's apprentice. He "comes out of Moses's army," as Jackson put it. Barack Obama was not, in any sense, an apprentice to King—or to Jackson for that matter. *So just how does he become Joshua?*

Generation 1: The Fighters

I prefer to put the biblical allusions aside and to think of the generation of Jackson, John Lewis, and King as one cohort, as Generation 1—the generation that forced modern-day America to acknowledge that blacks are full and complete human beings. They were the beginning. They ushered in the new age. And they fought not only on the civil rights battlefield but in law firms, corporations, and segregated communities. The "Gen 1 Fighters" took on a society that was wedded to the notion that blacks, no matter how brilliant and highly accomplished, are lesser beings. And in breaking through the walls that Jim Crow had built, they did indeed get scars. Those scars, deep and painful, left many of them unwilling to fully trust in the kindness and goodwill of white folks.

They were born in 1944 or before—early enough to have become adults by the time Bloody Sunday rolled around in 1965. They are now in their late sixties or older. And whether they risked their lives or just their psychological well-being, they were fundamentally shaped by the age of untrammeled white privilege and by their rejection, sometimes in the most brutal way, by the country in which most of them were born.

They are essentially contemporaries of the so-called Silent Generation, a term popularized by a 1951 *Time* magazine cover story and later adopted by authors William Strauss and Neil Howe (who define "Silents" as those born between 1925 and 1945). Most Silents, said *Time,* "want a good job with a big firm, and with it, a kind of suburban idyll." I doubt that anyone black was interviewed for the *Time* article. Certainly no one black is identified within it. It was written in an era when magazines such as *Time* felt that blacks had nothing useful to say. Had they included African Americans, I doubt that they would have concluded that "today's young people already seem a bit stodgy. Their adventures of the mind are apt to be mild and safe. . . . [Educators complain that they] seem to have no militant beliefs. They do not speak out for anything. . . . Today's generation, either through fear, passivity or conviction, is ready to conform."

The fact is that some members of that generation—at least those who were black—had all kinds of "militant beliefs," the most militant of which was the simple certainty that they were entitled to equal citizenship. Their conformist white peers, for the most part, were on the opposite side of that issue. Silents, steeped in the culture of white exclusion and fundamentally uncomfortable with blacks as individuals, were content with American apartheid. It was Silents who barred Gen 1s from universities in the South and from corporate jobs everywhere. To lump blacks of the era in with the Silents is to misunderstand both groups. They were opposites in many ways. While Silents dreamed of cushy corporate jobs, Gen 1s dreamed of throwing off their shackles and storming the corporate walls.

I acknowledge that my taxonomy, like just about any classification scheme, is arbitrary to some degree and that it does not encompass the full complexity of human beings—many of whom, in any generation, are capable of so much more vision and decency than their peers. I think it does give us a useful way, however, to think about the journey this country and its citizens have made over the last half century. To make sense of where we are now, we have to understand where we began. A natural place to start is with the Gen 1 Fighters: those who were witness to—and in many cases participants in—the tearing down of a legal framework that had supported the elaborate system of white supremacy that persisted for a century following the Civil War.

Among the people I met while researching *Rage* was Ulric Haynes, a Gen 1 who graduated from Yale University Law School in the 1950s. This is his story as I recounted it.

> Haynes sent off 135 job applications and succeeded in getting interviews with more than seventy white firms, none of which was prepared to give him a job—even though there were jobs aplenty, as the country was in a period of relative prosperity. At one of the firms, he did manage to meet the sole black lawyer who seemed to have cracked the white wall. As Haynes recalls, the now-prominent attorney "sat me down and said, 'There's only room for one of us here, and I'm it.'
>
> "I've never forgotten it. And, in my heart of hearts, I've never really forgiven it," says Haynes, who acknowledges that the man was doing him something of a favor by telling him not to waste his time. . . .
>
> Before Haynes could become a success, he first had to deal with his considerable anger over his rejection by the law establishment. When Haynes got his law degree from Yale in 1956, he thought the world was his for the taking: "I got suckered into believing that because I performed as well as anybody else . . . opportunities were going to be as available to me as they were to them." He still keeps a packet of the turndown letters he

received from major law firms, just to remind him of what those days were like. "The excuses were standard. The nice ones were, 'Oh, you wouldn't be happy with us.' The nasty ones were, 'Well our clients would feel uncomfortable dealing with someone of your race.' In between were those that said, 'You're certainly overqualified for anything we have to offer.' . . . To finish the sentence, *'anything we have to offer someone of your race.'*" . . .

Haynes naturally found the experience painful, and he was forced to turn his back on the legal career he had planned to pursue. But in the midst of rejection, he also found the instrument of his deliverance: "Fortunately, the one job offer I got came from Averill Harriman, who was then governor of New York State, and it was through him that I embarked on a career in international affairs. . . . It was very important to me, given my frustration in my own country, that I get out of my country. And I joined the staff of the United Nations secretariat in the European office in Geneva, Switzerland. . . . Then, from there, I went to the Ford Foundation in Nigeria, and then in Tunisia, at a time when both of those countries were newly independent. It was not by accident that I stayed abroad as long as I did. Or that I still frequently seek opportunities to go abroad. Living and working abroad helped me to come to terms with the disappointment I had known in my own country. And to turn what might have been self-destructive rage into rather more productive energy."

"Instead of self-destructing," I noted, Haynes "found himself vowing, 'I'll show the sons of bitches. I'll distinguish myself where they can't touch me.'"

Relatively few members of Haynes's generation fled overseas to escape racism at home. But virtually all, at one point or another, had to deal with the reality that, at some fundamental level, white American society would never treat them as it did its own.

Perhaps the first time I reflected deeply on this was when I was in college and had brought a white female friend home. My mother leapt to the conclusion that something romantic must be brewing, and she pulled me aside to warn me, "Her people will never accept you. They don't care anything about you." My mother was not, by any reasonable definition, a racist; she was merely speaking from her experience coming up in the segregated South—where black boys got lynched for looking at white girls and no white family would dare welcome a black boy as a mate for a southern belle.

When Gen 1s went out into the work world, many were met with rejection—particularly if they were trying to get jobs that were considered, in those days, suitable only for whites. Even those who were not rejected outright typically found their progress hampered by bosses who were unwilling to promote them above a certain level.

Discontent is palpable among my MBA Gen 1 respondents. One acknowledged that though he owed his considerable success to his Harvard degree, there was still an "attainment gap between where I am versus where I could be as a Harvard MBA because of race." Another wrote, "I still do not play golf based on exclusion [in the old days] from the private clubs." What one takes away from many of their comments is the same sense of frustration I detected in my friend so many years ago as he credited his Harvard MBA for opening certain doors but insisted that he deserved—and had been denied—so much more. And one is left with the question I found myself asking in regards to Jesse Jackson: what could they have become had they really been free, had they not been forced to fight so hard for a chance to prove their worth?

One Gen 1 MBA enjoyed a career as an educator before heading off to Harvard, but even that path—a somewhat traditional one for educated blacks—was not free of obstacles.

> When I applied for a teacher's position in Berkeley, California, in the late 1940s, with a bachelor's degree in mathematics, I was informed that the school district did not hire Negroes at the secondary level. After obtaining other employment and taking classes at night at the University of California at Berkeley that

would earn me an elementary teaching credential, I reapplied and was hired in 1954. I advanced through the school system from teacher to vice principal, principal, director of elementary education, to assistant superintendent for instruction before leaving the district in 1973. When we desegregated the Berkeley school system with two-way busing in the 1960s, the Berkeley Board of Education had to withstand a recall election.... People are often surprised when I tell this story because Berkeley was perceived to be such a "liberal bastion."

Among the prominent public officials I interviewed for *Rage* was Basil Paterson, now known as the father of David Paterson, New York's fifty-fifth governor. Basil Paterson was a force in his own right long before his son entered politics. A former deputy mayor of New York and a former New York secretary of state, Paterson was a longtime leader of the fabled Harlem political machine. When I interviewed him in the early 1990s, he was in his sixties and beginning to look back on his distinguished political and legal career. What he said was both unexpected and poignant: "Every day I realize that I'm further ahead than I ever thought I would be in my life," yet "by any standard that is uniquely American, I'm not successful. It's too late for me to get rich because I spent too much time preparing for what I've got. . . . Most of us are ten years behind what we should have been. We couldn't get credentials until we were older than other folks."

That sense of lost possibilities and unfulfilled potential is typical, I believe, of members of the Gen 1 cohort, and perhaps not surprisingly, they tend to doubt that things will be much better for those coming behind them.

When I discussed this book over breakfast with Paterson, he immediately took issue with the idea that America has made much progress. "You've had one [black] president in the history of this nation since 1789. We've had three governors. . . . We haven't gotten anywhere to speak of."

Just the previous day, he said, he had seen two young white

males secure jobs at two different major law firms simply because they had connections. "That has been going on for the other folks forever, and still goes on. [But] too few of us have an uncle or a father or a mother or an aunt who can put them someplace. *Too few.* And that's part of the entire commercial scene."

He personally had been very lucky, said Paterson. At the age of sixteen, after graduating from high school, he went to work in the old Port Authority building in New York "loading trucks and doing all kinds of things." One of his coworkers, a young black football player sporting a college sweater, asked why he wasn't in college. Paterson told the young man that his family could not afford it, and his new friend asked the manager, "Could you give him the same deal you gave me, where he can come in after school?" Because of that gesture, Paterson went to college.

That kid, George Fleary, later became a lawyer and then a judge. "I went out and campaigned all over the place for him and kept telling that story," said Paterson. "I've never forgotten that—that a kid eighteen years old would be concerned about another kid a couple of years younger. . . . How often do we see where somebody's in position, one of us to help the other?"

Paterson conceded that Obama's election is a step forward: "Anybody who says that wasn't progress is an idiot." But "there is no question that there was a price we paid." For Obama's victory has convinced many whites that blacks are getting too much power:

> Now, I think with a lot of younger blacks, they don't look at it that way. They think we have reached—not race-neutral or postracial—but they think things are really very different. And they are. But they ought to be very careful. The further up we go, the more of a target we become—not always just because of race, but because we're more identifiable as we move up the ladder of success. And everybody thinks that the more we make, the less they get.

Derrick Bell, a New York University law professor and Paterson's contemporary, is a brilliant scholar—the father of critical race theory—and one of the most principled, gracious, courageous, and bighearted people that I know. He is so principled that he walked away from a tenured professorship at Harvard Law School because at the time, 1990, the school had not seen fit to hire a woman of color on its regular faculty. When it comes to race, his view is even bleaker than Paterson's.

He agreed that progress has been made, "but it's not eliminated the deep-set sense of superiority that so many whites have and the willingness to let black folks who are threatening go down the tubes."

Over breakfast, Bell and I discussed a range of things, including his son, now middle-aged, who, as a youth, couldn't understand why Bell harped so much on race. "Mom, Dad, you all keep talking about this racism stuff. What's that have to do with me?" he would ask. Bell smiled. "Now he can kind of name off what it has to do [with him]."

In 1992, Bell published *Faces at the Bottom of the Well,* a book that spells out his view that black Americans must accept and cope with the permanence of racism. "African Americans must confront and conquer the otherwise deadening reality of our permanent subordinate status. Only in this way can we prevent ourselves from being dragged down by society's racial hostility," he writes.

I asked Bell whether he would write that same book today. "I don't think I would write the same book," he replied, "but it wouldn't be any more optimistic." Later in the conversation he added, "I'm waiting for someone to convince me that I'm wrong, [that] it's not permanent."

Paterson and Bell have earned their right to skepticism. They are both cosmopolitan, highly educated men who count many whites among their close friends, but they have seen enough of the ugly side of racism to be leery that it will ever stop being a governing force in the lives of African Americans. It is a mark of a generation that lived through lynchings and Jim Crow, of a generation that knows from personal experience what it means to be stymied and excluded at every turn. ("At Christmastime, they used to pay us not to come to the Christmas party," Paterson said, recalling the job of his youth.) In reflecting on Barack Obama, Bell observed that the president had grown up with a supportive white family: "Now, they did things that upset him or what have you, but they basically loved him. He didn't have our experience of growing up and coming to see how mean white folks can be on the issue of race."

In his memoir *Dreams from My Father,* Obama essentially confirms Bell's point. In describing his interactions with Ray, a black childhood friend in Hawaii, he writes that occasionally the conversation would turn to white folks,

> and I would suddenly remember my mother's smile, and the words that I spoke would seem awkward and false. Or I would be helping Gramps dry the dishes after dinner and Toot would come in to say she was going to sleep, and those same words—white folks—would flash in my head like a bright neon sign, and I would suddenly grow quiet. . . . It was obvious that certain whites could be exempted from the general category of our distrust: Ray was always telling me how cool my grandparents were. The term white was simply a shorthand for him, I decided, a tag for what my mother would call a bigot.

Obama also writes about how, at the age of nine, he discovered the power of race-based self-hate while browsing through a copy of *Life* magazine in the American embassy in Indonesia. He stared at a photograph of a man with ghostly, pale skin, a thick nose, and crinkly hair and initially thought he might be an albino or perhaps a radiation victim. Upon reading the article, he learned that the man had paid for treatments to lighten his skin so he could try to pass as a white person. Thousands of black men and women back in America had done the same thing, he read.

The picture, he writes, was a revelation:

> My mother had warned me about bigots—they were ignorant, uneducated people one should avoid . . . I could correctly iden-

tify common greed or cruelty in others, and sometimes even in myself. But that one photograph had told me something else: that there was a hidden enemy out there, one that could reach me without anyone's knowledge, not even my own. When I got home that night from the embassy library, I went into the bathroom and stood in front of the mirror with all my senses and limbs seemingly intact, looking as I had always looked, and wondered if something was wrong with me. The alternative seemed no less frightening—that the adults around me lived in the midst of madness.

I asked Obama about that story when I interviewed him in 2006. "Up until that age, I didn't think about race that much. I didn't have to," he said. He had been raised in Hawaii and Indonesia—not in Alabama—and reading that article in *Life* magazine was "one of my first memories of thinking not only of the issue of race, but also of how it can insinuate itself inside of you." Bell, like most members of his generation, did not have the option of not thinking about race. And certainly, as he made clear, he was not surrounded by loving white people. Indeed, to the extent that most blacks of his generation encountered whites at all, those whites tended to be anything but loving.

This is not to say that Gen 1s are invariably pessimistic, but as Jesse Jackson and John Lewis said, in almost identical language, they bear the scars and the pain of racism and segregation. And like adults who were brutally abused as children, many never fully learn to trust those identified with the former abuser. Even Lewis, who is one of the least pessimistic people I know, seemed a bit puzzled by the seeming naïveté of the coming generation, even as he expressed his appreciation of it.

> I have a great deal of admiration for these young men and young women on the rise. . . . They didn't grow up every day . . . seeing those signs saying "White Only," "Colored Only." So they come out here with a sort of different attitude. And [they can] go off to these unbelievable colleges and universities. They're somewhat

> freer and a little more liberated. And I've heard it said from time to time that when some of these young men and young women go off to these schools, they never come out straight. They never come out right—that it sort of messes up their mind.

I was not entirely sure what to make of Lewis's observation of the younger generation, but he seemed to be saying that their liberation has come at something of a price, that their sometimes rosy view of the world is perhaps a bit too benign, too innocent, that their experiences in those "unbelievable colleges and universities" have left some of their minds so messed up that they cannot see how far we still have to go.

Generation 2: The Dreamers

I think of the generation that followed Lewis, Jackson, and King as Generation 2. Many were old enough to have witnessed Martin Luther King in action and to be inspired by the movement that he led, but for the most part, its members were too young to have played any real role. This generation began to come of age as the legal apparatus supporting discrimination was tumbling down. With the Civil Rights Act of 1964, the Voting Rights Act of 1965, and the Immigration and Nationality Act of 1965, America was formally embracing the notion that bigotry should no longer be the guiding force behind its policies and laws.

Born between 1945 and 1969, Gen 2 "Dreamers" are the counterparts of baby boomers (born between 1946 and 1964) and the older members of Generation X. Although they did not play the leading role in the civil rights movement, they were, without question, the children of "the Dream." They took Martin Luther King's words fully to heart and pushed America to make them come true. One of my ABC respondents, born in 1957, wrote:

> I hearken back to August 1963 when Martin Luther King gave the speech at the [Lincoln Memorial]. And I think about being

> accepted based on the content of your character as opposed to the color of your skin. I think that unquestionably in the United States of America, race still matters. And if I could magically change things, I would [make America] a true color-blind society [where] race wouldn't matter.

The Gen 2s were not just children of "the Dream"—they were also children of the riots. Older Gen 2s lived through—and some of them participated in—the urban explosions that stunned and shook America in the 1960s as angry black communities rose up to demand an end to their oppression.

Gen 2s are the first and second waves of African Americans to pour into universities, corporations, and other institutions that previously had been almost exclusively white. At a conference on race and the law in 1996, Clarence Page, the syndicated columnist, talked about one effect of those riots:

> People ask me, "Have you ever benefited from affirmative action?" I answer boldly, quite rightly, "Yes, a program called urban riots." . . . Thirty years ago, in 1965 to '68, we had over four hundred urban riots in this country. . . . I came along . . . in the late sixties at a time when the newspapers of this country and the news rooms decided, "Maybe we ought to have a few people we could send out to the ghetto without looking too conspicuous." . . . My newspaper, for example, hired one black reporter in '67, Joe Boyce, a former Chicago cop. . . . It took over two years to hire another one, me. Joe helped to pave the way, you know. But these things happen very slowly.

Page is a friend of mine, and I have heard him make the same point in various venues. It is a story that many Gen 2s could tell, with appropriate revisions for specific companies and industries. Many ended up working for companies that really didn't want them but that felt, because of the tension in America's streets, that they needed a black face—and often it was only one black face—to show the world that they cared. It didn't matter very much that these African American employees sometimes had no particular training for the jobs they were getting, since most of their employers had no intention of having them do anything important. They were funneled into functions—community relations, public affairs, philanthropy—that were far removed, in most instances, from any real control over most corporate resources.

Sharon Collins, a sociologist at the University of Illinois at Chicago and author of *The Making and Breaking of a Black Middle Class,* has spent years studying African American executives in major corporations. In her research, she has found that those in the first wave of black executives were, for the most part, extremely "race-conscious. They all understood who they were in these organizations. . . . They understood they were unique. Some of them thought they had a community to pay back. Others said, 'Well, let the community look after itself.' But they were conscious of who they were historically." And many saw their job as being "kind of an advocate for the external community."

The second wave of Gen 2s, those who came armed with impeccable credentials, having integrated some of the nation's best schools, often fared not much better than the first. They aimed for the stars but generally fell short—rarely receiving the benefits and perks of whites with comparable credentials.

Audrey Franklin,* an ABC alumna born in 1952, responded to one of my survey questions with, "It is not enough for me to be as good as my white counterparts. I must be better, much better." When I asked her to explain what she meant, she said:

> One of the things I've always encountered was the fact that, in whatever job I've been in, [white coworkers never had the] educational qualifications that I did. They would hire people for the same positions who came from far inferior schools. And I thought that was always interesting. . . . I always have to be the sharpest around. I have to be the quickest, the most creative, and pretty much ahead of my white counterparts in order to at least be abreast of them.

Once, said Franklin, she was up for a promotion, and her boss told her, "I don't know how we couldn't give it to you." Franklin did not see that as a compliment or an altogether positive sign: "Basically what he was saying is, 'I *have* to give it to you,' not that 'I want to give it to you.' . . . I think the double standard is still pretty much in effect."

Attitudes like Franklin's were not cut from whole cloth. They were the result of interactions with whites in authority who could not see beyond stereotypes, who were simply incapable of treating black people in the same way they treated whites. Not that those whites were actively hostile. More often than not they were simply limited. Not having grown up among blacks, having no blacks in their lives as close friends or neighbors, they could not view them as anything other than foreign.

I remember some years ago an encounter with an older white man, a member of the Silent Generation, that came about because a white journalist friend wanted me to meet her boss. We got together for drinks in a well-known Washington hotel. The man was so discombobulated by my presence that he was reduced to babbling, and he proceeded to reel off the names of all the black people he had met—even though I had not asked him anything about black culture or about whom he might know. It was clear to me that he simply had no idea of how to engage a black person as a fellow human being, and that often was the case with members of that generation. It took a while for whites to begin to get comfortable.

Even for many liberal whites, embracing blacks was not necessarily natural, as *Guess Who's Coming to Dinner,* the 1967 movie starring Sidney Poitier, comically demonstrated. When the doctor played by Poitier suddenly appears in his white fiancée's San Francisco home, her liberal mother, played by Katharine Hepburn, is shocked speechless as she realizes that her daughter intends to marry a black man. The stammering woman finally recovers enough to say, "I suppose it would be all right if I said, 'My goodness.' Wouldn't it?" The father, played by Spencer Tracy, is even more astonished. "The doctor [Poitier] says you have a problem. You certainly have," he tells the young couple at one point. Later, in summing up the events of the day, which began with him learning that the two plan to be married, he says, "I think it's fair to say that I responded to this news in the same manner that any normal father would respond to it unless, of course, his daughter happened to be a Negro too. In a word, I was flabbergasted." Everyone's initial trepidations are rapidly overcome (in part, because Poitier's character is both a genius and a saint) as love triumphs over intolerance. It is, after all, a Hollywood movie. In the real world, acceptance did not always come so quickly.

"I was in an interracial marriage for eighteen years, from the 1970s. . . . I used to say it was people overcoming racism one family at a time," former senator Carol Moseley Braun told me in 2010 over lunch in an Italian restaurant in her Hyde Park neighborhood in Chicago. "I think we have to remind ourselves on a regular basis of that progress, and we have to celebrate it every chance we get," she added. "It's important to let whites who have made this transition, who are pushing for the elimination of racism, to let them know that their efforts . . . are appreciated."

Braun, born in 1947, was among the early wave of Gen 2s who seized the opportunities suddenly available to well-credentialed children of "the Dream." She spent several years as a prosecutor in the U.S. Attorney's Office in Chicago, after which she leapt into elective politics, becoming in 1992 the first black female U.S. senator in history.

She was acutely conscious that even though she had become a U.S. senator, some people would strive to put her in a black box—and she endeavored to change those expectations. "I made a public statement when I got elected to the Senate that I did not want to be 'Oprah gone to Washington,' and I didn't want to be 'Jesse [Jackson] in a skirt.'" She recalled that Oprah Winfrey got miffed at the line, "but what I was trying to say was, 'I'm here to represent the whole state of Illinois. I'm not a civil rights leader. That's not my job. On the other hand, I'm not here to entertain and nurture you either.'"

In the end, she thought, people got it and calibrated their expectations accordingly: "I think that if one is astute enough to read the cultural cues properly, then those expectations can be met and can be flipped on the positive side." But doing so, she believed, is harder for females and minorities than for white males.

> I mean, there is no set of negative expectations for white males. . . . My ex-husband used to tell me, "If I walk into a room and tell people I'm a brain surgeon, everyone says, 'Yes, doctor.' But if you walk into a room and tell everyone you're a brain surgeon, they want to know where'd you go to school, where were you on staff, how many brain surgeries have you performed, and did the patients live."

Moseley Braun dreams of a day when blacks will no longer have to overcome negative expectations, but she believes we are far from that day. "The demonization of blacks, the demonization of color," she argued, goes back to stereotypes created centuries ago when it was thought that blackness "was related to evil and the loss of God's love." To change that, she said, means "tackling a lot of history and a lot of very ingrained culture," and getting rid of "residual stereotypes having to do with criminality, . . . sexuality, lack of intellect," and with assumptions that "the dumbest white guy in town is smarter than the smartest black guy."

Rage detailed the price that many Gen 2s paid because, in their view, corporations were not ready to consider black guys as smart or competent as whites.

> Wallace Ford, a graduate of Dartmouth College and Harvard Law School, is characteristic. Comparing himself to whites with similar skills, experience, and education, Ford concluded, "I should probably be doing more than I'm doing now." At the time he was New York City's commissioner for business services and, though only in his early forties, had already held a series of impressive-sounding positions: president of the Harlem Lawyers Association, first vice president at Drexel Burnham Lam-

bert Inc., president of the State of New York Mortgage Agency, and others. Still, by his lights, he had underachieved, whether because of "bad luck, bad decisions, race," or "a combination of all three," he wasn't sure. But wherever the primary fault lay, he was certain that race had played a role.

"It's always a factor somewhere," said Ford. "It may not always be up front. It may be in the bushes, or lurking in someone's mind, but it's always there." Not that in the circles he frequented people were likely to vent racial animosities freely. "But you look at a situation and say, I know. By having gone to places like Dartmouth and Harvard . . . working with the governor, working with the mayor, [working with] people who are moving up . . . you realize that there's no magic." Yes, some of the stars who had briefly flickered near him before shooting high into the sky were brilliant and extremely well educated, but never so bright that he was "blinded from across the table." So he found himself asking: *Why can they do fifty-million-dollar deals with little more than projections on the back of an envelope?* And why were others, blacks who were "offering to give up mom, dad, and all their kids," able to get only crumbs? "You realize that a lot of it has to do with a lot of factors, race, who you know. Certain people are accorded the opportunity to do X. As you go up the ladder, much is made available to a few."

When I asked Ford recently what reception a young black person graduating with his identical academic credentials was likely to receive today, he agreed that things have changed radically. "I think that the near-term prospects for a young black man or woman coming from an Ivy League background would be excellent. Many institutions—law firms, investment banks, consulting firms, corporations—are much more attuned to diversity. And the prospect of highly educated black men and women walking the corridors of power is no longer revolutionary."

He was less certain about what would eventually become of those hired:

> Certainly there is a very real opportunity for these same men and women to stay the course and follow the rules, and they will be very successful by almost any standard—financially, professionally, personally. [But] for those who aspire to the highest rungs on the ladder, there are still very calcified points of view that have survived the generations. . . . A black president, a black chairman of American Express, a black CEO of Xerox, et cetera, has not changed the American way—at least not yet. I would advise any of these young men and women who aspire to the highest rung to look beyond the borders of the U.S. International trade and commerce is the way to go in almost every line of work. Prejudice and bias—against blacks, against Americans—will certainly be encountered, but it is a larger playing field, and someone with agility and flexibility can be very successful in the long term if they think globally and not parochially.

When I asked about prospects for his thirteen-year-old son, Ford was decidedly upbeat:

> I do believe that in his adult life there will be more opportunity for him in the global space that awaits him. I also know that there will be more competition that he will face, more than you and I ever encountered as young adults. Hundreds of millions of Chinese, Indians, Brazilians, Japanese, and Europeans are in the global marketplace. Technology will trump proximity, and Wally will have to be adept enough to adjust to dizzying changes in geopolitics, economics, and culture. But I think that he will embrace those dizzying changes and the fact that yester day doesn't control today and today may not predict tomorrow. In that sense, I welcome the changed world that awaits him.

Ford's guarded optimism is characteristic of Gen 2s, who acknowledge their own disappointments even as they concede that things may be changing for the better. They are much less likely than Gen 1s to have seen racism in its most virulent guise, and they are much more likely, during their formative years, to have had honest and close relationships with whites, Latinos, and Asians. They know, in short, that "calcified" views are less common than they once were. And they have seen, sometimes at very close range, how those views can change—and how, as a consequence, opportunities can open up.

"The difference between my generation and the generations ahead of me is that blacks in my generation succeeded more," said the Reverend Al Sharpton. And that success—a legacy, in many ways, of the Gen 1 civil rights leaders—is one reason, among many, that his job is not quite the same as that of the civil rights heroes he idolized as a youth and why he takes a different approach to it.

"There were the kids in my school that went to Ivy League schools, and there were the kids in my school that went to black colleges, whereas people fifteen years ahead of me, everybody had to go to a black college," said Sharpton.

> So I saw the world differently than Jesse [Jackson]. I didn't come out of the civil rights movement. I came out of the northern urban movement, which [focused on] racial profiling and police brutality. . . . I didn't grow up in the South. So, unlike Jesse, I never drank from a colored water fountain. I don't know about the back of the bus, but I knew about cops shooting you fifty times. I knew about going to the store and they follow you around. So it was another era, but fighting the same thing.

Younger Gen 2s—those in their forties—are, of course, even further removed from the racial rigidities that defined the world of Generation 1. And because of that, they are more likely to have formed trusting relationships with people of other races and less likely to see the world in stark racial tones.

James Howard,* born in 1965, works in Japan for an American technology company. Like many of his generation, he has grown weary of the racial dialogue in the United States, which, particularly when viewed from the vantage point of Asia, seems both overheated and outdated.

"Looking at the U.S. from the outside, I'm shocked at the degree of preoccupation Americans have over race," said Howard.

> At the same time, however, I can understand where that comes from. At times, I find myself doing the same thing, then trying to explain to my wife, who is Japanese, why I'm yelling at something on CNN. I know there is still racism in the U.S. There is also plenty of racism here in Japan, or anywhere else you go for that matter. What we tend to do in the U.S., unfortunately, is focus on the negative a bit too much. There isn't a lot of discussion about what works and why. And the focus is still heavily slanted toward black-white relations, when the demographics of the U.S. are changing in many more complex ways. In some ways, the public dialogue is still twenty or thirty years behind the times.

Howard saw color blindness as an impossible goal. Nonetheless, he argued, people of color in the United States should "adopt an attitude that says they won't allow themselves to be defined by their skin color—or by what people think should or should not be associated with that skin color. I've always thought this way, but living here has taught me what that actually means and how far [you] can go once you decide to see your life in these terms."

Barack Obama is obviously the most prominent example of a person who refuses to be defined by America's notion of what a man of African descent should be. And as Derrick Bell observed, Obama's world was never narrowly defined in racial terms. He was not forced into a black box of stereotypes, and his early understanding of whites was not rooted in experiences of exclusion and rejection but rather in love, acceptance, and support. All of that, no doubt, helped shape him into what he is today.

Obama is only half a generation older than Moseley Braun, but he came up in an altogether different world. "I know for a fact that I have memories of segregated water fountains and bathrooms," Moseley Braun said during our lunch.

> I had to sit-in at a lunch counter here on Stony Island in the late sixties, marched [as a teenager] with Dr. King when he came here to march in Gage Park, witnessed the riots. I was working at CHA

> [Chicago Housing Authority] when the riots broke out on the West Side in the sixties. So I've been there. I've seen that in my lifetime, [and] these are things that my son has no comprehension of.

Moseley Braun collects black memorabilia. Included among her acquisitions is a WE SERVE COLORED, CARRY OUT ONLY sign that hangs in her kitchen. Her son, Matt, born in 1977, "thought it was a joke. This was not a reality for him. I could've had a Roman artifact up there," she said, and it would have had just as much relevance to his universe.

Her son, of course, is a member of Generation 3, a group I think of as "the Believers." They are the group that Charles Ogletree had in mind when he observed:

> They are in this very unique, sequestered community at Harvard. And that gives them a sense that anything and everything is possible. It is not unusual for them to see . . . a female, an Asian or African American standing in front of them and teaching a class. . . . So they know that their environment has transformed. . . . And they are the answer to King's dream. They are being judged, in their minds, not by the color of their skin but by the content of their character. And that makes them conscious of the fact that they have opportunities others don't have and that race is not as much a barrier.

When Obama was his student, recalled Ogletree,

> Barack was the smartest kid in the classroom, but he was unique in that he was not the typical gunner—a student that tries to eat up all of the airtime to show how smart they are. He was much more of a conciliator. When he spoke, he was trying to bring out people in the conversation and to give them credit. . . . And I noticed that right on. And with respect to Barack . . . I said, he was so smart, so talented, I was convinced that when he grew up he was going to be the best damn mayor in the history of America. And when he hears me say that, he asks [addressing Ogletree by his nickname], "Tree, *mayor*?"

Ogletree's story neatly traces the arc of possibility as seen from the very different vantage points of those born near the beginning of the Gen 2 era and those born closer to its end. It was the difference, in short, between those who dreamed of conquering City Hall and those who set their sights on the White House.

Generation 3: The Believers

Gen 3s were born between 1970 and 1995. They overlap with the younger members of Generation X and the older of the Millennials. Separate water fountains and back-of-the-bus seating have about as much to do with their lives as troglodytes hanging out in caves. They came of age in an America where Jim Crow was ancient history and explicit expressions of racism were universally condemned. They grew up in a time when (as I put it in *The Envy of the World),* "white kids in the suburbs want to talk like us, want to walk like us, want to dress like us."

Many of the more privileged among them were raised in predominantly white neighborhoods and, from the beginning, attended predominantly white schools. Competing with other racial groups is nothing new to them.

Of that group, sociologist Sharon Collins said:

> They are operating like a white person would operate in an organization. They see themselves as entitled as anybody else in the organization. They have a pedigree just like the CEO over there. They went to the private schools. They have the network. . . . And I don't think race to them means the same as, say, race means to me, whose mother came from Mississippi and whose father couldn't be valedictorian because he was black. . . . I don't think race is a struggle for them.

The identifying characteristic of Gen 3s is their fervent—if not totally universal—belief that they personally can overcome whatever obstacles prejudice might set in their way. They don't believe America is color-blind, race-neutral, or "postracial." They do believe, however, that the old racial limits no longer apply and that the old racial boxes cannot contain them. And some of them are a bit fed up with the advice—and views—of their elders.

"My personal take [is that many members] of the civil rights generation have two models for corporate business success," said Simone Jenkins,* the thirty-year-old MBA who directs strategy for a major hotel chain. She argued that they either advocate "complete assimilation" or adopt an "I'm successful but I'm still down" persona, flaunting their ties to the "hood" even as they carefully try to navigate the corporate terrain. "Neither model works very well for those of us younger than Obama who don't have the same personal history of dealing with hard-core institutionalized and blatant racism," said Jenkins.

"Most of my peers have grown up with the recognition that we can be CEOs of Fortune 500 companies, managing directors on Wall Street, et cetera," said Jake Green,* who, at thirty-one, works in the health care industry.

> This belief and a better understanding of "the game" will help us create and capitalize on opportunities. However, we will also face headwinds the previous generation didn't experience—namely, the anti–affirmation action movement and disadvantaged white male sentiment, lack of a nearly twenty-year-plus bull market that the previous generation experienced, and the flattening of the global workforce. . . . My generation will have more opportunities, but they will be of a different kind.

"Of course, my generation has been the [beneficiary] of many gifts," says Ebony S. Morczinek, thirty-one, the Harvard MBA who works in the food services industry in Frankfurt, Germany.

> We are able to walk into jobs that previously were out of reach. We are also able to take the salaries that come with those positions and invest them in our families, churches, and communities. We are very well aware of our rights, despite not always

being willing to fight for them. We are also more comfortable in a white or mixed setting than other generations. This is the obvious by-product of integrated schools and allows us into the network of jobs that are never publicly advertised but passed along informally through word of mouth. However, there is much work to do. There are many senior-level roles where we are not considered, and we continue to be pigeonholed into "diversity" positions.

"My impression is that for older generations of black people, especially in the corporate world, there was a sense of 'I am an island,'" said Amara Baillie,* the twenty-eight-year-old MBA who works for a strategic consulting firm. There is no such sense of social isolation today, she believed. "For people of my generation, the biggest challenge is to adapt yourself to 'the norm.' If you're willing to talk like a white guy, if you're willing to completely assimilate, you will be successful. People will overlook that you're from a minority. [But] what I think we've missed is that people shouldn't have to mold themselves.

"Young people are much more meritocratic," said Baillie.

So I would hope that when I have children, they won't relate to anything that I'm saying. . . . It will be similar to the way that rural people get stereotyped against by urban people. You don't really hear about rural people support groups. It's much more subtle and, for the most part, manageable. . . . I am very hopeful about the future. . . . In the 1960s, when my parents were dealing with discrimination, they could point to really tangible, obvious wrongs. And even to some extent in the eighties, I feel like there were really clear instances of racism. . . . Overtly racist or sexist comments in my firm [are] almost unimaginable. I could not imagine a coworker speaking to me in an overtly racist manner.

Nonetheless, said Baillie, people have biases.

Your perception of my performance is very much shaped by your general overall impression of me. So whether you think I

> have client relation skills is going to be shaped by whether you think I'm a "sociable person," whether I'm someone the clients would want to hang out with. You're not going to think, "Oh, she's black," . . . but often those thoughts and perceptions are in the background.

"I think, even ten years ago, if you saw a face of color, a lot of folks wouldn't say it but they would think, 'Aw jeez, am I going to get stuck with that affirmative action person who can't pull their weight?'" said Angela Ndiaye,* thirty-one, who earned her MBA in 2007. She believed that her young cousins, who are nineteen and twenty, will not have to deal with that. "They genuinely believe they belong. And there isn't the self-doubt. . . . [Young people today] are just not plugged into the effort it took to get people where they are now. But in many ways that lack of knowledge is freeing, because it means . . . you aren't limited by these negative perceptions. You just 'do' and the results come."

Courtney Bass, twenty-nine, class of 2010, is a second-generation graduate of Harvard Business School (her mother earned her MBA in 1977), and she too is optimistic about the future: "My mother is in business, and I am going into business, and I think I will have more opportunities going forward. And I think that is because there's a lot more structure around opportunities. There are organizations that help minorities get job or nonjob opportunities. And those just hadn't been developed for previous generations."

Many Gen 1s and Gen 2s think the Gens 3s live in something of a fantasy world—that at some point, when they are older and more experienced, they will realize that the workplace is not nearly as fair as they believe it to be. When I asked Sara Scott,* the fifty-two-year-old utility executive, whether she thought the Gen 3s were naive, she replied:

> *Extremely!* I have two myself. And I talk incessantly about my family history and remind them of how contacts and networks have helped position them where they are in their very short

lives. However, they look at me as if I am speaking Greek. Their responses sometimes make me believe they think I am an angry black woman. I am—angry that because I and so many other parents have tried to give them a better quality of life, they are further removed from the poverty I recall and the bias that my parents endured. In trying to give them more, we have shielded them from many of the hardships we endured. It isn't real to them. They understand it intellectually, but they don't fully get it emotionally because they haven't endured as much. They have had the occasion to be followed in a department store or overlooked in an integrated classroom or not quite make the roster for extracurricular activities in sports when less athletic or articulate whites made it, but I am not sure they realize that this is a bias that starts early and will continue in some form or fashion throughout their lifetimes because of their exterior packaging—irrespective of their internal characteristics or qualities.

Charles Chisholm,* the sixty-something business consultant, was similarly concerned about the younger generation.

You can make a lot of money and have a lot of sway—more so than ever before. I think, however, as you know and other people know, there is what people call unconscious bias. The unconscious bias can in many cases be as bad [as conscious bias]. . . . People don't realize they're anti-black, anti-Hispanic, anti-woman. But it plays out in terms of evaluations, in terms of who you recruit, in terms of who you mentor, in terms of who gets the best assignments. And it's very, very subtle. And I think the younger blacks don't understand it. . . . I think the younger ones don't know it. The smart ones who can play the culture do very well. Now the issue there is, are they going to be sensitive enough to help other blacks move up the corporate ladder? Or are they just going to be that one black [at the top]?

The sharply different takes on the role of race were evident in my Harvard MBAs survey when I compared the Gen 1s and the

Gen 3s. On many questions looking at racial discrimination, they were worlds apart.

I am not suggesting that these results are definitive. The survey did not consist of random samples, and even if it did, the cohort of Gen 1 respondents (sixteen in total after I eliminated one white respondent who, for unknown reasons, had joined the black alumni association) was too small to allow for drawing any scientifically supportable conclusions. But given the consistency of the differences, I seriously doubt that they are just a function of happenstance.

When asked how much discrimination blacks face, 75 percent of Gen 1s said "a lot," compared to 49 percent of the Gen 3s. When asked, "Do you believe your educational attainments put you on an equal professional footing (in the eyes of employers or prospective employers) with white peers or competitors with comparable educational credentials?," 25 percent of Gen 1s said yes, compared to 62 percent of Gen 3s. When asked whether there is a glass ceiling at their current workplace, 93 percent of Gen 1s said yes, compared to 46 percent of Gen 3s. In response to the question "When competing professionally against white peers with comparable educational credentials, do you believe your race is a disadvantage?," 63 percent of Gen 1s said yes, compared to 42 percent of Gen 3s. "Would you be as successful if you did not have a Harvard MBA?" elicited a response of "no" from 94 percent of Gen 1s, compared to 67 percent of Gen 3s. All of the Gen 1s (100 percent) said that they had been discriminated against in the workplace, and 60 percent thought that discrimination had had a significant impact on their careers. For Gen 3s, the numbers were 68 percent and 20 percent, respectively.

As I said, I am not about to make a statistical argument based on these numbers, but the message nonetheless seems clear: generations matter—deeply—because experiences, and hence expectations, differ profoundly depending on the era in which one came of age.

In the time since the "Silents" came on the scene, a revolution has occurred in the United States. Those uptight suburbanites who couldn't imagine socializing with, working for, or marrying a "Negro," who thought that blacks existed in an altogether different dimension, who could no more see dining with a black person than dining with a giraffe, have slowly given way to a new generation that embraces—at least consciously—the concept of equality. And that process has cleared the way for a generation of black Believers—people who fully accept that America means what it says when it promises to give them a shot.

I cannot help but wonder about the generation to come—the Gen 4s—to which my young daughter belongs. If they are lucky, they will be the Reapers, the post-post-post–civil rights generation that harvests the crops from the seeds sown by those who came before, the generation that finally makes ours into an America in which race is no longer an acceptable reason to leave anyone behind.

When I asked John Lewis his thoughts, he replied:

> Your daughter is going to grow up . . . in a time when a black man, a man of color, was president, when there was a woman as secretary of state. So the whole question of race and gender—and hopefully the question of class—in a matter of a short time will be different. And she will grow up in a society where America will no longer be a white majority. . . . That's a different world. . . . [She will grow up] in a world where color no longer [will] be the issue.

I suspect that will not quite be the world she inherits, but it is nonetheless a beautiful thought.

Chapter Five

Hostiles, Neutrals, and Allies

Sarah* doesn't have any specific recollection of her first encounter with a black person, but she figures she must have felt a certain amount of trepidation.

> I just thought that they were really different, and because they *were* different, there was a barrier of not feeling really comfortable. . . . You have to consider, as a child, when we recited ring-around-the-rosy, it didn't end with "Ashes, ashes, we all fall down." It ended with, "Last one down is a nigger baby!" Brazil nuts were called "nigger toes," and slingshots were called "nigger flippers."

Her uncles, said Sarah, routinely referred to blacks as "niggers." She didn't think of it as a term of disparagement, however, because blacks were considered hardworking people: "I grew up with the impression that maybe they had a stronger physical endurance than some of us."

Her great-grandfather, a southerner, was much beloved by his slaves, said Sarah: "I've been told that when slavery was abolished, they actually cried because they felt like they were family."

Generation 1: The Hostiles

Sarah is a member of the Gen 1 generation. That generation, made up of Americans born prior to 1945, largely corresponds to what William Strauss and Neil Howe call "the Silent Generation." I call the whites of that era "the Hostile Generation." I do not mean to imply that most Gen 1 Hostiles were actively oppressing black people, burning crosses, or wearing white sheets over their heads, though some members of that generation did indeed do such things—just as some members of that generation fought courageously for racial equality. For the most part, however, this generation saw blacks as a race apart—as unworthy of full inclusion in the American community—and therefore entitled to neither the respect nor the consideration routinely accorded whites.

These were the people whom Young & Rubicam executives worried about offending in 1968 when they complained about British singer Petula Clark touching Harry Belafonte's arm during a duet they sang for her NBC special. James Baldwin was thinking about Gen 1 Hostiles when he wrote in 1974 in *No Name in the Street,* "A civilized country is, by definition, a country dominated by whites, in which the blacks clearly know their place. This is really the way the generality of white Americans feel." Hostiles were the people the Dreamers, particularly the older ones, had to deal with: bosses who were perfectly happy to hire blacks, but who had a hard time seeing them as senior managers; fellow workers who were perfectly happy to have blacks as associates, as neighbors (provided there were not too many), and even as "friends," but who could not really imagine them as family.

Sarah was born in New Mexico in 1941. When she was four, she moved with her family to Salt Lake City, Utah. There her parents raised seven children, imbuing them with strong Christian values. The first time Sarah recalled thinking seriously about race was during her teens, when the South exploded over desegregation: "I felt sad for Martin Luther King and them. They had to fight so hard for the rights [that they] should have had after slavery was abolished."

Sarah had six children of her own, including one who died young from leukemia. She and her husband ran a photography studio and several other businesses. Race rarely came up. But in 1965 she and her husband went to Los Angeles for a business conference and found themselves in the middle of Watts as one of the most violent race riots in American history was taking shape. "As we were talking in the car, we looked out the windows to see fire and smoke billowing from buildings on both sides of the street. The driver told us to lock our doors, that he needed to get out of there as quickly as possible. It felt like we were in the middle of a war."

When my interviewer asked Sarah whether she ever would have considered marrying a black person, Sarah seemed shocked: "No! *Definitely not*. That was entirely unacceptable. *Out of the question*. You just did not marry interracially, especially a black person. That was taboo."

Sarah is one of several whites interviewed for this book—usually by white associates, whose shared skin color, I thought, might encourage candor—who are voices of their respective generations. The mind-sets of Gen 1 Fighters, Gen 2 Believers, and Gen 3 Dreamers, as I've noted, did not arise in a vacuum. They were a response to the America and the prevailing ethos and prejudices of their times. Segregated as America was in the 1940s and 1950s, blacks of that era were acutely aware of how their white countrymen viewed them—even if those countrymen rarely gave them a second thought.

To watch virtually any movie or TV show made in that era is to enter a world where blacks, excepting the occasional servant or performer, seem not to exist. James* was a child of that age. He was born in Denver, Colorado, in 1941 and as an infant moved to Oak Ridge, Tennessee, where his father worked on a military project. After World War II, the family moved to a ranch in South Dakota, which he called home until he graduated from college.

James's first exposure to racial discrimination was through a story his father told of an incident on a Tennessee bus. "This black guy didn't go to the back like he was told to, and the bus driver pulled out a blackjack and just beat the crap out of him and kicked him off the bus. The next day Dad reads that he was killed for not obeying."

James remembered "walking down the street with my dad, and black people stepping aside." Of the blacks who worked for his dad, "it was always, 'yes, sir,' 'no, sir.'" After the family moved to South Dakota, blacks faded from his consciousness. "There wasn't a black person within fifty to a hundred miles. So all the way up through college I didn't have any association with black people."

He married in 1963 and honeymooned in the South, arriving in Birmingham, Alabama, in September—the day before the Ku Klux Klan bombed the 16th Street Baptist Church. "I could feel all the tension as we drove through." He decided to leave: "We drove on down to New Orleans, and it seemed like the blacks there were more subservient, so the unrest wasn't as noticeable."

In New Orleans, James and his bride decided to attend church.

> I was always a practicing Catholic. So we just looked through the paper and found where this "Saint Somebody's Church" was. And we went a little early because we thought that we might have trouble finding it. We saw the priest and he was white. As the church started filling up, I started to notice we were the only white people there besides the priest. Little black kids were pointing at us and giggling. Some people were smiling. And some of them were looking at us like, "What are you doing here, honky?" So we got our taste of what it's like to be a minority. Living in South Dakota, we never had.

Despite his relative lack of exposure to blacks, James was certain that he is not a racist.

> I never have had any prejudice. But I do know this. Well, I feel this—that the culture has created the challenges that the blacks have today. They have the opportunities, but they are so used to being screw-offs and lazy and getting government checks. I just heard on a talk show the other day where this gal just had

her fifth child. And she said that she would have to have nine to be able to get them checks enough to have everything that she wanted. That's sickening!

Asked about the civil rights movement, James conceded that "it was probably a good thing," though he thought "it could have been done better. . . . But who am I to say when I wasn't a part of it and I wasn't against it?"

He does not believe that America is yet an egalitarian society, since people (presumably meaning whites) still see blacks as different: "You notice when a black person comes into a room, where you don't if it's a white person. I think a white person would always describe their [black] friend as being a black person. I wouldn't say, 'Mary, a white girl.'"

Sarah and James both share an apparently heartfelt conviction that they are not prejudiced. They also share a profound belief that blacks are fundamentally different than they are. Both beliefs are typical of Gen 1 Hostiles. It is not an attitude that blacks—or enlightened whites, for that matter—have found easy to deal with. And in matters of race, it defines their age.

In 1951, only months before *Time* proclaimed the arrival of the Silent Generation, *Harper's* magazine published an essay entitled "My Daughter Married a Negro."

The editors introduced the article with the following: "What can a girl's parents do when their daughter decides on a mixed marriage? Without blame or prejudice, a father tells how his family tried to deal with a problem which has arisen more widely and more often than most of us realize."

The editors obviously assumed that typical readers would agree that the prospect of an interracial marriage constituted a "problem." And the anguished tone of the clearly liberal author made it clear that he felt the same. He spoke of the awkwardness of confessing this news to relatives and friends. It was better, he concluded, to keep some people in the dark: "I have business friends who, I hope, will never hear about it. With knights of the white supremacy I keep my mouth shut and calculate the explosive effect, in their company, of a few words dropped from our annals."

The writer recalled, with a mixture of pride and bewilderment, his country club's decision, apparently made in his honor, to admit

> members of the Jewish faith and Negro race . . . upon his or her merits as a person. "The news" was a stunning surprise. Nothing like it was mentioned in my presence nor had I ever talked with any of the board about my daughter and her husband. It is quite unlikely that Negroes will apply for membership for some time and when they do, the screening by any membership chairman now in view will be close.

Some relatives, he wrote, suggested that he take his daughter to a psychiatrist: "They reasoned that a good-looking girl who passed up members of her own race for a colored boy was mentally ill. While not professional it seemed a plausible diagnosis." The daughter eventually did consult a psychiatrist, who, to the father's apparent disappointment, found her to be of sound mind.

After trying without success to persuade the couple to break up, he ultimately accepted that the matter was out of his hands: "Two years ago all which we were wise enough to offer Anne was our sometime benevolent opposition. We thought we knew best, perhaps we did. Now, it is not so clear."

It is a beautifully written piece, rendered in a spirit of compassion and understanding. Yet even though the anonymous author strains to hit the right notes, what comes through is his certainty that, in choosing a Negro, his daughter has done something irremediably shameful—along the lines perhaps of becoming betrothed to a convicted rapist. What is also apparent is the clear presumption by the *Harper's* editors that the magazine's audience shared that view. And that was no doubt a fair assessment. It is not that Gen 1 Hostiles hated black people; in their view, that would have constituted racism. They simply felt that blacks ought to stay in their place, which was nowhere near white society—and certainly nowhere near anyone's white daughter.

Gallup's pollsters were quite familiar with that sentiment. In 1958, when the Gallup poll, for the first time, asked whites about black-white intermarriage, only 4 percent of respondents approved. By contrast, when Gallup asked the question of blacks—and the first such poll that identified black respondents was done in 1968—a majority (56 percent) approved of interracial marriage. By then, more than a decade after the Supreme Court had mandated desegregation of public schools, only 17 percent of whites approved.

The South, of course, was particularly hostile to anything that smacked of race mixing other than in a context where blacks were totally subservient. E. Dan Jordan, an Alabama native and former captain in the Jefferson County Sheriff's Office in Birmingham who was born in 1929, makes that point in *No More Hiding Under the Bed,* his self-published memoir chronicling his path to racial redemption. He tells of a 1960 incident during which a nineteen-year-old white woman was dragged from her aunt's home in Alliance, Alabama, in the dark of night and beaten by four men who had heard that she might be dating a dark-skinned person. The men subsequently were found innocent of the assault and the woman became the object of scorn and unflattering news coverage. "It was the southern way of life," writes Jordan, "and most readers liked it that way. Niggers, or maybe in this case, just dark-skinned people, had to be kept in their place."

The bulk of Jordan's book is devoted not to wrongly victimized whites (and he makes it clear that he presumed the woman innocent of interracial dating), but to his life and eventual racial redemption.

"A lot of poor whites and poor blacks lived near my family," he writes. "Of course, the black people lived in the alleys mostly, not on the front of the street. No one ever called them Negroes, or blacks, it was always niggers, no matter who it was.... I knew it was wrong, but I didn't care, no one else cared, why should I? White kids laughed when they said, nigger. I was never told it was wrong in my whole life by anyone."

Despite being raised in an atmosphere of casual racism, Jordan had something of a yearning to connect with blacks. He recalls noticing, as a preteen, a seemingly friendly black kid who routinely hung out with his buddies near a local drugstore. He takes considerable pride in having discreetly learned the kid's nickname. "I didn't intend to call him 'Jolly Boy' or make friends with him, I just wanted to know who he was. I imagined that 'Jolly Boy' would have something funny to say to me one day, and we could share a joke or two." The contact meant so much to him, Jordan told my interviewer, because it occurred at a time when "friendship or respect for black kids" was not permitted. "I was just happy to know who he was."

Though as a young man Jordan never questioned segregation, he was not a fan of the Ku Klux Klan. He dreamed of becoming a cop, since he considered the police to be the good guys. Following military service in Germany, Jordan achieved his goal. He became an officer with the Bessemer Police Department. Early on, a superior took him aside and announced his disdain for "niggers, Catholics, and Jews." He also instructed Jordan that, in Bessemer, "niggers" were not allowed on the sidewalk after dark. They had to walk in the middle of the street with their hands visible so as to make it clear they were not up to mischief.

Jordan credits the civil rights movement with forcing him to rethink things. His role as a lead detective in the case of Virgil Ware—a thirteen-year-old boy shot and killed by two white teenagers on the same day, in 1963, that four blacks girls were murdered in the 16th Street Baptist Church bombing—moved him to indignation. The white teenagers, who were returning from a segregation rally when they shot Ware, were found guilty of manslaughter instead of murder and given a suspended sentence. Jordan was "discouraged" by the outcome. He was also moved (again, in 1963) while escorting a busload of black grammar school and high school children to jail for marching in a civil rights demonstration. The kids reminded him of his young daughters. And to help allay their fears, Jordan—as he tells the story—quietly hummed "We Shall Overcome" loud enough for them to hear. During that bus ride, said Jordan, he realized that his badge "did not really stand for justice for *all*."

At one point, during those days of protest, Jordan was assigned to escort Martin Luther King to jail for marching without a permit. He took advantage of their brief time together to challenge King on his commitment to nonviolence. Eventually he came to deeply admire King and also to take a certain satisfaction in the fact that they were both born on January 15, 1929.

"I wish he could have lived, so I could have shared some of that with him. We were not on the same side," Jordan said when interviewed. Jordan's fantasy of sharing a birthday celebration with King seemed to me just as surreal as his dream of sharing a joke with "Jolly Boy," and rooted in the same sense of connection to someone with whom he probably could never actually have connected. White members of his generation typically did not have intimate, honest relationships with blacks. The power dynamic was too skewed for that, and the risks on both sides—but particularly for blacks—were way too high. Decent instincts and good intentions could not close the gap. So white Gen 1s were left with self-flattering fictions about happy slaves, complicit coloreds, and nonexistent interracial friendships as they viewed blacks from across an unbridgeable divide and told themselves, in different ways, that the status quo was not quite as bad as it was.

Katherine's* Gen 1 experience was very different from Jordan's, even though she was born in the same year, 1929. She insisted that blacks, at least in her part of the country, were better off before the civil rights movement came along. Katherine, the daughter of Austrian immigrants, was raised in western Pennsylvania: "The first black person I can remember was in the sixth grade, when a black boy appeared in school."

Katherine lived two miles from school and walked the distance every day. The black boy walked with her. "We'd walk two miles, then he'd walk back home. There was another girl that walked with us too. And they'd both walk me home, and then they would go home. I don't know whether the other kids didn't accept him or what, but he just became an instant friend."

She remembered no racial prejudice in her home: "The only thing I remember is my father didn't like Lithuanians. I didn't know what a Lithuanian was. And I didn't think you could tell by looking at them. It wasn't until I was sixteen, when I had a Lithuanian boyfriend, [that] my father's ire against Lithuanians came out in the open."

She recalls her hometown as

> a microcosm of the United States. Everybody moved in there. You had Italians, and Polish, Jews, and even a few Arabs, a very few blacks, and a few Jewish people. There were all kinds of people there. So if you weren't English, you were called "Hunkies." It meant foreigner. I think there was more discrimination at that time, there, toward those who didn't speak English.

She believes the civil rights movement and the violence that often accompanied it obliterated something of a racial paradise that existed in northern communities such as hers: "The times that I grew up in, we were all alike; all sharing. . . . I think the only ones who came out of it really well were the leaders of the blacks. And I think that they are still better off than the average black person. It's just too bad. See, we didn't have discrimination in schools. . . . They were just ordinary citizens like we were."

Her husband's ancestors, she said, were among the founders of the Underground Railroad and led escaped slaves to freedom. "We've always been on the side of freedom and also personal responsibility." But she was disturbed at the swing of the pendulum: "I've had experiences [with] professors who say, 'I am forced to give grades to black people who have not earned them.' And they refused to do so, and they had to leave."

In many respects, Dan Jordan and Katherine, despite sharing the same birth year, were a universe apart. Katherine would never have called a black person a nigger. She saw the South, with its rigid caste system and racial violence, as a mysterious, scary place. And while she would never have considered dating a black man ("That was not done in the society I was raised in, but it wouldn't bother me at all if one of my granddaughters did"), she claimed to have never harbored a prejudiced thought. Still, what Jordan and Katherine had in common with most of their fellow Gen 1s was a sense that certain racial boundaries could not be crossed. They also tended to see blacks more as abstractions than as real, and individual, human beings.

Generation 2: The Neutrals

Gen 2s (born between 1945 and 1969) came of age in a world forever changed by the counterculture, the Vietnam War, Martin Luther King, and the end of "Camelot." The oldest of them saw John F. Kennedy assassinated in 1963, the Civil Rights Act enacted in 1964, the Voting Rights Act passed in 1965, the Black Panthers appear in 1966, and the "Summer of Love" proclaimed in 1967. At the time, some believed America to be in the throes of a revolution that would wash away social conventions, racial boundaries, and preconceived notions of sex and gender. It was fashionable in certain circles then to believe that people could quickly shed prejudices and attitudes they had spent a lifetime acquiring. Not everyone, of course, was a flower child.

Gretchen,* born in 1947, was among that first wave of Gen 2s. But she was defined less by the antics of blissed-out hippies than by the midwestern farming community she called home: "I never saw anyone who was black or Hispanic or Asian in the streets. For rural and small townspeople like my family, who were mostly of German descent, the Italians who had come to work in the coal mines in the nineteenth century were practically a race apart." The largest black population was in a city half an hour's drive away, and they stayed pretty much on their own side of town: "I remember being told that blacks, like Jews, were different. They had their place; we had ours. We didn't mix."

Her father was proud that he was not racially prejudiced like their neighbors. He would often boast of his black podiatrist friend.

He had met the man in college and welcomed him as a partner in a chemistry class when no one else would have him. "My dad was his patient, one of his very few white patients." And the doctor would sometimes visit to fish in the family's well-stocked little pond. "My major memory is of him being extremely well dressed, even for fishing, but more importantly, I remember his attitude. He was overwhelmingly polite, excessively so, particularly with my dad. I was embarrassed by both his behavior and my dad's, who always talked about him as 'Dr. So-and-So, the black man.'"

It was not until college that Gretchen came into close and regular contact with people of other races. Her first college boyfriend was Middle Eastern. After that, "almost all my boyfriends were Jewish. They were alluringly different to me. My relatives didn't know how to talk to them when I brought them home. My father—a usually quite loquacious storyteller—was never able to talk at all with any of my Jewish boyfriends, including the one who became my husband." She recalled there being mutual attraction with a black fellow student, but things never turned romantic: "I think for me, at twenty-two, that racial divide was too daunting. We never spoke about it. . . . When I was growing up, race was a barrier that was insurmountable."

A close friend did date a black man: "Her father was a Holocaust survivor, and when he found out about the boyfriend, he came and carried her home screaming. I had nightmares for a long time with the sound of her screaming."

Gretchen's parents raised her to be tolerant. But "you also had to be careful and stay safe, which precluded going to the black part of town and subsequently getting close to any black people." Her Methodist church encouraged her to fight racism, "but in my life I didn't see any place or time for it. My college years were consumed with the Vietnam War. My boyfriends were all focused on the draft."

In some ways, Gretchen was more representative of her generation than the over-the-top crowd breaking taboos and burning bras and draft cards. Hers was a world where racial barriers still stood but were beginning to come down. And though she was happy to see them fall, that was not really her battle. Gen 2 Neutrals, in the main, were well-intentioned people who were not looking for trouble and had no desire to shake things up in a way that would result in fundamental change. They were not nearly as racially conservative as their parents, but they were not totally at ease with black people either—at least not initially. And that was partly because they knew so few nonwhites personally, and partly because the signals they were receiving from mentors and parents were rather mixed.

Frances, born in 1947 in North Kansas City, Missouri, was told by her dad that all people are equal, but she was also told that "blacks were not welcome in the small town of North Kansas City. They could work in that town during the day, but they better be off the streets when the sun went down." She recalled reading, as a youth, about school integration: "I also remember when the swimming pools in Kansas City were closed rather than allowing blacks and whites to swim together. I could never understand why it was even an issue because my parents had always taught me that everyone was the same regardless of the color of their skin."

Martha,* born in Peoria in 1945, recalled realizing at the age of four or five that people come in different colors and deciding she needed a black sibling:

> I must have said something to my mother, because she said something about black people having their own particular smell about them. She didn't say it negatively. It was just a marker, an indicator, with everyone having a smell and black people their own. That summer we went to Rockford to a family reunion in a park. I went on the swings with other children, and there was this little black girl my age and my size, and we talked, and she told me her name. She was very shy, but I remember trying to get close to her to get her smell and couldn't get any. . . . Otherwise, I grew up totally without any contact, any knowledge, any comments about black people.

I asked a longtime friend, Ieva Massengill, who came of age in the early seventies in a working-class white suburb of Chicago, how she would characterize her Gen 2 cohort. She observed, for starters, that most whites "hadn't even met a black person before they finished high school and ventured out of their neighborhoods to go to college or get a job. Their main source of information about blacks came from TV."

Much of the information, initially, was about Dr. King and his movement, which Gen 2s—those up north at least—generally didn't have a problem getting behind, especially since it seemed to be all about things happening in the South. But when marchers were supplanted by rioters and nonviolence gave way to black rage, blacks suddenly got scary: "They were people who didn't share white suburbia's values, people who, whatever their grievances, were not 'like us.'"

This view, of course, is a composite and something of a caricature, and it certainly does not represent everyone who happened to live in a white suburb—a population that certainly contained its share of relatively unbiased, decent folk—but I think it fairly reflects how a large number of people felt. They recognized that racism was wrong but were not really capable of seeing the world in a nonracial way—not because they did not want to be fair, but because the novelty of the notion of blacks as equals had not yet worn off. In other words, enlightened Gen 2 Neutrals saw the value of tolerance without realizing that tolerating is not exactly the same as welcoming.

There were some individuals who transcended the predominant characteristics of their generation—who had black friends who were more than symbolic, who not only tolerated difference but embraced it, even reveled in it. But if you were an up-and-coming black striver, the odds were overwhelming that you would find yourself with a white boss who was not comfortable mentoring you, who was incapable of imagining himself in your shoes, and who was simply mystified at your frustration when you didn't progress as quickly or as far as you thought you should, even though many such bosses considered themselves rather enlightened—as they were, by the standards of the day.

Nonenlightened Gen 2s, of course, were a different matter. In all relevant respects, they had more in common with Gen 1 Hostiles than with their more liberal generational counterparts. One white Birmingham native recalled civil rights demonstrators there as objects of derision. After Birmingham public safety commissioner Theophilus Eugene "Bull" Connor ordered his troops to battle marchers with attack dogs and fire hoses, this interviewee remembered, a friend gleefully poked fun by fashioning a sign reading: FREE BATHS DOWNTOWN. SPECIAL TODAY.

Nacogdoches, Texas, where Carlos Dews, chair of the English Department at John Cabot University in Rome, was born in 1963, was neither as violent nor as notorious as Birmingham, but segregation there was almost as deeply entrenched. In an article published in 2009 in the journal *Aspenia* ("Barack Obama and *To Kill a Mockingbird*"), Dews describes what it was like growing up in East Texas "during the ragged end of the Jim Crow era." Signs still designated certain water fountains as WHITES ONLY, though others were permitted to drink from them. Many school library books were stamped COLORED SCHOOL—having been brought over when the white school was forced to integrate. And a balcony in the local movie theater, once the "blacks only" section, was still referred to as "nigger heaven," wrote Dews.

> I remember my mother telling me to wait until we were inside the county courthouse to use the "white" toilet rather than the "colored" one outside, at the edge of the parking lot. I recall my parents instructing me, before my first day of elementary school, not to sit in a chair where a black child had sat and not to drink from the school's drinking fountains after a black child. I recall my parents carefully sorting through the box of Valentine's Day cards I was addressing to my classmates to make sure that I didn't inadvertently give a card with an overly affectionate sentiment to a black child.

I met Dews for lunch in a café in London and asked him to tell me more about his upbringing. His father, a jack-of-all-trades, worked primarily in the cattle and timber businesses. During downtime, his parents, particularly his father, schooled Dews in the southern racial folklore on things such as black people's smell and lack of intellect. "I never believed what they were talking about. It felt like they were trying to indoctrinate me," said Dews, who credits his maternal grandmother with helping him resist. She pointed out that his father's nonsense on race "had come from his own father."

He recalled a black employee with whom his father seemed to have a special rapport. But that man, who helped in the logging business, "never set foot inside the house." He would always come to the back to collect his salary outside from Dews's mom. "I think in my entire lifetime, a black person never set foot in my father's or grandfather's house."

Dews's was the first generation to attend integrated schools, though the kids still self-segregated on the playground. And dating outside the race was absolutely forbidden—"not because we didn't find each other attractive but because we knew the consequences." Dews's father made his own views totally clear. There were not many things that could drive him to kill his own son, but dating a black girl or becoming "queer" were among them.

One white girl, a couple of years older than he, had risked dating a black boy, creating a huge scandal. "The entire family was kind of demoted" and ended up taking refuge among African Americans.

As Dews wrestled with his own sexuality, he found himself attracted to a classy, well-spoken girl. She came from a highly esteemed black family "seen by white people as playing the role absolutely perfectly." But he never worked up the nerve to ask her out or tell her how he felt. Admitting he was attracted to a black girl, said Dews, would have been even more "frightening" than confessing his suspicion that he might be gay. "My fear . . . was strong enough, I didn't do anything about either one." Eventually Dews came to accept his sexual orientation. But when he was young he sometimes wondered, "Would I have been gay if I had been able to have a relationship with her?"

He conceded that East Texas is different now than when he grew up there, "but these differences are not as marked as one might think." He did see some hope in the fact that when the daughter of his sister's best friend married a black man, there were none of the hysterics that would have ensued a generation ago. Still, Dews's father "shakes his head and rolls his eyes whenever that situation is brought up." But his father's time, he knows, is quickly passing, and as he looks at the Gens 3s now coming out of college, "I see they are less anxious about race in general than my generation . . . in the same way they are less anxious about sexuality," said Dews.

Generation 3: The Allies

"Anxious" is not a word you would use to describe Russell Lacy. Born in Raleigh, North Carolina, in 1981, he gives off the calm, cool vibe of the jazz musician that he is. Though a southerner, Lacy came along a generation too late to personally experience segregation, but he is quite familiar with the history. His grandparents were educators (his grandmother was a schoolteacher, and his grandfather was the school board chairman) in the mid-1960s when their rural village in central Virginia acquiesced to court-ordered desegregation. They were proud that their schools, unlike many in the state, opted to admit black children rather than to shut down.

By the time Lacy started school in Raleigh, everyone pretty much accepted that black kids were part of the mix. Indeed, he considers himself fortunate to have attended schools that were incredibly diverse. His high school, a magnet school known for its academic and music curricula, was located in a predominantly black area of the city and took 50 percent of its students from the neighborhood. So there were many black students along with middle-class whites and others.

Instead of going to a predominantly white college, Lacy opted to attend North Carolina Central University, a historically black institution located in Durham: "When you say you went to college in Durham, of course people expect you to say Duke. And in sort of the most literal way, Central is across the tracks from Duke. It's really like [going from] the expensive white school to the downtrodden, African American school."

His decision to attend Central had nothing to do with race and a lot to do with music: "It had a really good jazz program. It was inexpensive because it was a state school. It was not a particularly hard school to get into academically, and . . . I didn't have a lot of options because my grades were so bad from high school."

Central was perhaps 96 percent black when Lacy attended, but he didn't feel isolated: "It was really a positive experience for me for the most part. Most of my classes were in the music department. And I was really close to all my professors." Even in courses such as African American history, he was never made to feel as if he didn't belong.

He recalled only one vaguely racial incident during his time there: "I don't really remember exactly how it all came to this point, but myself and the bass player were both white . . . which is a sort of funny paradox, to have the bass player and the drummer both be white in an African American school in an otherwise completely African American band." The bass player, who "had a pretty explosive personality," managed to annoy the trumpet player, who turned to him and declared, "This music doesn't belong to you. You really have no right to be playing this. And you'll never be able to do it properly because you're not African American."

The outburst had a strong impact on Lacy, even though he wasn't its target. And he found himself pondering the trumpet player's point:

> I mean, jazz is definitely a by-product of the pain and suffering of African Americans. . . . I'm very aware of that. But at the same time, I do feel like I have a right to play jazz. And despite the

> fact that it came from such adverse circumstances, it's a great art form. And not only that, it's a great American art form. . . . And I feel like we should all take part in it and be proud of the beautiful art that it is and be cognizant of the adverse circumstances which it came from.

While in college, Lacy dated a Chinese American woman he had met in high school. One day—he thinks it might have been during Black History Month—they went to a forum on interracial relationships. There he realized that, in their two years of dating, they had never considered themselves an interracial couple, "because in both of our minds 'interracial relationship' purely meant a black and white couple. . . . And both of us were like, 'Wait a minute, we're actually in an interracial relationship.'"

Lacy noted that his sister was currently dating a black man she had known for several years:

> And she knew my parents would be completely accepting of that relationship . . . as long as they thought it was a healthy relationship for her and that he was a decent guy. . . . I'm sure at some point people give them weird stares in certain circumstances, but for the most part, not so much. Whereas if you take it one generation further back, if it had been *my* mom, her mother wouldn't have been accepting. In Sanford, North Carolina, in the late sixties, it would have been much more awkward.

But today, said Lacy, "there aren't the kinds of limitations that there were." America, in his view, "is further along in the right direction than a lot of people of the older generations [know]."

Lacy is not exactly typical of Gen 1 Allies (those born between 1970 and 1995). Not many whites of his generation—even aspiring jazz musicians—decide to attend historically black schools. But he is absolutely right that his generation has considerably less anxiety and discomfort around race than Gen 2s and especially Gen 1s. Their world is not the world of *Guess Who's Coming to Dinner.* When that movie came out in 1967, the question was, "How could such an attractive, well-to-do white girl possibly be interested in marrying a black man?" These days, a viewer—particularly a young viewer—is more inclined to wonder how such a handsome, brilliant doctor, one apparently on the short list for the Nobel Prize, could find anything remotely interesting in such a silly girl. In interpersonal relationships, race is becoming less and less of a factor—not just because of the passage of time, but because of the rise of a generation whose experiences have been fundamentally different from those of their elders and who received very different messages growing up. These are the young people who studied the civil rights movement as history but cannot recall a time when blacks were not full members of the American family. They rallied around Barack Obama and never questioned the correctness of different races sharing a common space. Many have interracial friendships that go back to childhood and that were not abandoned in adolescence (as many Gen 2 friendships were).

For Lori,* a twenty-four-year-old New York actress, being racist was never much of an option. Her physics professor father and schoolteacher mother were "kind of like hippies," she said. They enrolled her, at the age of four, in Manhattan Country School, a private academy founded in the 1960s with a mandate to imbue its students with a commitment to equality and social justice. "I don't know if other schools teach you about Emmett Till [the young black boy murdered in Mississippi in 1955 for supposedly flirting with a white woman] when you're eleven and show you images of him in his coffin," said Lori.

When Lori brought a black boyfriend home, she knew it would be no big deal. And she knows the same would be true if one day she decides to start a family with someone outside her race: "I mean, if I met someone who I wanted to have a kid with and if he happened to be black . . . I'm not going to not be with that person because of [his color]."

Ashley Broas, a twenty-year-old University of Michigan student from Grand Haven, Michigan, is also a member of the "no big deal" generation. She looked forward to enrolling at Michigan in part because it was so much more diverse than the largely white, Christian community in which she grew up. In her Grand Haven schools, "we always had, like, the diversity day, but it was a group of white students and a white teacher telling us about diversity." She knew Michigan would be different.

Her current boyfriend, she noted, "is a quarter black and half Jewish. . . . And I don't see it as a problem at all from my group of friends." Nor, she said, does she get any objections from her parents—although, she noted, her boyfriend happens to look white. But "if I were to bring home a person of color, I think they would react the same. They'd be welcoming, but I think they'd be curious."

Gens 3 are far from color blind. But they obsess a great deal less over color than did their parents and grandparents.

Lauren Branchard, another Michigan student, hails from Traverse City, Michigan, and is a self-described conservative Christian. Her mother is from New York, and her father is from the South, and she can see the evolution of attitudes in her own family: "My grandma is really bad about it. When she'll see something on the news, she'll instantly blame it on race." Her parents, said Branchard, will sometimes leap to racial conclusions, "but they're very much more accepting. . . . And then with my generation, my brothers and I, we're much, much more open to different ethnic types."

Because Gen 3 whites come with a lot less racial baggage than their parents carried, it makes it easier for Gen 3 blacks to see them as allies rather than as obstacles. The generation coming up behind them (Gen 4 Friends) presumably will carry even less racial baggage and be even more capable of relating to their black counterparts (Gen 4 Reapers) as equals in every relevant respect. Certainly, Gen 2s and even Gen 1s often had deep and caring relationships that crossed racial lines. But those relationships were considerably more likely to have an explicitly racial edge. Even the hipsters and hippies of those past eras, who made a point of proclaiming their love for blacks and black culture, typically did so in a very self-conscious way. It was often as if they were shouting to the world, "I'm going to prove how open-minded and inclusive I am by showing you my black friend, by demonstrating, in the most blatant way, how racially transgressive I can be."

For Gen 3 Allies, interracial friendships, including romantic ones, are not acts of racial transgression; they are simply, and increasingly, *no big deal*. And that makes it easier for their black counterparts, Gen 3 Believers, to trust them and to trust that, whether they encounter Gen 3 Allies in school, in a bar, or on the job, they will be seen by them as a real person—not simply a color or a symbol to which they need to respond.

Chapter Six

Reaching Across the Generational Divide

Most Gen 1 Fighters and many Gen 2 Dreamers never expected their country to give them a totally fair shake. Their aspirations, however high they might have soared, always had to be carefully calibrated to account for the possible exigencies of color. For Gen 3 Believers, the calculations are, in some respects, more nuanced and complex. They—at least the most privileged and well educated among them—have been primed for a world where color no longer matters even remotely the way it once did. So they are not always sure whether the lessons and experiences of their fathers have much relevance to their own lives. Their world, many seem to be concluding, operates under an altogether different set of rules. In this chapter, we meet some young people, along with their fathers, as they struggle to make sense of this new state of affairs.

The Sociologist and His Son

Elijah Anderson is the William K. Lanman Jr. Professor of Sociology at Yale University—a post he has held since 2007, after spending most of his career at the University of Pennsylvania. His books—including *A Place on the Corner* and *Code of the Street:*

Decency, Violence, and the Moral Life of the Inner City—are considered classics in ethnography.

In one generation, he has made a remarkable leap across the class divide. He was born in 1943 in Hermondale, Missouri—a tiny, poverty-ridden town in Pemiscot County, near the Arkansas and Tennessee state lines, about eighty miles north of Memphis. His grandmother, a deeply religious folk doctor and midwife, brought him into the world. He was named for the Old Testament prophet who was carried to heaven in a whirlwind inside a chariot of fire drawn by flaming horses.

He comes from a family of sharecroppers. But his father, Leighton, found a way out. He signed up for the Army during World War II and ended up in Paris driving trucks. He was so moved by the appreciation and deference shown to black soldiers by Europeans—in contrast to the contempt and scorn showered on them by whites in the South—that he considered not coming home. But he did return—to a place with very few options for a black man with a fourth-grade education. So he moved to South Bend, Indiana, where there were relatives to help him get situated and a Studebaker automobile plant ready to offer a job.

When we talked in late 2010, Anderson had recently come from a family reunion, during which he and his wife had considered stopping in Hermondale. They found the dirt road turnoff but decided not to go down it for fear of getting lost. Instead, they continued on to Blazer to meet the relatives and to reflect, among other things, on their collective journey.

Anderson, who studies race, class, and social mobility, sees his own story as characteristic of the journey made by many upwardly mobile blacks of his generation. He was part of what he calls the "incorporation" process, a beneficiary of the programs and policies put in place to bring African Americans—marginalized for so long in American society—into the so-called mainstream. The opening up of institutions—schools, companies, clubs, communities—previously closed to people like him "really produced the black middle class as we know it," Anderson observed.

For Anderson, who was both a good athlete and student, the ticket from poverty to prominence was education. He got his bachelor's degree from Indiana University, his master's from the University of Chicago, and his PhD from Northwestern.

He joined the Swarthmore College faculty in 1973 and was hired away by Penn two years later. By 1980, when his father visited him for Thanksgiving dinner, he had become an established star. "We were sitting around drinking beer, listening to the blues," recalled Anderson, when his father turned to him and said, "You're teaching at this university now. And you have white students and white colleagues and all of that. Now tell me one thing. Do they respect you?"

Anderson immediately understood. "He's curious because where he came from everybody knows that white people don't respect black people." So his father wanted to know just how different was this world that his son had managed to infiltrate. "He doesn't have a sense of Ivy League or whatever, [but he knows] I've got a big job." But what could such a job mean for a black man? Could it conceivably come with respect from whites?

The question, said Anderson, "stopped me in my tracks. You don't lie to your daddy." So he gave the only honest answer he could. "Some do," he replied. "I'm sure *some* do."

In *Dreams from My Father,* Barack Obama tells the story of Toot, his white grandmother, who worked in a bank in Texas following World War II. She struck up a friendship with a black janitor. One day when the two of them were chatting in a hallway, a secretary overheard his mother address the man as Mr. Reed. The secretary stormed up angrily and told Toot to never "call no nigger 'Mister.'" Sometime after that, Toot found the janitor in a corner weeping. "What have we ever done to be treated so mean?" he asked.

The story was one example—out of millions harbored by blacks of a certain age—of the lengths to which whites of that generation would go to disrespect blacks. And that generation, of course, was the generation with which Elijah Anderson's father was most familiar.

I told Anderson that his story reminded me of a visit to the University of Hyderabad in India during which I had a long and pleasant meeting with an economist who belonged to the Dalit—or so-called untouchable—caste. He was an impressive and very accomplished man who, I imagined, commanded great respect from his students. But being familiar with the humiliations imposed by caste, I wondered whether he ran into problems with higher-caste students. So I asked him if he found it awkward to be the thesis adviser for upper-caste PhD candidates. *Do they respect you?* was the essence of my question. He laughed loudly and replied, "Oh! That *never* happens."

In the United States, Anderson observed, "we don't have a caste system. It's castelike. . . . And it was more castelike a long time ago than it is today. . . . Even in the days of Jackie Robinson, it was not completely caste." And Obama's election, he said, has changed things. More people now believe that "there's a place for them. It says that we're at the table. . . . He has helped just by rising."

That powerful symbolism, he observed, has a potential drawback. "One might even argue that Hillary [Clinton] might have been a better president for blacks in the sense that blacks could petition her. They can't petition Obama."

So what does Obama's election ultimately say about the full integration of at least well-educated blacks into American society? "We're not there, but we're closer than we've ever been," said Anderson.

And how does the world of Anderson's now grown children differ from the one he had to conquer as a young man? "My kids don't have the same issue that I had. They have been the beneficiaries of private schools. They are well educated. They got high board scores—high enough to qualify [even without affirmative action] for many Ivy League schools. They know all kinds of people." Anderson's children are not likely to face anything like the bigotry and racism that people of his generation dealt with. Nor are they much in need of any sort of special help. "They are more like Obama's kids."

So does that mean that their options and opportunities are essentially equivalent to those of upper-middle-class whites? "It's complicated," Anderson replied. "There are certain places that are really trying very hard to be egalitarian, to focus on how good a person is," as opposed to their physical attributes. More and more whites and blacks are forming real friendships. "But it only takes one or two or three people who are racist to upset the whole apple cart. . . . All it takes is one ethnocentric person in that workplace to make a really bad day for a black person, or a gay person, or a Jewish person." The continuing challenge, said Anderson, is to "keep the ethnocentrism in check."

The Son

Luke Anderson was raised in West Philadelphia just eight blocks from the campus where his father taught sociology. He attended a nearby public school popular with Penn faculty and recalled having mostly white kids as friends. "It's a function, I think, of having a white mother [in that] she probably gravitated toward the parents who were white."

Luke, who was born in 1981, became aware of class differences when he was quite young: "When you're playing football on the street in West Philadelphia when Southwest Philly [a much tougher neighborhood] is just over the bridge, certain boys would want to hang out with us. And often they had no football of their own. So it was an issue of how do we negotiate with these boys who, in a way, we were wary of."

In middle school, race suddenly became extremely important. "You had kids from all over the city of Philadelphia—blacks, Puerto Ricans, white kids. That setting is where I really first noticed that the black kids hang out with the black kids, the white kids hang out with the white kids."

He was made aware that he didn't talk like a lot of other black kids. At one point, when he showed confusion about a term relating to hair ("edge up"), a schoolmate dismissively told him that he did not "deserve" to be black.

He attended Germantown Friends School, a Quaker high school. There, race was also important, but the dynamics were totally different. He went from being "the inauthentic black person at my [public] middle school" to being a "cool black person—the person that everyone looks to when issues of race come up." He liked the attention. "It was something I think a lot of black students go through at places like GFS."

After graduating, he went to the University of Pennsylvania, opting to live in the W. E. B. DuBois College House, established in the 1970s as a nurturing refuge for blacks at Penn. Living there, Luke reasoned, would strengthen his ties to other black students. Most were from affluent backgrounds, and many were African or Caribbean, yet some of them felt compelled to adopt street personas in certain settings: "Around each other, they would sort of put on this whole veneer of, 'We're black,' using the N-word, cursing, dressing a certain way." The persona changed whenever they played basketball at a gym where they encountered real kids from the street. "Then they straightened up. You didn't hear them putting on what they perceived as this image of blackness."

For Luke, the DuBois House presented something of a dilemma. "It's like I felt pressure to kind of fit in with black folks at DuBois House. On the other hand, I was going to be myself." Luke eventually moved off campus. "I kind of removed myself from that black kind of scene. My best friend from Penn actually ended up being a North African French guy."

He thinks his family background makes it easier for him to navigate various worlds:

> My father's family is southern, relatively underprivileged, lived in places like Arkansas, Missouri, southwest Indiana, whereas

my mother's relatives are relatively upper-middle class, well educated. I feel like I'm super-nonjudgmental. I think my experience and my foot in these two worlds has really helped me kind of understand some of the ignorance I see out there.

After graduating from Penn in 2003, Luke enrolled in the PhD sociology program at Northwestern. "I figured, I can go and get my PhD in five years. I'll be twenty-seven and have a doctorate from Northwestern. Also, there was my father's influence. I'd seen his lifestyle and his getting summers off and being kind of in control of his own time. Also, I had an innate interest in sociology—maybe not innate, but it was bred into me growing up around my dad." But after two years he opted out of the PhD program, having realized that he was less than passionate about the subject.

He had always been drawn to issues of social justice and had even spent a summer as a union organizer. As he pondered what he could do, he connected with a friend involved with NFTE, the Network for Teaching Entrepreneurship. NFTE is an international organization that tries to foster entrepreneurship among students in low-income communities:

> Basically we'd go into the schools and say, "Do you want to start an entrepreneurship program? We're going to provide you with all these resources. All you have to do is pay for the teachers to get certified in our training [and] pay for half the curriculum." My job as program director was to go in and make about ten site visits per year in each school to help get the program off the ground.

He loved it: "My favorite part of NFTE was being in these communities, being in these schools, and trying to create something positive out of these really tough environments." That was not easy. "To me the biggest thing was just the apathy." Many of the teachers didn't really care about the kids, and many of the parents were unengaged. "The really tough part was seeing what these kids' home lives were like. I had sixteen-, seventeen-year-old kids telling me that they can't wait to turn eighteen because they know that when they turn eighteen they qualify for their $685 a month housing voucher. That's when they can go get a little apartment in this really terrible community."

He pondered how he could help change such attitudes and decided that teaching was one route, so he signed up for a master's in education. He student-taught—and later accepted a full-time job—at North Lawndale College Prep, a charter school in a poor, predominantly black Chicago community that claims that over 90 percent of its students graduate and 100 percent of its graduates go to college: "I think the reason why this school is effective is we spend a lot more money on staff, in the sense that we have counselors, social workers, school psychologists. We have small classroom sizes. I have no more than twenty kids in any one class."

He nonetheless worries about what happens to them when they are not in school.

> Gangs are a huge, huge issue here. . . . Our boys will walk home, and there will be Vice Lords or Gangster Disciples out there. And these gangs will try to "shake up" with them. . . . And these boys, these fourteen-, fifteen-year-old boys, tell me that they have a couple choices. They could either shake up with these boys—do the gang handshake [which is considered a sign of affiliation and respect]. If they don't do it right, they get beat down. Or they can just not shake up, which is disrespectful; you can get beat down for that. Or you can just run and maybe they'll chase you, maybe they won't. So this is what's going through their minds every day when they leave home. It's this obstacle course.

Luke thinks that he may teach for five years or so and then get a PhD in education. His dream is to start his own charter school—"a school with small classes, intense instruction, sky-high expectations."

The Journalist-Politician-Businessman and His Daughter

Randy Daniels was born in 1951, the seventh of ten children. His mother, a seamstress, had migrated from Tunica, Mississippi. His father, a hat maker, hailed from El Dorado, Arkansas. They eventually found their way to Altgeld Gardens, a housing project in Chicago, where Randy was born. His father owned a dry cleaning shop and, at one point, a canteen truck—in which Randy sometimes worked with his siblings.

When Daniels was eight, the family moved to Markham, a tiny suburb on its way to becoming predominantly black. He remembered a house they would pass on their way to school where little kids were hiding in the window behind the curtain and saying, "Nigger, nigger, nigger." In high school, blacks and whites were friendly, but "we didn't hang out." Interracial dating was uncommon.

The black power movement was flowering, and Daniels aligned himself with student efforts to get more black teachers hired and became so wrapped up in his activism that he flunked senior English. Instead of barring him from graduation, the principal offered to let him march with the proviso that he would receive his degree only after he had made up the course in summer school. His parents said no: if he hadn't done the work, he didn't deserve to march. "That day I promised myself I would never ever in my life be unprepared for anything."

He attended Southern Illinois University, with dreams of becoming a journalist. The first interview he recalled doing was with Jane Fonda: "She was beautiful. I couldn't remember my questions."

The only black network newsperson whom Daniels was aware of was George Jackson Foster, a correspondent for CBS. Nonetheless, as graduation time approached, he sent letters to all the networks. CBS was interested enough to send him to the Chicago affiliate with orders to shoot an audition tape on gas gouging. "I had no fucking idea what to do," he remembered. A black cameraman took pity on him, filmed the scene on location, and told him, "Just write something to sum this up."

The story became part of the local newscast, which led to a job as a copyboy and later to his promotion to "broadcast associate," a title then given to young black recruits. After completing a CBS training program, Daniels got a shot at writing. When Chicago correspondent Bill Plante noticed that Daniels was floundering, he told the young man, "When you write something, let me see it before you turn it in." Plante would discreetly edit Daniel's copy, explain what he had done, and tell him, "Now go show them this." Soon Daniels was promoted to reporter and then to correspondent, a title that came with a big pay raise. "I was one of them. I was in their club."

The next year, Washington bureau chief Bill Small became president of CBS News. He asked Daniels what he wanted to do, and Daniels replied that he would like to cover Africa. "Do you know anything about Africa?" asked Small. "No, but I've read a lot," Daniels replied. A few months later, he was en route to Nairobi to open a CBS bureau.

Around that time, Ed Bradley, then a rising star at CBS, told Daniels, "Don't come home for a long time." There was no way that Daniels, a black man with no fancy pedigree, was going to become a White House or Pentagon correspondent. His only shot at stardom, Bradley was telling him, was overseas—the route Bradley had taken.

Nairobi had its frustrations. It was impossible to get a satellite signal, so all film was shipped to London, which meant that the news was old on arrival. But Africa was also educational. He learned to mine the African press corps for information—a resource that many of his white competitors ignored.

Daniels returned to the United States in 1980 but left CBS two years later when the Nigerian government hired him to upgrade its television news operation: "I ended up, over a two-year period, recruiting fifty people." A military coup canceled his contract, and he came back to the States to sort things out. "I had some money . . . and I'd always wanted to own a television station. So I hired a communications lawyer and started competing for television licenses."

That venture was only marginally successful. So he took a job as communications director for the president of the city council, leaving two years later to become press secretary for Lynden Pindling, prime minister of the Bahamas. Daniels's main challenge was dealing with the public relations crisis that resulted when the Pindling administration was accused of facilitating drug trafficking—a challenge he faced head on. "Before I was done, *60 Minutes* did a profile on the guy and said that the government of the United States [had] no evidence to support any allegation of drug trafficking by [Pindling]." Nonetheless, Pindling lost his 1992 reelection bid. In the interim, New York mayor David Dinkins had invited Daniels to come aboard as a deputy mayor: "They wanted me to . . . help to streamline the administration and project a more dynamic image for the guy." But before he could start work, Daniels was awash in scandal. A woman accused him of sexually harassing her, and her accusations were leading the news.

Daniels resigned and immediately filed a lawsuit against the woman, who ultimately recanted. She had a history, it turned out, of such accusations. But his vindication came far too late to save his job. "I had to start over again," said Daniels.

As he gathered the pieces of his shattered life, he heard from real estate developer Donald Trump. "This is bullshit," said Trump. "You're too hot. I can't give you a job. But if there is another way I can help you, I'll help you."

"I don't want a job," replied Daniels. "I want to bring you a deal."

Daniels knew that Trump had once owned Paradise Island in the Bahamas. He also knew that Carnival Cruise Line was selling its hotel and casino complex there. He figured that Trump could get it at a discount. Soon he was in Florida, negotiating with the Carnival team: "I said, 'Donald, how do you place a value on this thing?' He said, 'Listen. The value of any property is what I say it is.' I never, ever, ever forgot that." The deal fell through, but Trump sent him a check anyway.

Slowly, Daniels rebuilt his credibility. In 1994, with the gubernatorial election looming, he met with George Pataki, the Republican candidate, and agreed to become an adviser to the campaign. When Pataki won, he gave Daniels a job in economic development, which Daniels eagerly accepted. He needed to prove, said Daniels, that the scandal "had not defeated me."

He worked in the Pataki administration for five years, leaving at the end of 1999 to join a real estate investment company. A year and a half later, Pataki called him, this time offering to make him secretary of state. "I was floored because I hadn't expected it. . . . There had only been one African American secretary of state [previously], and that was Basil Paterson."

He was the third-highest constitutional officer in the executive branch, the head of the cabinet, and responsible for a dizzying array of projects, including waterfront development: "Now I could make a difference. Now I had the power to direct resources. I had like $30 million a year to give out in environmental grants for municipalities and counties. And I used to go to every one of them and hand them the check personally." He became one of Pataki's closest aides. And one day the governor called him in and said, "I think you can succeed me as governor."

Daniels began organizing a campaign, but before long "I found myself being undermined by people around the governor." Pataki's people were worried that Daniels's candidacy would divert money that could otherwise fund Pataki's nascent presidential aspirations. So they were quietly promoting William Weld, the former governor of Massachusetts, who they thought might help fund his own campaign.

"When I started out, I had twelve upstate counties that were ready to endorse me immediately and six more in the center of the state," said Daniels. But once word got out that the governor was backing Weld, support dried up. Daniels, furious, dropped out and threw his support to another candidate, who lost the election to

Eliot Spitzer. As for Daniels's relationship with Pataki: "We always sort of pretended that he had clean hands in it because that made it easier for us to be friends."

Daniels decided to opt out of a political career. "I don't want to spend my life in that environment where people lie straight to your face every day," he said, his voice cracking. "You can't imagine what that's like."

He became vice chairman of Gilford Securities Inc., a boutique investment banking firm, and now travels the world putting deals together.

Charmed as his life has been in many respects, it has not been free of racial incident. In the mid-1970s, his home in Itasca, Illinois, was firebombed before he and his wife could move in. "That was searing. You remember that." And he occasionally is reminded that stereotypes still carry power. "I have a major client in Singapore. I just spent a week traveling across the U.S. with them, visiting investors." The trip took them to San Francisco, where he and his Asian companions rented an SUV. After Daniels turned the keys over to the hotel valet, the man—assuming Daniels was the chauffeur—told him to be sure to give the ticket to the passenger he assumed was the boss. "He's the driver," Daniels shot back.

Though a Republican, he believes that Obama's presidency is changing things for the better. "When I travel abroad . . . I'm received and looked at differently. I'm taken more seriously. They no longer see us as just an isolated minority in America that has no power."

He acknowledged that his three daughters face different challenges than those of his generation.

> We were trailblazers. We had no expectations of everything going smoothly. They're going to have to learn to deal with the subtleties and nuances . . . with the covert undermining.
>
> They're going to have to be better prepared than we were because the competition is fierce. And the competition is more international. . . . I think they need the understanding that they

have to work harder than the other guy, not the same, because the same is not going to get you what he got. With all [the progress] that has happened, there's an expectation that it's going to be okay. Well, it's not going to be okay. If we've still got a third of our people who have lost hope and do not see opportunity and are trapped in despair—if that exists, how can you have an expectation that it's going to be all right for you? As long as that's there, you have to assume that these problems are going to touch all of us, just in differing degrees. I don't care how wealthy you are, you will be reminded at some point that you're black. The question is, how will you deal with that?

The Daughter

There were always questions about living in a house in a city of apartment dwellers. Teachers were forever asking Asha Daniels for her apartment number. "I'd say, 'There's no apartment.' And they'd be like, 'You don't have an apartment?' And then I'd have to explain that we had the whole house. Kids would hear that and go, 'Wow, you have a whole brownstone.'"

Asha, a striking, stylish woman, was not raised in luxury, but she is a daughter of privilege. "My parents were these upper-middle-class people who bought a brownstone literally in a neighborhood [in Harlem] that was surrounded by a lot of drugs."

Born in 1981, she attended private schools her entire life. And those schools generally had few black students. "I remember my parents always making it a point to become friends with the other black children at the school." If Asha made a playdate with a white kid, "my mom would make a playdate with a black boy." And because she was so aware that she was different from many of her friends, she felt compelled to show that she was not *that* different: "I think it always created in me a feeling that I had to prove myself or prove that my family's just like yours."

When the family moved to the Bahamas, her school, being

exclusive and private, was mostly white. Nonetheless, it was a happy period. Returning to New York was tough. "Back in the city, rap was really taking over. I didn't know what was going on. I was scared to go outside, scared to do things, scared to take public transportation. . . . Once you get assimilated into popular culture, it definitely makes it easier."

Her assimilation largely took place in her Catholic school, which she attended through the twelfth grade. But she wanted something different for college. Her mother had gone to historically black Spelman College, which was one reason, assumed Asha, why her parents had so many close black friends. She wanted that as well. So she chose Spelman, the largely black, all-female school in Atlanta:

> I just loved the prestige of the school. I loved womanhood and that big sorority. And I loved the fact that Morehouse [the historically black all-male college] was across the street. . . . I loved just being able to knock on someone's door and have someone do your hair. I loved being able to walk around with a head scarf on in the dorm and have no one ask you why you were wearing that.

It was Asha's first time attending a predominantly black school, and the experience was revelatory:

> One of the biggest things it taught me was how different we are. I mean, you had everything there, from people whose parents were poor—they could barely afford to be there—and people who came from the elite. It was my first sense also of how we look at each other. It was the first time people would say, "Oh, light-skinned Asha." I'd never identified myself that way. I'd always been black.

She didn't worry about how the degree might be perceived in a predominantly white world. "I always knew I could go wherever I wanted to for grad school."

She majored in political science but discovered her passion in fashion, particularly the business side of it. She worked for Estée Lauder in London during her junior year abroad and upon graduating in 2003 took a global marketing job with Avon.

Because of her upbringing, racial issues have always loomed in her mind. "I have always felt a sense to prove that I was just as good." She now feels the same need to establish the bona fides of her fiancé, who is black. She tells people that "he works on Wall Street, he went to Kellogg [Graduate School of Management], so they don't just assume he's some okie-doke guy."

What impact will race have on her career? "I think it's definitely an issue when you work at a company that doesn't have a lot of senior black executives." But she assumes that whites will be comfortable with her because she is well dressed and upper-middle class. Also, her aspirations are not all that high. Though she is earning a master's degree at the Fashion Institute for Technology, she doesn't see herself running a big company: "To be a mother and a wife will probably be the most important [things in] my life. I think that I'll always have a career, but I don't need to be a CEO. I want to be able to spend time with my family and my children. I see it in women who lead my division. They really don't see their kids that much. They travel a lot. I don't know if that's what I would want."

When she thinks ahead to the time when she will be raising a family, her father's voice plays in her head. He never talked much about race, "but he always pushed us. I think it was always in our mind that 'You're going to have to prove yourself. You're gonna have to always be better.'" She expects to impart that same lesson to her own children. She and her fiancé "talk about how our child's going to take Saturday-morning math class so they can be just as good—be all those things, learning a different language."

She doesn't think the basic lesson for blacks has changed much from her father's generation to hers. "Look at Obama. He had to be triple what John McCain was to get to where he is. I'm not naive to the point where I'd believe that an average black guy can become president. He had to be the best of the best of the best. He needed to have the perfect academic record. He had to have a perfect wife."

She does concede, however, that the racial challenges she and her friends are likely to face will be different from those that confronted her parents—and not just in the workplace. With highly educated black women vastly outnumbering well-educated black men, "a lot of my friends now are dealing with the fact that they're probably not going to be married to a black man. . . . I have a friend who said, 'Okay, if I marry this [white] guy, what can I do to keep my kids black?' It shows that race is still an issue, even if you're choosing someone who's not black as your mate. It's still in your mind." Her friend is

> the last person I'd ever thought I'd see with a white guy. But it just happened that way. She even says it to this day, "I really always wanted that black power-couple type of situation." But here's a great guy who worships her, is smart, went to business school with her, and it just happened that way. Her dad did say, "We'll always support you. But I wish you would've given it up to a brother."

Relationships in this age and in her circle have less and less to do with race. "My best friend at work is white and southern. And we just really bonded. . . . And my fiancé's best man will probably be this white guy that he worked with at Merrill Lynch. It's just the way it is. We don't feel the need to explain that."

That reflects, in her mind, a healthy larger reality. "Before, when you saw a black man with a white woman, you'd think, 'He just doesn't like black women.' But I think today that's not necessarily the case. I mean, people working together and going to school . . . things are happening that you never thought would happen. It's a different time."

The Civil Rights Lawyer and His Son

Theodore Michael Shaw was born in 1954, just months after the Supreme Court handed down *Brown v. Board of Education*. That decision forced schools in the South to desegregate—albeit reluctantly, belatedly, and in many cases far from completely—and ultimately brought the curtain down on Jim Crow. If civil rights was not in Shaw's DNA, it was very much in the air when he was coming up.

One of his early memories is of people lying in the street. "They had newspapers with them. Buses and cars came right up to them, and they were blocking traffic." For years Shaw thought those were images from a dream. But in college, while researching a paper, he stumbled across a newspaper story about Harlem residents blocking the Triborough Bridge to protest merchants who would not hire black workers. The "dream," he realized, was not a dream at all but more likely a half-remembered incident from childhood. "I figured that I might have witnessed that with my grandmother."

He has an earlier, even stronger memory—from shortly before his mother died in 1957. She had been hospitalized, but that night she came home to Harlem.

> My father used to make the bed military-style. You could drop a coin on it and it would bounce. And I couldn't find my way out [of the bed]. I was screaming and crying, and my mother came and pulled me out of the bed. She was comforting me, holding me. She was also laughing a little bit. She obviously thought it was very funny. And I remember looking over her shoulder and there was a full moon.

Shortly after that, Shaw's mother died—from complications of pneumonia and tuberculosis—while pregnant with what would have been her fourth child. Life became unstable. For a while, he and his two siblings moved in with his maternal grandmother. She was middle class by African American standards of the day, having been one of the first black secretaries of the New York City board of education. His father was not around very much. Soon after his mother's death, his dad remarried and moved the family to a public housing project in the Bronx. There, Shaw's dad and his new wife had two more children. "My father and stepmother remained married for maybe six, seven years, and then divorced. And my stepmother, who was overwhelmed, kept all five of us."

Much of the responsibility for raising the brood fell to his paternal grandmother, a deeply religious domestic worker who occasionally brought home clothes from the families who employed her. In retrospect, he thought that her dedication to the family was penance for having had a child out of wedlock. "I think she was punishing herself for being a single mother when she was younger. She lived the rest of her life for her son and grandchildren."

When he was not yet nine, his grandmother offered to take him to the March on Washington for Jobs and Freedom, the 1963 mega-event that would become the biggest demonstration ever seen in the nation's capital. Shaw's stepmother, fearing violence might break out, refused to let him go. "I have always regretted that." He watched the demonstration on television. Like millions of others who heard Martin Luther King challenge America to "transform the jangling discords of our nation into a beautiful symphony of brotherhood," he was moved. His grandmother brought him a small package of mementos—including a handbill from the march that he framed and keeps in his office.

Attending Catholic schools, Shaw believes, saved him from the fate of so many of his friends: "I was hanging out with all of my buddies, and I was in [the depressed inner city] but not of it." As a Catholic schoolboy, "I caught hell sometimes. I'd be called 'faggot,' 'punk,' 'chump,' all those things. [But] when the people I grew up with started using hard-core drugs, I wasn't about sticking a needle in my arm. . . . Catholic school education gave me a different sense of what the possibilities were."

He attended Cardinal Spellman High School in the Bronx (where he became fast friends with Sonia Sotomayor, the future Supreme Court justice and a fellow member of the class of 1972). It was at Spellman that he came into his own, thanks largely to a special leadership program for young black men started by the archbishop after Martin Luther King was assassinated in 1968.

The original plan was to develop potential priests, but the program quickly evolved into something broader—with weekend retreats, cultural events, and readings in black history. "We had to read a book every week. We used to have [to make] speeches. And we went to see plays. And a lot of black theater was around. We were just immersed in all of that." His program peers became lifelong friends, and the white priest who ran it "is still one of the closest people to me."

Without the program, he doubts that he would have gotten into Wesleyan. Nor would he have gone to Columbia Law School, which he completed in 1979, intent on becoming a civil rights attorney.

After graduation, he joined the civil rights division of the U.S. Justice Department. He was thrilled to be part of a government division working for civil rights. With Ronald Reagan's election in 1980, the division suddenly shifted focus. Instead of promoting desegregation, it was opposing "forced" busing. And it reversed the previous administration's stand against a tax exemption for Bob Jones University, which prohibited interracial dating.

"I had a lot of conflict with the people and their point of view—particularly with the head of the civil rights division," recalled Shaw. "I was spending more time in conflict with them than litigating my cases. And [while] I was trying to figure out what to do. . . . Jack Greenberg called me out of the blue."

He told Greenberg, then head of the NAACP Legal Defense and Educational Fund, that he was about to resign. Greenberg offered him a job in New York with the NAACP LDF. Shaw stayed for twenty-five years—except for a three-year period when he taught at the University of Michigan Law School—and served his last three years in the top job, as director-counsel. He then became a law professor at Columbia University and of counsel to Fulbright & Jaworski, an international law firm.

He credits his success to many things: his Catholic education, his love of reading ("I never got on a plane until I was twenty years old and I was on my way to Tanzania as a junior in college, but I traveled through reading"), and even his light complexion: "Even within the African American community, light skin means more privilege—or has meant more privilege." Though in his majority-white Catholic schools he would occasionally be called "nigger," he is "conscious of the fact that I was the beneficiary of privilege too—undeserved, unearned, and wrong, but nonetheless there."

Like many, Shaw is struggling to put this present era in context. Cleary, Obama's election was a milestone—"for our nation and for African Americans in particular." Yet even though it was "psychologically liberating" to see Obama elected, most schools in black communities "are exactly what they were on January 19 of 2009: they're failing schools. And [black] neighborhoods are neighborhoods in which there's violence and poverty." While Obama's election proves that blacks can be anything, "your realities are still a challenge. And that's a tough one to explain, either to our children or to explain in public discourse in a way that most Americans are going to understand."

His dad "wasn't much of a father," said Shaw, "but I remember my paternal grandmother would say, 'Get your education. It's the one thing they can't take away.' My maternal grandmother was similarly very strong in her emphasis on education. . . . They were trying to prepare us for a world in which everything wasn't fair. I think the message to our children now changes."

The message now, he said, is that "you can't blame white people for whatever failures you may have. . . . It's what you are capable of doing. It's what your values are. It's how hard you work."

I asked him about his own children—a son in his twenties, a teenage daughter, and a toddler. He would want his youngest child

> to think that she's living in a world in which no one will ever treat her unfairly because she's a woman or a person of color. I would say to her, "You may run up against those kinds of people, but less and less do they define the world." . . . The first president she's going to know is Barack Obama. Think about the psychologically liberating effect of that for a child who is African American—really for all children.

His son went to Andover.

You don't get much more privileged than that. Did he live in neighborhoods where many of his contemporaries were unprivileged and impacted by poverty and lack of opportunity? Yes. But my message to my son is, he's been blessed. My message to him is, "Just be the best you can be, and give something back." But all things are possible for him. For my sixteen-year-old, my message would be the same. Would I tell them that there's inequality in the world? Yes. Does it affect them tremendously? Not as much as it affects that boy or girl growing up in [the projects]. Will that define their lives going forward? I don't think so. Will it define my daughter's life? I don't think so—well, in the sense that identity does and culture does, yes. I mean they're growing up as African Americans.

The Son

Theodore Winston Shaw goes by the name of Winston. The physician who delivered him suggested the name, saying the wrinkled baby reminded him of Winston Churchill. Born in 1986, Winston spent his early childhood on both coasts, in New Jersey, Harlem, and then Los Angeles, where his parents separated when Winston was three. Shortly after that, his mother, a TV reporter and writer, moved with him to Jacksonville, Florida, then St. Petersburg. He lived there for the next few years, spending summers largely with his father, primarily in New York. Then they moved west again, to his mother's hometown of Richmond, California, and later to San Diego, before heading to Chicago.

Early life, as he recalled it, was one big series of moves. "I was always bouncing back and forth between New York and wherever my mother was. I lived in over twenty-five different homes. I was always readjusting." For the most part, he attended public schools. "The times that I went to private school, it was usually when we moved [in] the middle of the year. So I would go to private school for the rest of the year until she found a good public school or a public school with a magnet program."

Sometimes the good programs would be in dicey neighborhoods, but "I was always in gifted programs." He was also a standout athlete—in football, basketball, and baseball. Sports invariably opened doors. Nonetheless, "I was always feeling like I was living in two worlds—just feeling like either I was going to be misunderstood or going to be trying to explain who I was."

He recalls being in St. Petersburg in October 1996 when riots broke out. They were sparked by the fatal police shooting of a black teenager in a car mistakenly thought to be stolen. Winston was staying with a neighbor at the time, and he remembered worrying about his mother, who was covering the violence. Later, he found out that his mother was fine. The riots, nonetheless, made a big impression: "It just made me realize at a young age the importance of race."

He would sometimes go on trips with his father.

> He took me to Europe one time—Paris, London. It was always one or two days at a time because he was going for conferences. So it wasn't like I really knew the place. But I would get a taste. And it was always in the context of, like, race in this place or, you know, Roma rights in Europe. . . . We went to Budapest and Prague. It was all in like a week and a half because he was speaking places. He took me to Brazil. . . . And always in that light of the importance of civil rights.

Even though he was traveling the globe and immersed in magnet programs, he was surrounded by kids far less privileged. "None of my friends from San Diego that I was close with went to college. None of them." He knew enough to realize that he needed to leave his San Diego neighborhood and go to a really good high school.

His father talked up Phillips Exeter Academy. Someone in his middle school suggested Loomis Chaffee. A Better Chance event in

Los Angeles introduced him to Phillips Academy in Andover, and though he was not eligible for ABC's program, he was intrigued by the school. Winston applied to—and got into—all three: "I chose Andover because it was the one that I felt was most open-minded."

The transition was hard: "I did really poorly my first year—really, really poorly. Culturally, I didn't fit in. A lot of people didn't like me." Part of the reason, he concluded, was the way he dressed. Also, the vibe was so different from what he was accustomed to.

> There weren't a lot of kids from California there. There were all these kids from New York. Most of the Hispanic kids were Dominican. And most of the black kids were African or Caribbean. . . . One of the reasons I went to Andover is because they talk about how it's like a microcosm of the world. But in the world that I lived in—Florida, Chicago, San Diego—the majority of Hispanic kids were *not* Dominican.

Sports had always provided a way to fit in, but not at Andover. "I tried to hang out with the black jocks, and I just felt like they were full of it, to be honest with you." So many were trying to act like bad boys from tough neighborhoods when in reality they were anything but that.

Over time, he adjusted: "I was used to adapting. It just was a bigger adaptation than I had ever made." The friction with fellow students gave way to friendship and intellectual curiosity. His arguments with black and Latino students fueled an interest in Latin America and Afro-Latino studies. He also came to appreciate Andover's refusal to coddle him: "I was able to get away with a lot at my middle school because I was smart and black." He couldn't at Andover. "And I'm glad for it."

During his senior year, he starred in a performance of *Things Fall Apart,* a play adapted from the novel by Nigerian author Chinua Achebe. The group was invited to perform the play in Grahamstown, South Africa, and some nearby townships: "I had been to South Africa before with my dad but couldn't remember much of it. . . . My dad took me there, and I met Nelson Mandela. But I was young, like five or six." When he returned, he was old enough to savor the experience. "I was amazed at how much it had in common with the U.S. [and at] how easy it was to speak with some of the friends I met there."

His father pushed Wesleyan as a college choice, but Winston was not convinced. He was hesitant to volunteer for what he saw as a collegiate version of Andover. So he applied to Morehouse, which came through with a full scholarship: "I weighed the fact that it was an HBCU [historically black college or university], the fact that I would be going there for free, the fact that it was in the South and I hadn't gone to school in the South in a long time. And I said, 'Well, if I'm going to school for free, why not!'"

He discovered that, in certain respects, Morehouse was much like Andover. There were people there, as at Andover, who judged others on the basis of their appearance and clothes. There were also many students with a great deal of family money—which they brandished much more blatantly than the kids at Andover: "Andover is insulated because we're all boarding school students who don't have cars there. You don't really see the money that much. . . . It's not in your face, taunting you every day. But at Morehouse, people are riding around in Hummers."

Morehouse gave Winston the same insight Spelman gave Asha: "It taught me how diverse we are. When you go to an all-male African American school, none of your identity has to do with being black and male anymore, because everyone's black and male. . . . Outside of Morehouse, if you're a black male, that's how you're defined by the rest of the world."

He majored in Spanish and international studies, spending his junior year abroad with a Catholic outreach organization that worked with black Ecuadorians. Following graduation and an internship in New York at ESPN, he moved into his mother's home in Philadelphia. He was interested in law but reluctant to commit to—and incur student debt for—a profession he was not sure he was passionate about. He discovered a program—Philadelphia Teaching Fellows—that would allow him to earn a teaching certificate while working as a teacher in "high-need" schools.

Teaching was "something I care about, but at the same time it's something that's possible." It also put him in touch with a population—young, urban black males—that he thought were in crisis.

Law school may be an option eventually, but for the moment he is determined to do what he can to help young people—who remind him of himself a few years back—get to where he is now. "Once you've gotten to the age of twenty-three and you don't have a record and you have a college degree, you're probably in a pretty good position." The challenge for young black men is getting to that point.

He has a certain reverence for what he considers to be the age of candor, which happens to overlap with the age—in many urban areas—of raw, openly expressed black rage: "I look at the sixties and seventies as kind of like a really great time because black people were honest and they were listened to because they were honest." Now, he believes, Americans are more interested in self-delusion: "All that we've achieved . . . is being reversed because of the whole colorless society conversation, because we think we're somewhere we're not."

Chapter Seven

A Place to Call Home

As we have seen, African Americans are increasingly optimistic. But is that optimism justified? In this chapter, we look a bit more deeply at that question—and at some economic realities (the Great Recession among them) underlying it.

Most Americans never saw it coming. We certainly weren't ready for the good times to end. We were so busy enjoying our new acquisitions that it never occurred to us that perhaps we couldn't pay the bills. So we continued to buy cars, homes, and whatever else we could pay for on credit—confident we were doing the right, and fiscally sensible, thing. No one, after all, was making new land. So why not snatch up what was left while we could? Home ownership, however financed, was inarguably a good thing. Or so it seemed during those happy years when the bank vaults swung open and money rained down on virtually anyone willing to hold out his or her hand.

Between 1994 and 2005, home ownership rates increased by nearly 8 percent, with the biggest jumps among Latinos (20 percent), Asian Americans (17 percent), and blacks (14 percent), according to U.S. census statistics. While ownership rates among minorities remained far behind those for whites, all ships were rising and minorities were closing the gap. The "incorporation process"—to use sociologist Elijah Anderson's term—seemed to be working. Formerly excluded people of color were moving into the mainstream and buying heavily (albeit with borrowed money) into the American Dream.

When the U.S. economy tanked in late 2007, people of all colors and classes saw their dreams—and rosy assumptions—crumble as their equity shriveled. Between 2006 (the prerecession year) and the end of 2009 (when the recession reached its nadir), household real estate in America dropped $6.4 trillion in value, according to the Federal Reserve.

In the last few years, numerous experts have weighed in on what caused the mortgage market meltdown. In *The Subprime Solution,* economist Robert Shiller explained it this way:

> Mortgage originators, who planned to sell off the mortgages to securitizers, stopped worrying about repayment risk. They typically made only perfunctory efforts to assess borrowers' ability to repay their loans—often failing to verify borrowers' income with the Internal Revenue Service, even if they possessed signed authorization forms permitting them to do so. Sometimes these lenders enticed the naive, with poor credit histories, to borrow in the ballooning subprime mortgage market. These mortgages were packaged, sold, and resold in sophisticated but arcane ways to investors around the world, setting the stage for a crisis of truly global proportions.

New York Times economics writer Edmund Andrews was blunter. The crisis, he wrote in *Busted,*

> would not have been possible without breathtaking cynicism on the part of the brainiest people and biggest institutions in American finance. For all the baffling complexities at work—"collateralized debt obligations," "conduits," and computer-run risk models—this is a fairly simple story about how a lot of really smart people embraced and proselytized for a lot of inexcusable hogwash.

Certainly, as the crisis unfolded, one thing became quite clear: using complex financial instruments that no one seemed to understand and loans for which no one took responsibility, banking institutions and affiliated companies had taken advantage of borrowers' naïveté and sucked them dry. And minority communities were among the primary targets—especially for the near usurious loans that came to be called subprime.

"From big cities like Chicago and Cleveland to Stockton, California, the patterns were strikingly similar. African-Americans and Hispanics were several times more likely than whites to get subprime mortgages, even when the borrowers had comparable incomes," Andrews pointed out. And many blacks and Latinos, whose grasp on middle-class life was tenuous to begin with, quietly slipped into poverty—helping to push the official U.S. poverty rate to its highest level since before the dawn of the new millennium. The tragedy devastated not just individuals but entire communities—and ultimately the economy as a whole.

Although the recession caused hardship across the board, it was particularly distressing for black and Latino communities. Most blacks and Latinos were less likely than non-Hispanic whites to have garnered the resources to weather an economic storm. They also were disproportionately targeted for predatory loans. So they were particularly at risk of losing their homes—and therefore their claim to middle-class status. The Center for Responsible Lending estimated that property depreciation related to foreclosures between 2009 and 2012 would end up costing black communities $194 billion and Latino communities $177 billion.

In *Black Wealth/White Wealth,* published in 1995, sociologists Melvin Oliver and Thomas Shapiro make an important and underappreciated point—that income alone is a deeply inadequate measure of economic wherewithal. Wealth, often transmitted down through generations, is what allows people to get a decent start in life, invest in their children's future, and survive financial setbacks. They find that whites—regardless of their income level—have, on average, much more wealth than blacks. Indeed, whites from even the "lowest status families" have more wealth, on average, than blacks employed as professionals. The reason, they argue, has a lot to do with an array of policies that have prevented most blacks, until very recently, from accumulating anything like the resources that whites routinely pass down to their children.

Even before the Great Recession, the gap between blacks and whites had been growing, according to research by Shapiro and his colleagues at Brandeis University's Institute on Assets and Social Policy. The gap between the accumulated wealth of an average white family and that of an average black family, excluding home equity, stood at $20,000 in 1984. By 2007, it had grown to $95,000.

> The growth of the racial wealth gap significantly affects the economic future of American families. For example, the racial wealth gap in 1984 amounted to less than three years tuition payment for one child at a public university. By 2007, the dollar amount of the gap is enough to pay full tuition at a four-year public university for two children, plus tuition at a public medical school. The gap is opportunity denied and assures racial economic inequality for the next generation.

The racial wealth gap, they argue, is due to many things, including tax cuts and other policies that disproportionately benefit the wealthiest.

> At the same time, evidence from multiple sources demonstrates the powerful role of persistent discrimination in housing, credit, and labor markets. For example, African-Americans and Hispanics were at least twice as likely to receive high-cost home mortgages as whites with similar incomes. These reckless high-cost loans unnecessarily impeded wealth building in minority communities and triggered the foreclosure crisis that is wiping out the largest source of wealth for minorities.

Even high-income African Americans were doing poorly relative to whites: "Middle-income white households had greater gains in financial assets than high-income African Americans. By

2007, they had accumulated $74,000 whereas the average high-income African American family owned only $18,000." But since then, argue Shapiro and his colleagues, things have only gotten worse. From 2007 to the end of the first quarter of 2009, low-income black families (those with an annual income of $40,000 or less) found their "asset securities . . . reduced from about a thousand dollars to about two hundred bucks," he told me. In other words, if they suddenly lost their income and had to rely on savings, their financial reserves would run out in less than a week.

For Shapiro, such statistics raise the troubling question of whether America's racial progress will collapse under the weight of financial insecurity. That is a critically important subject—one that could easily fill several books on its own, and I will not explore it in depth here. But amid all the financial wreckage, it's impossible not to wonder how the banking industry managed to pull it off. How, to be more precise, could a country that was making such strides toward equality allow lenders, with impunity, to cynically target minority communities with their flimflam?

The short answer is that because of segregation, poverty, and a hunger for credit that dates back to the days when redlining was rampant, poor black and Latino communities were ripe for the taking.

No one is suggesting that any group of bankers ever convened and essentially agreed to screw over minority home owners and would-be home owners. But as Tom Rudd of Ohio State's Kirwan Institute observed, "Greed motivates you to look for people who are most vulnerable. And in our society those people tend to be people of color."

> You had this transition in the mortgage market where the profit incentive was how many mortgages you could process. It wasn't long-term sustainability. So you look then for untapped markets that you could proliferate with as many loans as possible. You also had in some communities—at least we have anecdotal evidence of this—refi's [refinanced loans] . . . targeting particularly the elderly—folks who had some equity but were cash-poor.

Some mortgage bankers who had front-row seats to the crisis gave depositions in 2009 in response to a suit filed by the city of Baltimore against Wells Fargo Bank. Among those deposed was Elizabeth Jacobson, who was hired by Wells Fargo in 1988 as a loan officer and was subsequently promoted to sales manager. Jacobson worked, for the most part, out of an office in Federalsburg, Maryland, and was responsible for making subprime loans in an area that included Prince George's County and Baltimore. She was apparently very good at it. According to her sworn statement, she was always among the top three Wells Fargo loan officers in the country. In 2004, when she grossed more than $700,000 in commissions, she was number one. Between 2003 and 2007, she made loans valued at $50 million.

The subprime market was so profitable that even loan officers responsible for so-called prime loans sent their customers to her—including customers who qualified for better terms—since the referring loan officers got a share of the commissions. They would use any number of ploys to convince their customers to go along. They would tell customers that the only way to get the loan processed quickly or to avoid onerous paperwork requirements was to go the subprime route. Or they would advise customers to put no money down, which would automatically push them into subprime territory—along with its sky-high interest rates. But no one would tell customers about the added costs. And no one seemed to care what was in the customer's best interest.

Sometimes, said Jacobson, loan officers actually falsified applications: "I was aware of A reps who would 'cut and paste' the credit report of a borrower who had already qualified for a loan into the file of an applicant who would not have qualified for a Wells Fargo subprime loan because of his or her credit history. I was also aware of subprime loan officers who would cut and paste W-2 forms."

Once the transaction was consummated and the fees received, the loans were sold on the secondary market—thereby ending Wells Fargo's exposure.

There were numerous efforts to target the black community with donations to churches and other incentives: "Wells Fargo hoped to sell the African American pastor or church leader on the program because Wells Fargo believed that African American church leaders had a lot of influence over their ministry, and in this way would convince the congregation to take out subprime loans with Wells Fargo," said Jacobson. The bank also conducted so-called wealth-building seminars whose only purpose was to market subprime loans to blacks:

> I remember preparing to participate in a wealth-building seminar that was to be held in Greenbelt, Maryland. It was understood that the audience would be virtually all black. The point of the seminar was to get people to buy houses using Wells Fargo loans. At the seminar, the plan was to talk to attendees about "alternative lending." This was code language for subprime lending, but we were not supposed to use the word "subprime."

Among her colleagues at Wells Fargo, said Jacobson, any reference to churches "was understood as a code for African American or black churches." Jacobson, who is white, estimated that "a large majority" of her customers were black. Managers, she said, called predominantly black Prince George's County the "subprime capital of Maryland."

Tony Paschal, a black native of Muskegon, Michigan, who worked in the Annandale, Virginia, office of Wells Fargo Home Mortgage, corroborated what Jacobson had to say. A large part of Paschal's job was attempting to get existing Wells Fargo customers to refinance their homes. He was also specifically charged—in his role as a "community development representative"—with working with community groups to expand Wells Fargo's business, particularly in minority communities, said Paschal in his deposition.

Paschal said he became uncomfortable with what he perceived as "deceptive and discriminatory" practices—in particular the custom of allowing white customers to benefit from drops in market rates prior to a loan closing when black customers were routinely told that the original rate was locked in. He left in 1999 to work for another firm, but returned two years later when that firm went under. Again, Paschal was in the business of soliciting customers to refinance their loans. Many of those customers ended up in the Mortgage Resource (MORE) division, which exclusively offered "higher-interest-rate subprime loans." MORE specifically went after minorities, said Paschal.

> The MORE division targeted zip codes in Washington, D.C., east of the Anacostia River, Prince George's County, Maryland, and the city of Baltimore, with predominantly African American populations. I heard employees in the MORE division comment that Howard County was not good for subprime loans because it has a predominantly white population. . . . They referred to subprime loans made in minority communities as "ghetto loans" and minority customers as "those people who have bad credit."

The bank also developed special materials aimed at blacks, said Paschal. "For example, if a Wells Fargo loan officer anywhere in the United States wanted to send a flyer to prospective customers in an African American neighborhood soliciting their business, he could access software on his computer that would print out a flyer to persons speaking the language of 'African American.'" Wells Fargo also created an "Affinity Group Marketing" team in Silver Spring, Maryland, consisting entirely of black employees, which "targeted African American churches." Those employees were only authorized to offer subprime loans. As a result, they pushed into the subprime market black customers "who could have qualified for a lower-cost prime loan."

When groups such as the Association of Community Organizations for Reform Now and the Center for Responsible Lending complained about the discrimination, said Paschal, Wells Fargo responded with superficial measures "for public consumption only" but did not "actually restrict discriminatory practices."

The bank fired Paschal in September 2007, claiming that his

productivity was low. "My loan production was lower than many other loan officers because I tried to do the right thing by Wells Fargo customers by putting them in loans they could afford," said Paschal. "If a customer did not qualify for a loan or could not afford an estimated monthly payment, I did not originate the loan."

Paschal is an athletically built and soft-spoken man in his early fifties, but he is nobody's shrinking violet. When I interviewed him in Washington, D.C., over breakfast, he elaborated on the allegations he had made in his deposition.

Paschal, a Howard University alum, began his career in insurance. He switched to mortgage banking after a family friend offered to hire him into his brokerage business, promising to teach him everything from the ground up. Paschal was an eager student. Mortgage banking seemed like a good way not just to make money but also to perform a valuable service: "You could . . . empower someone [through] home ownership." After working for his friend for a few years, he took a job with Norwest Mortgage, which was then the eleventh largest bank in the United States. Within months of his arrival, Norwest merged with Wells Fargo, and the combined company took on the more recognized Wells Fargo name. Paschal became a loan officer in Wells Fargo's sales and marketing section.

At that time, 1998, the company was not yet a significant player in the subprime market. Indeed, virtually no major banking enterprise was. But with the merger, Wells Fargo acquired an entity called Directors Acceptance Corporation, whose primary function was to make subprime loans. Paschal ended up working with that unit. In the early days, he said, they were not targeting any particular race. They were simply going after people who were not eligible for more conventional, lower-interest-rate loans—those with low credit scores (under 620) and high debt-to-income ratios (over 36 percent). "If you look at any other company in the late nineties, they were all doing the same thing." The attitude was, "Let's test this thing out and see how it works."

During Paschal's two-year break from Wells Fargo, the industry radically changed. When he returned in 2001, the subprime market had taken off, and Wells Fargo had realized, as had other lenders, that black and Latino communities represented a great untapped market. Residents were hungry for credit, and thanks to residential segregation, they were easy to target. Moreover, those lucky enough to have homes had generally seen the value increase—making them ripe for refinancing schemes. And to make things even more tempting from the bankers' perspective, these potential customers, most of whom were relatively poor and financially unsophisticated, were not likely to have fancy lawyers or savvy financial advisers who would warn them away from toxic financial products.

Paschal believes that the way his bosses went after black customers was very different from the way they dealt with whites:

> Here in the D.C. metro area, the affinity group made an arrangement with African American churches. Now, I say "African American churches" because there were no Lutheran churches, there were no Mormon or Latter-Day Saints; there were Baptist churches in African American communities, D.C., Maryland, and Baltimore. So they offered these ministers a contribution if they could market to their congregations.

Borrowers were more than willing victims. With money dangling before them, theirs for the taking, they eagerly reached out:

> I had a guy over here at Northeast Washington who bought his house for $180,000 back in the seventies. All of a sudden the house was worth $380,000. So he calls me up and said, "Tony, I want to refinance my house and pay off some credit cards." The guy had about $70,000 worth of credit card debt. So he says, "I want to pay off these credit cards." . . . Then he says, "I want to buy a car." . . . This particular guy asked for an additional $40,000 to buy the car, "because I want to get a Mercedes." I said, "Well, I'm not going to do your loan."

Paschal explained to the man that if he loaned him the money, the man was likely to end up losing his house. Although the loan might start off with a 9 percent interest rate, in two years the rate would rise to 11 or 12 percent, and given the amount he was asking for, he would owe an additional $1,000 or so a month, which he could not afford.

> So I refused to do his loan. He called back into that office and got a white guy right down the hall [with] Mortgage Resources. He said, "Tony, I got one of your customers and I'm doing his loan." And not only did he pay off almost $70,000 credit card [debt], he gave him $50,000 [for the car]. These types of behaviors were rewarded. I was written up so many times for loans I thought it was not prudent to do as far as the customer was concerned . . . because the result, you could see it coming.

In that era, Paschal recalled, people came to believe—and were encouraged to believe—that money essentially had become free. One guy called and asked for a "coffee-on loan," which the man's friend had told him carried only a 1 percent interest rate. Paschal asked the man if he had any idea what he was asking for. "It's a mortgage based on coffee rates," the man replied. Paschal explained that there was no such thing as a "coffee-on" loan. The man had to be talking about a COFI-ARM (cost of funds index, adjustable rate mortgage). Those loans, he explained, typically had a very low rate, but only for a very short time. The cost mushroomed after that, so much so that people often ended up owing much more than they had borrowed, even after paying a considerable amount to a bank. If he took such a loan, Paschal told the caller, he would probably lose his home: "That was almost [always] my bottom line with everybody."

Successfully peddling such products required not only unscrupulous bankers but naive and befuddled borrowers. And one thing that became clear to me while researching this book is that those borrowers, after finding themselves in foreclosure proceedings, are very reluctant to talk about what happened to them. They are ashamed of their own ignorance and gullibility. And because of that, they essentially collude with the bankers to keep what happened private. Many of those we approached to tell their stories said, in effect, that they were too embarrassed to talk. The couple whose story I will tell here insisted on anonymity. The wife was afraid of being looked down on in her church, and her husband didn't want his fellow Masons to know what happened to them. They are elderly—which is also typical of victims of this type of financial abuse, for older people are particularly likely to have accumulated the resources that make them tempting targets for all manner of charlatans and schemes.

I will call them the Johnsons, Percy and Sylvia. She was born in 1928. Her husband was born in 1930. They live in the same house in Bedford-Stuyvesant that Sylvia moved into as a teenager.

Sylvia's mother died when she was eight. Her father, an immigrant from Barbados, raised Sylvia and her sister alone. He worked as a baker for the Ward Baking Company, a Brooklyn institution famous for its white bread and its state-of-the-art factory, built in 1911, that was filled with modern, meticulously crafted machinery.

Originally, Sylvia, her sister, and her father lived across the street from where she now lives. But sometime during the 1940s her dad managed to pull enough money together to buy the house. She has pleasant memories of that time. "The community was very good. We were the second black [family] when we moved over here. My father bought the house from a doctor."

In 1955, Sylvia, who worked as a payroll clerk, married Percy, another New Yorker whose parents had migrated from Barbados. Shortly after the marriage, he went to work for the New York City Transit Authority and stayed there for thirty-five years, retiring in 1990.

In 1978, Sylvia's father gave her the house, free and clear. He died a few years after that, and the Johnsons realized that their now ramshackle home was no longer in great shape. They were approached by various lenders eager to help them out. In retrospect, Percy conceded that they made some bad decisions. He also insisted that they were deceived: "They wasn't honest in the beginning. And when they came here, they hoodwinked us."

Their indebtedness started off relatively small. They had outstanding loans that needed to be repaid, home repairs that needed to be done. Their memories were somewhat fuzzy. They were no longer clear on precisely what the initial loan was for. Sylvia believed that it was to "help pay off some loans and help repair the house. . . . We figured we would get help." The record shows that they took out a home refinancing loan in 1986 for $25,000. "That was so long ago. All I remember is we went out to Flushing someplace and we got that loan," said Sylvia.

As time passed, said Sylvia, "we found that we still needed some more money to help repair the house. And we went off to somebody else." Over the next several years, they took out a succession of home equity loans—$15,000 in 1988, $50,000 in 1990, $36,000 in 1992, $115,000 in 1994—from various lending institutions. The money was needed, said Sylvia, for "house repairs, to help pay off our bills—credit card debts and whatever. And then we had to buy a furnace, and that really put us in the hole."

Loans continued to pile up: $33,000 in 1996, $180,000 in 1998, $260,000 in 2001. At this point, the Johnsons were on a treadmill, taking out new loans, on ever more onerous terms, to pay off old loans that were draining them dry. "All I know, we just figured we would get the money and we would manage to pay it," said Sylvia. "They never said, 'No, you can't afford this.' . . . Never said it. Never said it."

In February 2004, they borrowed $328,000, refinancing seven months later with a loan of $485,000. A year later, they borrowed $565,000. And in 2006 they borrowed $630,000. Every time the retirees refinanced, the amount they owed increased, while they remained on a fixed income. They became increasingly desperate as the numbers mounted.

After they took out the loan for $630,000, their monthly payment was in the neighborhood of $4,500. They could not come up with the money and eventually found themselves in foreclosure proceedings.

Frantic with worry, they asked for help. "We went back to Wells Fargo, and they said they can help us, but the monthly payment was going up a little higher. And I said, 'No, we couldn't do that.

No. No,'" recalled Sylvia. Happily, they came to an arrangement—or so they thought. "They claimed if we made three payments . . . then they will see if they can help us," said Sylvia.

So the couple scraped the money together and made the payments in the hope that the lender would modify the deal. "But when we made those three payments, then they turn around and say they couldn't help us. So then we were stuck again," said Sylvia.

"When they came in, they came in with smiles and everything," she observed, but once the Johnsons got in arrears, "they didn't actually care about the house or how we were going to pay off the loan."

The Johnsons went to a number of places seeking relief and finally ended up in a local legal services office. "We negotiated a modification," said their counselor, "but it fell apart. They never honored it. It was over the phone. We never had it in writing."

In 2010, with the legal services agency's help, the Johnsons began renegotiating terms. The $630,000 loan had, by then, ballooned to a $730,000 debt. Meanwhile, the legal services agency had an appraisal done. The house was worth roughly $600,000. "They knew they were writing a loan mod [modification] that had their loan . . . significantly underwater," said the counselor. "And they didn't care. They knew they were recapitalizing interest based on a loan they should have never offered."

Ultimately, said the counselor,

> I went to court. The attorney who represents Wells Fargo was there, and she called her person at Wells Fargo . . . and then the next day I got an e-mail [with] this terrible offer. . . . And I kept pushing back and saying, "At least if you're going to give them a massive loan that leaves their house $100,000 underwater, put that $100,000 as a balloon at the end, because they're never going to pay that back. *They're eighty*—forty years from now they'll be one hundred and twenty."

At the end of it, they settled on a barely affordable monthly payment of just under $2,500, which will rise gradually over the years, for a house that they once owned outright. When they die or can no longer afford to keep up the payments, the property will almost certainly pass into the hands of a lender.

"I get nervous and everything wondering where I'm gonna go at this age, because I'm eighty-two now," said Sylvia.

It would require a combination of cynicism and insensitivity that borders on the monstrous not to be moved by the plight of people such as the Johnsons—even if you blame their own stupidity for getting them into trouble in the first place. Yet it was on the equity of unsuspecting and vulnerable people such as the Johnsons that the subprime industry rose. In a relatively short time, it went from virtually nothing to the status of a major business. A complaint filed against Wells Fargo in 2009 by the attorney general of Illinois reckoned that subprime lending volume grew from $35 billion to $625 billion between 1994 and 2005. None of it required any form of explicit racism. It just required greed and a lack of compassion. All it required, in Tony Paschal's words, were lenders who "sit down and calculate how to rip off the least protected of classes in this country."

Black loan officers, said Paschal, were caught in the middle:

> Not a whole lot has changed for African Americans in terms of economics. I mean, we can sit at lunch counters and we can go to theaters. We can do this. We can do this. But when it comes to economic independence, or the ability to make our own decisions based on what we know is right, we don't have the ability. I say that because I talked to other African Americans at Wells Fargo who were going through some of the same things that I was going through. And they suffered in silence because they didn't want to lose their jobs.

I sent a very detailed e-mail to Wells Fargo, asking for the company's response to the allegations made by Paschal and Jacobson. I received in response the bank's "most recent communication on this topic"—a press release, dated September 14, 2010, and headlined "For the Second Time, Court Dismisses

City of Baltimore Lawsuit Against Wells Fargo"—which I reproduce here, and which answered none of the specific questions or allegations.

> Today U.S. District Judge J. Frederick Motz of Maryland dismissed, for the second time, the lawsuit that the City of Baltimore filed against Wells Fargo in 2008 alleging the company's lending practices led to foreclosures that harmed the city.
>
> "We have contended from the beginning that the challenges Baltimore faces cannot be attributed to the small number of loans Wells Fargo foreclosed in the city," said Cara Heiden, co-president of Wells Fargo Home Mortgage. "Even the city has acknowledged that long-standing crime, unemployment and socioeconomic issues have contributed to the city's problems. We remain committed to working with city and state leaders to help revitalize Baltimore by addressing issues related to abandoned properties. We also will continue to do our part to lessen the impact of foreclosures on communities in Baltimore and across the nation by working with our customers to reach affordable home payments wherever possible."
>
> On Jan. 6, 2010, the Court dismissed Baltimore's lawsuit for the first time, but provided the city with an opportunity to file a narrower, amended complaint that addressed only the economic impacts associated with Wells Fargo's foreclosures in Baltimore. In its original complaint, the city disclosed Wells Fargo was responsible for less than one-half of one percent of the 30,000 vacant properties in Baltimore. By comparison, Baltimore's own Housing Department has reported that 10,000, or one-third, of the vacant properties are owned by the city.

In 2010 the Center for Responsible Lending estimated that nearly 8 percent of both African Americans and Latinos had lost their homes to foreclosures, compared to 4.5 percent of whites: "The racial and ethnic disparities in these estimated foreclosure rates hold even after controlling for differences in income patterns between demographic groups."

The subprime story is one of failure at multiple levels, beginning with banking regulators who, in the 1990s, changed the rules in ways that made it easy—and ultimately irresistible—for banks to pass on the risk of their subprime bets by bundling them into mortgage-backed securities. It is a story about how easily people who had acquired the trappings of financial success can end up broke when financiers foster and prey on unrealistic expectations. It is a story about how, even in a postracist America, minorities can be disproportionately and systematically exploited. It is fundamentally, however, a story about a simple lesson that we never truly seem to learn: in America—and in the world at large, for that matter—our fates are interconnected, whatever the color of our skin.

Chapter Eight

Jail, Jobs, School, and Hope

How long will the hopefulness last? How deep does it run? According to a series of polls taken over the last few years, blacks are as upbeat as we have ever been. Our optimism is so high—and so out of whack with apparent reality—that it borders on the incomprehensible.

A year after Obama's election, as I noted earlier, blacks told Pew's pollsters that African Americans had progressed more in the past two years than during any other period in the past quarter century. Gallup reported in July 2010 that over 60 percent of blacks claimed that their standard of living was improving—a number much higher than Gallup recorded for whites. That same year, Hamilton College released a national poll of high school–age students in which some 69 percent of African American teenagers expressed the belief that they would be better off than their parents. Only 36 percent of white teenagers believed that they would be better off than their parents.

A poll released in February 2011 (conducted jointly by the *Washington Post,* the Henry J. Kaiser Family Foundation, and the Harvard University Survey Project) found that black optimism continued to soar. "Hopefulness among African Americans is evident across a variety of measures: 85 percent of African Americans are optimistic about the future, 62 percent say their personal finances will improve over the next year, 59 percent think America's best years are yet to come, and 32 percent say the economy is already recovering (a relatively low figure, but well above what whites and Hispanics say about the trajectory of the economy)," reported the *Post*.

What made the polls all the more remarkable is that they came out when foreclosures of homes owned by African Americans were at record levels, 32.5 percent of black workers between the ages of sixteen and twenty-four were unemployed, and unemployment for blacks overall was at a twenty-five-year high. We are in the throes of the worst economic environment we have seen in our lifetime, and one of every three black boys born can expect to spend time behind bars. So why are so many of us convinced that this is such a great time?

A lot of it has to do with the Obama presidency—with what Professor David Thomas termed "irrational exuberance." But it is not all about Obama. As societal barriers have fallen, it seems that we have undergone a once-in-a-generation reassessment—most significantly among the young—of what it is possible for a black person to be in this country. And the sense of hope unleashed by that reassessment seems not much affected—at this point at least—by the state of the economy. But while unbridled optimism may make sense for African Americans who are fortunate enough to hold a Harvard MBA, what of those who are not nearly so blessed? What of those who are much more likely to be languishing in prison than admitted to an Ivy League university?

That question led me to the Fortune Society, the nonprofit group that promotes alternatives to incarceration, helps reintegrate ex-offenders into their communities, and is run by JoAnne Page, the plainspoken daughter of a Holocaust survivor and a former legal aid attorney whom I would certainly not describe as irrationally exuberant.

A few decades back, she pointed out, an uneducated blue-collar worker could earn enough to raise a family and send his children to college. Even a few years back—until the mid-1990s, when the

Violent Crime Control and Law Enforcement Act essentially disallowed Pell Grants for prisoners—people behind bars could easily earn college credits, presumably facilitating their reentry into society. That is no longer the case, said Page.

> So I think the future is less open for folks coming through our doors now than it would've been ten or twenty years ago. . . . I see the rope getting tighter around the necks of the folks we serve. When we work with individuals, we can wiggle some of them through. But when you look at the broader picture, it's getting uglier. They're competing against people with more education and less stigma.

A now famous study done in 2004 found that young black and Latino males were stigmatized regardless of whether they had a criminal record. Princeton sociologists Devah Pager and Bruce Western made every effort to ensure that the make-believe job applicants in their study presented themselves as equal in every relevant way:

> Our research design involved sending matched teams of young men (called testers) to apply for 1,470 real entry-level jobs throughout New York City over ten months in 2004. The testers were well-spoken young men, aged 22 to 26; most were college-educated, between 5 feet 10 inches and 6 feet in height, recruited in and around New York City. They were chosen on the basis of their similar verbal skills, interactional styles and physical attractiveness. Additionally, testers went through a common training program to ensure uniform style of self-presentation in job interviews.

Nonetheless, Pager and Western discovered, race trumped "all else in determining employment opportunities." Employers overwhelmingly preferred whites, even when whites—by every relevant measure—were identical to blacks and Latinos. Blacks were roughly half as likely as whites to be considered for employment. Latinos, though not as favored as whites, were much preferred to blacks. White applicants with a felony conviction did just as well as or better than blacks with no criminal background. Glenn Martin, now vice president of development and public affairs for the Fortune Society, was a project manager for the study. "I was the one that sat there day after day and [saw] these guys coming back," he told me.

As a black man who grew up in Bedford-Stuyvesant, Martin "wasn't surprised, but [the study] did change the way I think about the work." In the past, he had been much more willing to ignore the possibility that race played a heavy role in the treatment of his clients. Many institutional allies, after all, were not particularly receptive to talk of racism. But the research made it impossible to ignore the reality that black men looking for entry-level jobs were at a decided disadvantage simply because of their race. And for those with a criminal record, the already bleak outlook became bleaker. "Here in New York, for instance, there are actually SUNY [State University of New York] schools, government-funded institutions, where you can't even apply based solely on having a felony conviction," said Martin.

The Fortune clients I talked to were under no illusion that they would have an easy time. In that sense, Barry Campbell was typical. He was born in England to Jamaican parents and came to New York in the early seventies as a child. He soon became what he called a "system baby": "foster care, boys' home, jail, and then prison." For most of his early life, said Campbell, he was "just hustling in the streets"—until he was sent to prison for second-degree robbery. Once out, he resolved to turn things around. After working for Fortune in various capacities, he decided to "break into corporate America."

Campbell, who had learned how to handle payroll at Fortune, applied for a payroll position at a major New York newspaper.

> It just happened to be payroll day. And I went into [the interviewer's] office, and she didn't know what she was doing. She was all over the place. And I said, "Look, ma'am, I know this is an interview, but get up and let me do the payroll for you." She

> got up. I ran her payroll, and she said, "Look, the job is yours. It's just the formality of some small paperwork. When you come back tomorrow, we'll do the paperwork." And I walked out of there and I said, "*Yes!* I'm in." When I came back the next day, she said, "I apologize," and she handed me a check for one day, and she said, "This is a union job, and we cannot hire formerly incarcerated people or people with a felony." I looked at her and my heart dropped. . . . "Have you ever been convicted of a felony?" Just asking you the question on a job application is enough to make people get up and walk out of the door.

Anthony Williams, a twenty-year-old convicted of robbery from South Jamaica, Queens, agreed that the job search was invariably hard. "Most jobs don't accept people with felonies." Security jobs, he noted, seemed to be the exception. Otherwise, "you can't do nothing with a record nowadays."

Because there are so few other options, resisting the pull of life on the streets can be difficult. Indeed, even without a criminal record, the allure can sometimes be overwhelming, as Mark Stewart, a twenty-five-year-old former drug dealer, pointed out. "I really want to play football," he said, but his father was a drug dealer. "So I was born into it. It was right there for me. . . . My father died from a bullet. Will I die from a bullet? I don't know." One thing he does know, said Stewart, is that changing direction is virtually impossible. "The block don't let you change. My community don't let you change. My friends, my peers, don't let you change. The system don't let you change. If I come back to the block, [with a] shirt and tie, a lot of dudes like, 'Yo. You's a punk man. Get out of here! What are you doing here with a shirt and tie, nine-to-five, working?'"

To escape such influences, said Stewart, he hoped to take his three children (ages five, three, and two) away from New York. Once he was off probation, they were all heading to North Carolina, where a cousin had recently opened a soul food restaurant: "I'm going to try to go back to college, but . . . I think my purpose is to raise my kids. I feel like I messed up my life already."

What I found striking about Stewart and the others I spoke with at Fortune was that they had not quite given up. They were acutely aware of the precariousness of their situation but still felt they just might be able to get their lives together.

Carl Dukes, originally of Jacksonville, Florida, was incarcerated for thirty-one years for felony murder. He was released in January 2008. When we met in the spring of 2010, he was preparing for his job search. "It don't make no difference what has happened to me in the past," he said. "I believe that I can talk my way through it."

Barry Campbell, then working at Fortune as a peer counselor, spoke poignantly of his commitment to carving out a decent life for himself:

> Every now and then somebody will come through the doors of Fortune who knew me from the street. They look at me and they're like, "Wow. If you can do that with your life after where you come from." . . . And I've run the gamut. I've been about as low as I can possibly go, from sleeping on the park bench to spending a night in the Waldorf [Hotel]. But everything that I've gone through in my little meager life has made me the man I am today. . . . And I wouldn't change a damn thing.

When he was released, said Campbell,

> I got a job working at Au Bon Pain. At the time, your uniform was an apron, a hat, and a name clip. Most people would carry their uniforms in the bag and get dressed in the store. I would purposely put mine on in the morning and walk through the neighborhood. And the reason why I did it is because it helped remind me that I was in this to win. I was going to put the work in to get what I wanted. There was going to be no instant gratification for me. And it really didn't matter what people on my block said. Some of them even pulled up to my job one day while I'm cutting the bread. And they're coming in with big pockets of money, buying sandwiches, laughing at me.

Campbell smiled:

> I still receive collect phone calls from those people who are locked up right now. I had to stay focused that I was in this working thing for the big money, for the big haul. I was going to get me a job, and I was going to work nine-to-five, regardless of what, because I knew what instant gratification would get me. They'd spread my ass cheeks [and order me to] "bend over and cough." I don't want that. So a lot of times you have to fight for the change.

The optimism expressed by Campbell and his colleagues, I knew, had at least something to do with the fact that they were in an institution—the Fortune Society—whose mission was reclaiming people whom society had already, in large measure, written off. So I was not particularly surprised to find signs of optimism in the small survey I did with thirty-six Fortune clients. I was, however, a bit surprised at its intensity. And of course, frustration came through as well.

"Law enforcement regularly targets low-income individuals. It almost felt like a setup," complained one respondent. Another wrote about applying "so many times" for jobs and never getting an answer. Yet another wrote about a prospective employer who "ripped up a job application in my face." Still, a stunning 92 percent—all but three respondents, in other words—said yes when asked, "Do you believe you have the ability and the opportunity to be a success in any field you decide to pursue?"

That hunger for hope, of course, is not peculiar to the folks at Fortune. It is an essential human trait—one that the ex-incarcerated are no doubt as likely to express as anyone else. And there may conceivably be a racial component to it. "It's become clear there's this thing called resiliency, where if it doesn't kill you it makes you stronger, and black people have that," observed Carl Bell, the psychiatrist from Chicago, as he speculated on why the black suicide rate was less than half that of whites. The Reverend Jesse Jackson told me much the same thing: "Our strength is measured by absorbing trauma without being embittered. Those who cannot survive trauma commit suicide or they use liquor and drugs to drown the sensation of pain." I have no idea if there is something in the African American experience and lifestyle that confers some protectiveness against despair, but I do know that those men at Fortune have a faith rooted in something deeper than logic.

Sean Joe, associate professor of social work and assistant professor of psychiatry at the University of Michigan, suggests that an important component of that faith may be generational. His research specialty is suicide. Although Bell is right in claiming that suicide rates among blacks have historically been much lower than among whites, for black males between fifteen and thirty-five those rates began to converge in the mid-1980s. That movement seemed to stop, at least temporarily, in the mid-1990s, but Joe nonetheless thinks the convergence may reflect a larger phenomenon.

"Young blacks cope differently than older blacks in terms of how they explain their life experiences," said Joe, in large part because their lifestyle and options are coming to more closely resemble those of whites.

> If you ask young blacks about how they explain blacks' experiences in America, they're more likely to point to individual factors. If you ask older blacks, they're more likely to point to external system factors—racism, things that young blacks will tell you they don't see as much. . . . Their dreams are truly unlimited. [They believe] that they have the ability to do anything they want, including [becoming] president of the United States. We always told them that. . . . At the same time, they have a social culture that's telling them that just their own ability will determine their future. . . . We left them bereft of an understanding that there are structural factors that might impact their lives.

Certainly, the ex-offenders I met at the Southern Center for Human Rights—an Atlanta-based organization that works on capital cases and fights for criminal justice reform—exhibited the same sense of optimism, of faith against all odds, as did the clients at Fortune.

As a teenager, Walter Rhone, now in his thirties, began stealing cars in his hometown of Bessemer, Alabama. He was soon dealing drugs. Rhone, a star football player, justified the illegal enterprise as a way of helping out his cash-strapped family, while satisfying his own need for fashionable clothes and shoes. ("I got tired of wearing my cleats. I didn't have a decent pair of shoes to wear to our engagements after the [football] games.") Even when he was shot and injured so badly that he was temporarily confined to a wheelchair, Rhone kept selling drugs: "I never gave up the dope game. I never saw another way. I never was shown another way." As a drug dealer, Rhone carried a gun and occasionally used it on people, but he ended up convicted—in 1999—for the murder of a man he claims he didn't shoot. His cousin did the crime, according to Rhone, and Rhone refused to squeal and ultimately was sentenced to life without the possibility of parole. With the help of lawyers from SCHR, he brought to light numerous irregularities by the prosecution and even by the jury, one of whose members made an unpermitted and unsupervised visit to the crime scene where the murder had taken place. In 2007 the state offered Rhone a deal for time served, and he took it. His lawyers promised to fight for his exoneration once he was out.

When we met, Rhone was living on disability payments of $674 a month, plus the occasional odd job, and focusing on being a positive influence on his three teenage children. "I know that God's got something for me," he said. "For me to be shot eighteen times—one of those in the head? I've seen guys got shot in the leg and died. I got life without parole. I stayed there nine years, I came out. I got half my leg cut off, but I'm still here. I'm still strong. I *know* He's got something for me to do."

Omar Howard's story is similar. Now in his thirties with two teenage sons, Howard also became a drug dealer as a teenager, which led him into armed robbery. The rationale, in his case, had to do with his kids: "Baby had to have diapers. Baby had to have milk. I had to have gas in the car." Eventually, he ended up in prison. During a robbery in which Howard was participating, an armed associate shot and killed someone—by accident, said Howard.

Nonetheless, in 1993 Howard got an eighteen-year term for manslaughter. "When those doors slammed behind my back, I realized [it was] serious. . . . I knew then I wanted to change my life."

Howard got his GED and found God before being released in 2007. Now he dreams of finishing his education and perhaps getting involved in a ministry working with young people: "I haven't given up hope. . . . I have to do everything necessary to make a better life for myself. I see a brighter future." But he worries about young black men coming up as he did getting caught up in the madness of the street: "I think it's very hard for a young black man to grow up in these times, because we don't have any solid role models anymore. . . . Probably one of the best things that happened to us was us getting a black president. . . . I think it has an encouraging effect. But it's an almost unreachable goal, because that's only one position."

Both Howard and Rhone are motivated, intelligent men who are clearly capable of something better than whiling away their time in prison cells. But their faith, perseverance, and optimism notwithstanding, they face a difficult road back. They remind me of dozens of young men I have met over the years who, given a different set of circumstances, could be thriving, well-respected members of society.

One such man is Walter Simon, whom I featured on my *Against the Odds* public radio program. Simon's father was a hustler in Detroit, and Simon was drawn into drug dealing himself after his parents broke up and his mother moved the family to San Francisco. Simon started selling crack when he was thirteen. He chose to ignore the one good piece of advice his father had given him: "Son, the worst thing you can have in this life is to have people fear you." By the time he was eighteen, he was a pistol-wielding tough guy feared by his rivals. One night one of them jumped out of the bushes and started shooting.

Simon recalled the incident:

> He hit me in the back a couple times—boom, boom. And my legs just gave out from under me. And I tried to get up, and I

> couldn't get up. And then a car pulled up on the side of me, and a door opened. Guy stepped out on the passenger side. And he just started unloading 'em, just boom, boom, boom, boom, boom. Just giving it to me. Then they tried to turn me over to shoot me in the face. . . . I was able to pull out one of my guns that was in my front pocket. So I hit one of 'em. And he dropped his gun. And the other one, or one of 'em, ran. And then some dude picked up his gun and jumped in the car—they smashed off. And I was laying there in the street. And all kind of people would just start coming from everywhere, trying to help me. And I'm pointing guns at 'em, so they can't really get close to me. I'm hearing like friendly voices, stuff like, "Simon, put the gun down, put the gun down, put the gun down, man, we trying to help you, we trying to help."

Simon spent six weeks in a coma and lost the use of his legs. But after his recovery he was back on the block, selling drugs from his wheelchair. Finally, he found his way to Joseph Marshall, a PhD psychologist and former schoolteacher who runs a San Francisco–based nonprofit called the Omega Boys Club. Marshall's mission is to help young people find alternatives to a life on the street. With his help, Simon embraced a different lifestyle and won admission to UCLA.

At one point during a lengthy conversation, Simon turned to me and said:

> Just because I'm sitting in this wheelchair and I'm hurt and I don't have my ability to walk anymore, I don't use that as a reason for me to sit around and say, "Oh, woe is me." Because there's a lot of people that's probably waking up right now that I caused a lot of hurt and a lot of trauma to in their lives. And so I'm appreciative of my existence. And even though I did get shot eight times, I still have the gift of life. And I have found some enlightenment in terms of why I'm here. I'm not here to sell drugs. I'm not here to shoot people. Not here to rob people. I'm here because I have something to contribute. I'm here because my life is salvageable.

It was a moving and powerful insight, and I recall thinking that it was a shame that Walter Simon didn't have it much earlier—before he got involved in the drug life, before he spent time in prison, before he started packing a gun, and before he ended up in a puddle of blood, paralyzed from the waist down.

After my meeting with Fortune's clients, I chatted with Page, who sighed and said:

> They're just so trapped. . . . They don't see an alternative. And we get a handful of minutes to try to change it around, and sometimes you can do it. . . . The amazing thing is how much people hold on to hope if they've got it. And sometimes we don't grab them hard enough. And it just makes me think, "What more can we put in the mix that increases odds?" They break my heart. They fucking break my heart.

Barry Campbell, the peer counselor, asked whether I had noticed the tattoo that one of the young men was wearing. One tattoo featured a gun held by what looked like two hands in the position of prayer. On the other arm, LIVE LIFE was spelled out in dice. Those tattoos suggested a gang affiliation, Campbell explained: "He doesn't mention it, but he was born into it. It's almost like he knows that he's doomed."

The work that organizations such as Fortune do is crucially important. If people whom society has thrown onto the trash heap have nowhere to go, there is no hope for us as a civilized nation. And yet, as Campbell implicitly was pointing out, Fortune is mounting a rescue mission—and one with an extremely high fatality rate. There is no getting around the reality of the odds faced by Fortune's people or the implications of the statistics regularly trotted out. Some 60 percent of those now in prison are black or Latino. On any given day, one of every eight black males in their twenties is locked down. Nor, in light of such statistics, is there any getting around the fact that the voices of the street—and the penitentiary—are the voices of a good deal of our future.

I thought it important to include some of those voices in this book.

Our future, of course, also encompasses others—people like Luke Anderson, the son of Yale professor Elijah Anderson, and Winston Shaw, the son of civil rights attorney Ted Shaw (whose stories are told in chapter 6), who have opted to work with young people and help them avoid the bad choices that land so many in jail. It is not surprising, given his focus on kids trying to survive on the tough streets of Chicago, that Anderson ended up working in a charter school. In recent years, it has become fashionable to put charter schools in so-called at-risk communities, neighborhoods that expose children—who are much too young to make informed choices—to drug dealing, drug money, violence, and the mystique of prison.

Charter schools, which operate independently of local school boards and are essentially free to make up their own rules, are more than just a fad. They are largely a response to the atrocious quality of so many inner-city schools. Harvard sociologist William Julius Wilson is a strong backer of such schools. They are much preferred, he told me, to the "inner-city ghetto schools [that] have become dumping grounds for inadequate teachers."

Many charter schools, he pointed out, have "dramatic, spectacular results" working with largely minority populations. In New York City, he observed, "kids in these schools outperform kids in traditional public schools. . . . And their scores on the cognitive statewide math and English tests match those in math of kids in upper-middle-class white suburbia." The successful schools have certain things in common, he added.

> They have an extended school day. They have a longer school year because they have a relatively short summer vacation, and we all know that's very, very important, because [during the] summer . . . poor kids, inner-city kids, go home and watch TV. Their parents don't have money to send them to camp. Kids from more privileged families go to enrichment programs, summer camps, and so on, so the gap between haves and have-nots widens dramatically—not so in these schools.

I took a look at the research that Wilson cited during our conversation. A 2009 report by investigators from the National Bureau of Economic Research, Stanford University, and the Wharton School of the University of Pennsylvania evaluated New York City charter school performance from 2000 through the 2007–2008 school year. The students in the charter schools that they studied were drawn from communities that are poor and largely black or Latino and where parents (typically single mothers) generally didn't have college degrees. Because there was high demand in those communities for such schools, students were admitted by random lottery—ensuring that a broad cross-section of the community enrolled, not merely the top students.

Despite arriving at the schools with severe educational deficits, the students did extremely well. They made great strides in closing the so-called achievement gap—even when compared to students in Scarsdale, one of the most affluent communities in the country. And the longer the inner-city students stayed in the charter schools, the more they improved: "On average, a student who attended a charter school for all of grades kindergarten through eight would close about 86 percent of the 'Scarsdale-Harlem achievement gap' in math and 66 percent of the achievement gap in English," concluded the researchers.

Another group of researchers looked at schools in Boston and reached essentially the same conclusion. The study, also published in 2009, looked not only at charter schools but at "pilot schools"—schools that are still under the local school system but have more flexibility than normal schools. The study found that charter school students showed marked improvement, especially in math. Middle school students had cut the black-white achievement gap in math in half. Pilot schools did not do so well. The "estimated impacts of Pilot high schools using the lotteries are not statistically significantly different from zero," said the researchers.

My sister-in-law, Diana Shulla-Cose, happens to be a cofounder of Perspectives Charter Schools in Chicago. She and her friend Kim Day were public school teachers who felt frustrated:

> We were two idealistic teachers on fire in a big school house that was sucking the life out of us. We wanted our kids to have access to the world outside of their five-block radius [and use] the city as a classroom. We wanted to provide . . . relevant and rigorous curriculum. We really wanted to enroll a diverse student body and create a place where students felt safe to be smart and where we were intentionally addressing social emotional development. . . . The social justice component driving our model and "a disciplined life" [remain] central to who we are today.

I decided to take advantage of a visit to my hometown to see what she and Day had wrought.

Chartered in 1997, Perspectives is one of the oldest charter schools in Illinois. It was originally housed in a warehouse and served 150 students. It is now a network of five schools with a combined enrollment of 1,700—projected to grow to 2,700 by the end of 2011. Three of those schools—a middle school and two high schools—are located in a South Side building that formerly housed a failing public high school called Calumet. Perspectives took it over in 2005. And that's where I met Rhonda Hopps, the CEO of Perspectives. The daughter of Jamaican immigrants who earned her MBA in finance and real estate from Stanford University, Hopps has held a number of corporate positions—portfolio manager for Allstate among them.

When the school was called Calumet, only one-third of the students who entered ultimately left with a degree. "This year we're looking at that being maybe 75 percent," said Hopps. And of those who made it to their senior year, all were expected to graduate. Virtually all were also expected to go college. The motto "college for certain" is backed by a requirement that each student apply to at least five colleges. "There is no magic bullet, it's a lot of really good, strong, consistent hard work," said Hopps.

Perspectives expects most kids to arrive with academic deficiencies, and the teachers are prepared to deal with that. But the school also tries to set "cultural and values-oriented norms for behavior in the school," said Hopps. So teachers work with a model for a disciplined life built around twenty-six principles, "things like perseverance, hard work, time management." These are principles, she added, that,

> when you look at the list, make flat-out common sense. These are attributes that you would want your child to have to be successful in life. The difference with Perspectives is that we acknowledge that those are the attributes and then we explicitly teach them. We don't leave them to chance, [or expect that] you will develop them on your own. It's going to be taught, and it's going to be reinforced throughout the curriculum. We actually have classes called "a disciplined life."

Staff members also make it a point to get to know their students. "I can't say that I know every intricate detail of every student, but there's someone on my staff that does. And I try to know as much of it as I can," said Glennese Ray, principal of one of the high schools.

Poor attendance is not tolerated. "I can remember that first year," said Ray.

> We had students who just weren't coming to school and [middle school principal] Tamara Davis and I rode out [to get] them. We'd go and knock on their door during the school day. There was one girl, we could hear Beyoncé playing outside her door, and we're knocking on the door and she comes. Her whole face drops [as if to say], "The principals of the school came for me." That child showed up in school every day after that. She even made honor roll at one point.

Later the girl told them, "I didn't think anybody cared. I was going to drop out. But you guys came and got me."

How, I asked Ray, do they compete with the street? She replied:

> A teacher that I interviewed said, "We can't be stronger than our kids. They've seen more and they know more [about] what's out

> there than we do." So we have to use that to develop them within our walls. We know that there's the street. The street cred is out there. We know you have to do what you have to do. But [we ask them to] respect what's in here. . . . Every night there's a shooting in [the] Auburn-Gresham [community]. There's a gang fight in Auburn-Gresham. And we all have gang members in our school. But we've made this into a unity zone. We don't tolerate gang representation at all. No hats to the side. No colors. No nothing.

Shawndra Pitts, a senior at Perspectives, told me her older brother was in prison. Her older sister had attended a neighborhood school, Chicago Vocational High School (CVS). Her two younger sisters had followed Shawndra to Perspectives. "When I was in eighth grade, I was headed toward CVS until this school had a lottery and I got selected," said Shawndra. "I really didn't want to go to CVS because [my] older sister . . . attended there and she dropped out." Her sister had also warned Shawndra about CVS. "She said, 'It's a lot of fights. And the teachers, they don't care.'" At that point, Shawndra was not so sure about Perspectives either. She realized that it was in the old Calumet High School building, and she had heard only awful things about Calumet. "I said, well, this is a bad school too. I had heard there were like shootouts and a whole lot of gang stuff."

Practically everyone she knew in grammar school went to CVS. Had she gone with them, said Shawndra,

> I know I would have been trying to hang out with them. A lot of them smoke. They have babies now. So I probably would have been on that same road, trying to be cool . . . 'cause, by it being a big school, you don't want to be the one that stands out. You want to try to fit in with everybody else. In my grammar school, the teachers, they actually told you, "You ain't gonna be nothing." They cursed at you. They told you [things] like, "I don't see you going nowhere." They didn't care about you. They didn't call home. [But at Perspectives] they make sure they call home so your parents can know. . . . They actually care.

At the end of her sophomore year, Shawndra went to Kenya on an archaeological dig paid for by Ernst & Young, one of Perspectives' sponsors: "I was so scared. I never thought [I would be] picked to go to Africa. And that was my first time on a plane, first time out of the country. It was great."

Charter schools, of course, are not the only institutions that can put inner-city youngsters on the road to success. I have long been a fan of the Harlem Educational Activities Fund, an after-school program founded by Daniel Rose, a New York real estate developer. I featured it on my *Against the Odds* radio documentary series.

HEAF has worked for over two decades to help young people get a decent start in life. It runs an array of after-school programs and support activities, identifying talented students from Harlem and the surrounding communities while they're still in middle school and then doing everything possible to make sure they get through a four-year college.

Danielle Moss, HEAF's president, has a bachelor's degree from Swarthmore and a doctorate from Columbia University. And she knows, from events in her own family, how easily the street can lead young folks astray:

> The day before I packed my bags and got on the bus to go to Swarthmore College, I buried my twenty-year-old cousin after a drug overdose in the Bronx. We came from the same family. The standard was the same, but he just didn't manage to overcome those neighborhood pressures. And I am here with a PhD, and I have a cousin serving, you know, a life sentence in Supermax in Maryland.

HEAF does not take on hard-core thugs. Nor does it focus on a handful of neighborhood stars. It targets those in the middle, kids who have talent and drive but are not obviously destined for success. Because HEAF tries to reach kids before they are seduced by the streets, its students' stories are not necessarily dramatic. Fausto Jimenez is typical of the type of student who ends up there. His parents moved to Harlem from the Dominican Republic when he was one year old. They were farmers looking for better opportunities. But Jimenez's earliest memories are of danger. "I remember not being able to go outside and play. I remember various times, while we were just walking down the block, having to scurry into a store or, you know, duck down because there would be cross-fire in the middle of the day," he told me.

Since Jimenez and his younger brother and sister were not allowed to play in the street, they only had "school friends," as he calls them, which was fine with him, since he liked school from the beginning. He ended up in a middle school for the gifted and talented. It was there that he encountered HEAF.

HEAF, he said, "introduced me to the world of higher education. Even though growing up the expectation was to graduate and have some sort of degree, I didn't have any direction." HEAF also helped to educate Jimenez's mother about a world of new opportunities. "I remember when I was applying to colleges," said Jimenez,

> she didn't want me to go anywhere. She was just like, you know, "City College is up the hill. You can go there and that's absolutely fine." But HEAF actually sponsored a trip for us to Pennsylvania. And we were able to visit Swarthmore and Haverford College. . . . And after that [there was] no problem with letting me go away anywhere. But I ended up deciding [on] Columbia.

In September 2010, I joined HEAF founder Daniel Rose at the organization's annual dinner at the Pierre Hotel in New York. At one point during the dinner, Rose brought over to the table a young HEAF graduate named Tanasha Bennett, who stood ramrod straight in military dress, and he suggested that we get to know each other. When I met Rose for lunch later in the week, he gave me a photocopy of a *New Yorker* article from 1997 by John Lahr headlined, "Speaking Across the Divide: What's Between Ebonics and the Mainstream? According to One Program for Harlem Teen-agers, a Better Way to Be Heard."

The article was, in part, a profile of two young HEAF participants, Tanasha and Yasmin Maya-Gutierrez. It opened with an anecdote about the two taking a subway from a speech class at the Juilliard School to their homes in Harlem:

> When they stepped off the subway and into the bright, dishevelled uptown day, they were entering not just a different community but a different community of speech. Yasmin and Tanasha are both in that sense bilingual; they know that they must simultaneously be cool and defeat cool as they maneuver through the gauntlet of street talk, which in some quarters these days goes under the name of Ebonics.

Tanasha was seventeen at the time and attending Brooklyn Tech. And she had already honed her "nobody-can-beat-me attitude," wrote Lahr, which he illustrated with the following quote from Tanasha: "Can't nobody beat me. Can't nobody do anything to me. Because somebody's always gonna try to challenge me." Lahr described HEAF as a program that took in young people who were the modern equivalent of Eliza Doolittle: "gifted students [who] have the intelligence and ambition to move beyond their community, but they may not yet possess the vocal or presentation skills that would enable them to move comfortably between worlds."

Rose was unaware that I had actually spent several hours with Tanasha a couple of years before he introduced her at the dinner. I had interviewed her for a possible profile in my *Against the Odds* radio documentary special but, for editorial reasons having nothing to do with her, had decided not to use the interview. After our chance meeting at the dinner, I reread the transcript.

Tanasha was born in 1979 in Brooklyn's Kings County Hospital to an unmarried eighteen-year-old. Eventually there were four other children, three girls and a boy (not including a stepsister and baby brother who died when Tanasha was two), all raised in Harlem and Brooklyn, where her father and grandmother lived.

Her mother, said Tanasha, had always been a hard worker. She initially worked with a program to remove lead-based paint from houses and later worked for a bank. "She took me to school with her when I was really young. . . . She's a very, very strong woman. . . . She always wanted me to do more than she did. And she just pushed."

That push propelled Tanasha into her school's gifted and talented program and into a variety of other programs assisting at-risk young people, including HEAF. "And once you got into these programs . . . you know you're going to college, there's no other option. I think before that . . . [when] nobody else in the neighborhood is going to college, it doesn't really seem like a viable option."

Money was always short, so she began working when she was fourteen to help out her mom. Her first job was with street vendors selling clothes on Harlem's 125th Street: "And my stepdad, who was living at home at the time, had a fit. 'Cause I was fourteen and a girl, you know, working on 125th Street."

At the suggestion of her HEAF advisers, Tanasha applied to Temple University in Philadelphia. "I thought Philadelphia was really far. I'd never left New York, really." She loved the school, but she was struggling financially: "I was paying for school myself. . . . And I had gotten to a point where something was going to have to give, because I wasn't making enough. [Even though I was working] forty hours, thirty hours, as much as you can work and still be a full-time student, I just wasn't making enough."

She decided to look into ROTC. "The ROTC recruiter asked me what my grades were, and my SATs were, and he was like, 'Okay, we have a scholarship for you.'"

The full reality of her decision dawned on her during her junior year: "It's not just ROTC, you know. Once you accept a scholarship, you accept [a military] obligation. . . . I struggled with that a great deal." But a mentor, a professor of military science, "sat me down and talked to me. . . . It took a lot more than talking to me to get my mind right and to get me back together. But it worked."

She was commissioned on August 31, 2001, and graduated a week later with a degree in marketing. Her first posting was in Germany: "I'd never been anywhere. You know, my first time on a plane was when the military had sent me my junior year of college. So I was going to live overseas. . . . I was looking forward to that."

When the war broke out, she went to Iraq, initially serving as her division's chemical plans officer: "That was a big thing, the chemical threat. . . . So I had a really, a really big role."

After returning to the States, she applied to a competitive Army program that would send her to law school while still on active duty. When we chatted in 2008, she was beginning her second year at Temple University Beasley School of Law and had extended her military commitment to a total of fifteen years.

I asked about her sisters. Three, she said, had children, and none had finished college. She was unsure why she had been so focused on school and they had focused elsewhere. "That's something that I discuss with my mom a lot. Like, why, you know, I went the way I did and my sister went the way she did." One of her younger sisters, she added, had gone to virtually all the same special programs she had gone to as a child, excepting HEAF. "I think that was probably . . . defining, I guess, for me. Had she gone that route, maybe . . ." Tanasha left the thought unfinished.

I asked her about other people she had grown up with. Many had not done so well.

> There's nothing different in how we grew up, or, you know, what our homes were like. . . . I don't know why some of us do what we do and others don't. . . . I think having an example of what you can do, what you can accomplish if you, if you're determined, if you're dedicated, if you're motivated. Having an example in front of you of—I think that is a profound thing. *Right?* . . . Sometimes people feel stuck. They feel like this is all they can do and this is all they are capable of. . . . I mean, this is the conversation I've attempted to have with my sister, just because it seems so crazy that we, she and I, brought up in the same house, and we've gone in completely different directions. [But] if you don't know what to do, you don't know what your options are, then you kinda get [stuck].

Along with the *New Yorker* article, Rose handed me a note mentioning that Tanasha Bennett was now *Captain* Tanasha Bennett and that she had already been vetted to become a major. Yasmin, the other young woman mentioned in the article, he added, "is today a Bryn Mawr graduate who teaches in the New York area."

A few weeks later, I e-mailed Tanasha and asked whether she had given any more thought to why she had been so successful and her sister, raised in the same household, had not. I also asked whether her younger siblings seemed bound for college.

"It is very hard to believe you can escape when everyone around you is so deeply ingrained with complacency and failure. It may seem easier to just fall in line than to dream and work at achieving that dream," she wrote back. "Unfortunately, my sister and I made very different choices and she wasn't lucky enough to have the same mentors I had."

As for her younger brother and sister:

> My two youngest siblings are somewhere in between the extremes that my sister and I present. My youngest sister (eighteen years) is enrolled in a community college. [She] initially planned to attend a four-year college to become a dentist. She seems to be straying from her initial vision. My youngest brother (sixteen years) appears to be on track to become a menace to society. He is a very bright young man, evidenced by his grades, but he repeatedly gets into trouble. I have and will continue to provide my siblings with guidance in the hope that they can follow their dreams and be successful.

She believes that her own success "was the product of the influence of mentors and my personal choice to be successful."

When I asked Dr. Moss Lee about outcomes for HEAF students, she replied:

> Thirty-five percent of black and Latino students nationally are actually graduating from college in six years or less. In HEAF, 90 percent of our kids go on to college and actually finish within

five years or less. And that exceeds rates for white students. You give them space to grow, but you also have to let them know, "I still expect something from you. And hopefully . . . you're not going to accept anything less from yourself."

It's not that students in Harlem or on Chicago's South Side lack ability or ambition; what they lack is knowledge, self-confidence, and a well-informed sense of the possible. What they need, in Lee's words, is "someone to say, 'You know, I can work with that student and help them to create the kind of future that maybe they haven't even considered.'"

The challenge is creating that atmosphere for everyone, not just for a few. Basil Paterson, the attorney and former politician, doesn't see that happening with charter schools. "I represent the largest teachers' union in the country, UFT [United Federation of Teachers] in New York," he told me. "I also represent the American Federation of Teachers nationally. I'm not optimistic. . . . If you believe in W. E. B. DuBois's concept of the talented tenth, you believe in charter schools. The population of charter schools in New York is thirty thousand kids. The population of our public schools is a million-one."

Not too long ago, said Paterson, he listened to a presentation from an expert on charter schools. "And we started asking questions. So afterwards, he comes to me and says, 'You don't like charter schools?' I said, 'Don't misunderstand. If my kids were coming up now, and I couldn't get them in a parochial school, I'd put them in a charter school.' . . . But the problem is all those left behind."

The reality of life, of course, is that someone is always left behind. But when it comes to black America, the numbers at risk—jobless, locked in prisons, trapped in no-way-out communities—are so huge that it's hard to see, absent a social revolution, how the soaring optimism sustains itself.

Chapter Nine

The End of Black Politics, Reconsidered

It was August 2006, and I was staying in the Serena Hotel, a peaceful five-star oasis in the middle of Nairobi. I had stopped by the modestly outfitted gym in the early evening to work off a bit of the jet lag from the transatlantic flight. A few others were also present. Among them, I immediately noticed the slim form of Barack Obama, the junior senator from Illinois.

Obama was not yet a declared candidate for president, so he did not have Secret Service agents protecting him. Nor did he have a large entourage. His wife, Michelle, and a few others had accompanied him. They were talking among themselves as the senator moved at a leisurely pace from one machine to another, never pausing long enough, it seemed, to get much of a workout at any particular station. After he dismounted some aerobic contraption, I greeted him with, "Hello, Senator. You seem to be having a hard time finding a machine you want to spend any time with." He smiled and replied, "I'm not very patient."

We chatted for a few minutes and resumed our respective workouts, but it was clear to me from even that brief encounter that he had a politician's gifts—a dazzling smile, effortless charm, the ability to make a listener feel at ease.

I had come to Africa to accompany Obama on a portion of

his multicountry trip. I was curious to get a glimpse of this rising political phenomenon whom people were already talking about as a prospective presidential candidate. As I followed him from one event to another, I quickly realized that he was not just a dazzling speaker but that he had the ability to connect instantly with either an individual or a crowd without revealing too much of himself. Traveling with him through Kenya was like watching a deity coming to earth. Wherever we went, people swarmed him. They stood in trees and atop cars, trucks, fences, and any other conceivable perch, eager to catch a glimpse of this exalted son of Africa who had come to visit his ancestral home.

A few days after I arrived, we met in the room of his press secretary, Robert Gibbs, for a previously scheduled one-on-one interview that ended up lasting roughly an hour and a half. It was the end of a long day during which Obama had spent a considerable amount of time in Kibera, one of the largest and worst slums in Nairobi. Pushing back against U.S. embassy types who thought it unwise to tarry in such a dangerous place, Obama had seemed to think it important to spend some real time there.

He seemed tired but fully alert as he proceeded to answer my first question: "When I made the commitment to make a long trip here, it made sense to come to the place where my father was from and to sort of reconnect and have a sense of who he was," he explained.

> Since I'm on the Senate Foreign Relations Committee, what I have tried to do is take a couple of trips a year. The first, last summer in August, was with [Senator] Dick Lugar to Russia. And that very much had to do with my long interest, dating back to the campaign, with issues of nuclear proliferation and the need to get a handle on not just loose nukes but also more broadly a lot of the weapons that remained from the cold war. In January, I traveled through Iraq and the Middle East. . . . So the question was, what would be the trip this summer. And it struck me that I've got a unique connection to Africa, that

Africa is often a neglected part of the world when it comes to U.S. foreign policy. So I thought that I might be in a position to uniquely highlight both the challenges and the opportunities of Africa.

As we talked about the speech he planned to give at the University of Nairobi, which would focus on corruption, Obama became more animated:

That's something I do feel strongly about, primarily because I think it is extraordinarily difficult to imagine how Africa is going to fully develop and meet its potential with corruption on the scale that you see on the continent. And this is an area where I do claim to have some knowledge because I have family members here who experienced it. I have uncles and cousins who explain to me we can't get a job unless we pay the head of the HR department a bribe. I have people who have tried to do business here and say that they've got to put up 15 percent or 20 percent of their profits. And in that sense I've got, I think, enough of a basis to suggest to the people of Kenya that this stuff matters.

Some of his more intriguing observations had to do with fame and his adjustment to it. Well before the famous Democratic Convention speech, he said, there was a point at which he began to get serious attention. "We just seemed to start striking a chord." But what helped to put it all in perspective was his run for Congress four years before his election to the Senate. "I got whipped by [Congressman] Bobby Rush," said Obama. It was "a dumb race," he added, one that had left him "flat broke" and with an angry wife.

After that disaster of a campaign in 2000, friends suggested that he cheer himself up by going to the Democratic National Convention in Los Angeles. He arrived at LAX international airport with maxed-out credit cards, which the rental car company initially declined. Only after he got on the phone and pleaded with them to relent did they authorize his charge. He arrived at the convention without proper credentials, so he could only circulate around the fringes. He finally came home in frustration. The trip, he had concluded, was serving "no useful purpose."

"I think about that . . . about my experiences four years later. I'm not that much smarter—maybe a little wiser, but not that much smarter. . . . This stuff is pretty fleeting, ultimately," said Obama. So he was not focused on his growing fame. His question to himself was, "Am I being useful? Am I doing good work?" He had noticed, with some satisfaction, that he had not lost his head to all the attention: "I find it less and less satisfying as time goes on. It's nice . . . nice precisely because it happened so fast and because I worked in almost total obscurity for most of my adult life. . . . I don't find that aspect of my work deeply satisfying."

I asked about the upcoming presidential election, and he replied, "The day I was elected, somebody asked me, 'Are you running in '08?' The *day* I was elected. And I said, 'No.'" Nothing had happened since then to change his mind, said Obama. But he was nonetheless very much interested in the debate around national politics and thought the time was ripe for "a pragmatic, nonideological but identifiably progressive politics."

As for his own success so far, he could not take sole credit for that. It was "a testimony to the sacrifices and struggles of previous generations," of people like John Lewis, Rosa Parks, and Martin Luther King. But as bound as he was to that generation, he was not of that generation: "A Harold Ford, Cory Booker, or myself don't feel a ceiling on us. . . . When people told me I couldn't win a Senate race in Illinois, I didn't believe them. And I didn't believe them because of the groundwork that has been laid by the previous generation."

He was not, he said, oblivious to race. Clearly race mattered. The "larger society makes snap judgments based on stereotypes." A young African American is likely to be viewed differently than a young white male. So it is not unheard of for a black man, stopped by police, to turn out to be an innocent Ivy League graduate. Such societal problems, he said, "are not going to vanish overnight." But he felt that it is important to note that "stereotypes can be overcome in a way they could not before." So one should "look at our race relations through a split screen"—by which he meant acknowledging "the reality of change" while not forgetting that race is still "a force in our society."

He was aware, he said, that people would point to him and his rise as a sign of racial progress. He was not uncomfortable with that. "I have a lot of different pieces, a lot of different people in me." And if some saw him and his success as evidence that "we can get along, I don't mind that. Maybe it's a simplification in terms of who I am, but there is something hopeful in that that is healthy."

We talked of his political heroes. Three stood above all the rest: Mahatma Gandhi, Martin Luther King, and Abraham Lincoln. But he also admired Franklin D. Roosevelt and James Madison—a "smart cat." What they all had in common was that they "didn't just practice politics. They changed how people thought about themselves and each other." Theirs was "a transformative politics. . . . They dug really deep into the culture and wrestled with it. I deeply admire that, because one of the things I think about today's politics is what is needed is not technical solutions to problems. . . . What's missing is the ability of . . . people to dig deep and step out of themselves."

I walked away deeply impressed, not just with his intellect, which I had known to be powerful, but with his style, his ease with himself, and what seemed to be his ability to calculate the impact of his words even before he said them.

Two years later, he had received the Democratic nomination and was on the verge of being elected president of the United States. That August, the *New York Times Magazine* ran an article by political correspondent Matt Bai whose headline asked, "Is Obama the End of Black Politics?"

The answer, in short, seemed to be yes—not that black politics, as such, was ever really defined. By inference, however, black politics seemed to be the politics of grievance, anger, and distrust—especially distrust of the good intentions of white folks. Bai wrote:

> For a lot of younger African-Americans, the resistance of the civil rights generation to Obama's candidacy signified the failure of

their parents to come to terms, at the dusk of their lives, with the success of their own struggle—to embrace the idea that black politics might now be disappearing into American politics in the same way that the Irish and Italian machines long ago joined the political mainstream.

His essential point was that Obama and a whole new cohort of young black politicians (Gen 3s and younger Gen 2s, though Bai, of course, did not call them that) represented something very different from the old generation. The essence of that difference (and he did not state this explicitly either) was that they were more appealing to white voters.

He told the story of Artur Davis running an uphill battle against Congressman Earl Hilliard in Alabama in 2000: "Davis lost that race, but he won in a rematch two years later. Now he's weighing a run for governor." And he quoted Davis observing that Obama's ethnicity won him points with at least certain white voters. "There's no question that some young cohort of white voters were drawn to Obama because they like the idea of a break with the past. A young, white politician from Illinois might not have gotten that support. So race probably cost Obama some votes. And it probably won him some votes. That's the complex reality we're living in." What he was sure of, said Davis, was that,

> if Obama is president, it will no longer be tenable to go to the white community and say you've been victimized. . . . I understand the poverty and the condition of black America and the 39 percent unemployment rate in some communities. I understand that. But if you go out to the country and say you've been victimized by the white community, while Barack Obama and Michelle and their kids are living in the White House, you will be shut off from having any influence.

From a parade of younger politicians the article singled out Davis, Newark mayor Cory Booker, Congressman Jesse Jackson Jr., Massachusetts governor Deval Patrick, and Philadelphia mayor

Michael Nutter. It was a standard list for articles on rising black politicians, which sometimes included Adrian Fenty, who was elected mayor of Washington, D.C., in 2007. Harold Ford of Tennessee was invariably on that list before he lost his bid in 2006 to become a senator from Tennessee.

In *The Breakthrough: Politics and Race in the Age of Obama,* Gwen Ifill profiles all of these politicians and adds several others, including Congressman Kendrick Meek, a 2010 candidate in the Florida Senate race, and Kamala Harris, the San Francisco district attorney who was poised to move up to attorney general of California.

The rise of this group of politicians, notes Ifill, has coincided with the rise of "an eager and growing audience among citizens of every race ready to embrace the notion that the end of race-based politics is near." Ifill leaves readers with an unanswered question: "Do these new leaders represent a fundamental shift in the way race politics has played out in the years since the Voting Rights Act took full root? Or are they merely the latest stage in a political evolution that has yet to fully unfold?"

Hanes Walton Jr. of the University of Michigan's Center for Political Studies argues that it is too early to say what these new leaders represent: "You can't define the era by five people, you know. We do not have enough examples to make the extrapolation that we are . . . on the verge of a new day."

And as for Obama himself, said Walton, about all we can assert for certain is that he ran a singularly brilliant campaign:

> Barack Obama has literally rewritten every single book on political parties, every book on campaign politics. . . . All of them say you can't raise enough money from small donations to win a presidential campaign. Now what are you gonna do with all those books? All those damn books need to be thrown in the goddamn [garbage]. . . . No one can take a book on primary politics and find anything in any of them about caucuses being important. There ain't shit in any of them that says, "Look, concentrate on caucuses." They say, very clearly, "Caucuses are

> too difficult to do and require too many hours and too much manpower to be bothered with. *And they don't pay off.*" . . . No one ever heard of superdelegates before Barack Obama ran for president. . . . You couldn't find a decent paragraph in any political party book on superdelegates. You may find a line, two lines, three lines at the most. . . . This boy has rewritten the book on this stuff, man.

Whether another black candidate can do something similar, said Walton, is anybody's guess.

James Jackson, professor of psychology at the University of Michigan and director of the university's Institute for Social Research, agreed that Obama's victory resulted from such an unusual confluence of factors that it's difficult to say just what it represents:

> Every single star had to be aligned: an awful Republican candidate; an incredible eight years in which . . . it became clear even to the American public that, indeed, this guy [George Bush] was an idiot and had done some really awful things; an awful economy, which is now, of course, kicking [Obama] in the butt. All those things lined up, and then an incredibly attractive, smart, accomplished man who was able to very quickly understand, when running against the establishment, one could reach out with new technology to harness [voter discontent]. It's just unbelievable all that came together. And it took all of that in order for him to be elected—and not by that great a margin.

Clearly, as events since Bai wrote his article have made clear, we can safely say that, at this junction at least, these politicians represent something far short of a fundamental shift—if only because some of the most promising fresh faces are having a difficult time fully delivering on their promise. Kendrick Meek's Florida Senate campaign never ignited; he came in a rather distant third in the general election in November 2010. Artur Davis's gubernatorial campaign never got past the Democratic primary. Thurbert Baker, attorney general of Georgia, also lost his state's Democratic primary contest for governor. Fenty, the much-touted face of the District of Columbia's future, lost his bid for reelection, a defeat widely blamed on hubris and political misjudgments. Jesse Jackson Jr. became embroiled in simultaneous and interconnected scandals, one involving money possibly promised to the former governor of Illinois if Jackson was named to Obama's vacated Senate seat and the other involving Jackson's relationship with a sometime swimsuit model.

Perhaps the most mystifying of all the meltdowns is that of Artur Davis, the Harvard-educated would-be governor of Alabama. Davis arrived at Harvard Law School in 1990—months after Barack Obama was elected president of the law review. And many, in Alabama and elsewhere, thought his political gifts rivaled those of the president himself. Charles Ogletree, his old law school professor, recalled him as "very smart, very crafty, but he seemed to be more, I would say, restrained and conservative. . . . He was an excellent debater, which is a skill that you needed in law school. And I thought that he would play some major role in politics, but he wouldn't be the predictable, traditional member of the Congressional Black Caucus. I just think he had a different vision."

I met Congressman Davis for breakfast when he visited New York in 2006, and I was impressed with his earnestness, his intelligence, and, most of all, his ambition. He made it clear that he was planning at some point to run statewide. So I was not surprised when he got into the governor's race. I expected him to do well—as did many others, including a substantial number of whites.

"A lot of people would have liked to have seen Alabama elect its first black governor, and a lot of people thought Artur could be that person," James Rotch, a prominent white attorney whose Birmingham Pledge Foundation seeks to foster interracial harmony, told me after Davis's defeat. "He just got on the wrong side, from a winning standpoint, of some of the major issues, and on the wrong side of some of the major political powers."

The forty-two-year-old congressman lost (by more than twenty points) a Democratic primary that had seemed to be his for the taking. "This is not exactly the speech I'd planned to give," he somberly admitted as he conceded to state agriculture commissioner Ron Sparks.

The *Birmingham News* spelled out just how devastating and curious Davis's loss had been. He was "the first African-American candidate in a statewide Alabama race to lose the black vote. And he lost it overwhelmingly." Davis even lost his home county, reported the *News,* with Sparks racking up 58 percent of the vote there: "Davis won only a single majority black polling place in all of Jefferson County. He even lost his own polling place—Southtown Housing Community Center—by a handful of votes to Sparks."

Davis was an early supporter of Obama's presidential campaign but opposed his health care legislation. That cost him dearly in terms of his credibility. Critics saw it as pandering to the white, conservative voters he would need to win the state. The Reverend Jesse Jackson, among others, slammed Davis, saying that he had voted against the interests of his own constituents. "That created real tension," Jackson told me.

The tension never went away. Jesse Lewis, publisher of the *Birmingham Times,* a black-oriented weekly, said most blacks in the state would have liked nothing more than to see an African American as chief executive but couldn't warm up to a candidate who didn't seem to have their interests at heart. State senator Sanders was more emphatic.

Davis's vote against health care was "a catalytic event," Sanders told me.

> The second thing was, he released a press release saying he was not going to enter the black voter [groups] to be screened, while he was still going to white groups. Artur was being perceived at that point as that he had the big head. He didn't listen to anybody. Nobody could really talk to him. And when appointments came, he insisted on being the only person to have any input in terms of appointments made by the president. . . . People began to see him as not only not trustworthy, but perhaps dangerous,

because he had changed so dramatically. And if he wasn't going to talk to us before the election, he certainly wasn't going to talk to us after the election.

What made the situation even more surreal, said Sanders, was that there was "a white candidate saying I'm glad to talk to anybody, anyplace."

Both Sanders and Davis are graduates of Harvard Law School, and neither is a child of privilege (Sanders attended on a Felix Frankfurter Scholarship targeted at "poor young men who show great promise"), but they are different generations. As Sanders pointed out, "I'm sixty-seven, he's forty-two." Sanders insisted, however, that his problems with Davis were not generational. Other blacks, he said, had run for statewide office without alienating their base: "I don't believe any of them attacked black leaders in the way Artur did. I don't think any of them said, 'I will not appear before black groups.' He was taking this to a whole other level. He could have said, 'I will work with these groups. I will reach out.' People would have given him space. They're not going to give him space to stomp on them." Sanders and many other prominent African Americans in Alabama threw their support behind Sparks.

Following the primary vote, *Birmingham News* columnist John Archibald wrote a column lamenting the result:

> The nation will read today that Alabama was not ready to nominate a black man as governor. Maybe not. But the nation will still be misled. For Artur Davis did not lose the Democratic nomination because he is black. Davis lost the nomination in spite of the fact he is black. Davis was perhaps the smartest, most able man in the race, but he forgot who he was. He lost himself so thoroughly in the campaign that he came off looking like a disingenuous opportunist.

Davis "shot himself in the foot," Archibald told me when I called to discuss his article. "Nobody thought he did the right thing. Davis's refusal to court the state's traditional black coalitions was clearly designed to establish his independence. It just backfired," said Archibald.

"I don't know if Alabama is ready to elect a black governor," he said in a follow-up e-mail.

> I know white Democrats in Alabama at the start of this campaign really looked forward to voting for a black candidate. They were eager for Alabama to break the color barrier, and let's face it—if you are a white Democrat in Alabama you have really thought about Democratic ideals.
>
> The problem came because Davis thought he was a shoo-in to win the nomination. Period. He ran his whole race as if it were a general election and he wanted to claim some conservative street cred. Alabama Democrats—blue dots in this big red state—have very little patience for that.

There were other factors at play. Davis and Sparks had different positions on many things—most notably on a rewrite of the state constitution, which Davis favored, and on the expansion of gambling in the state, which Sparks enthusiastically backed. Then there was Davis's reputation as something of an egghead. Alabama, Archibald wrote, "rarely accepts an intellectual candidate. Davis had big ideas. They just don't translate well on Bama TV."

But even had Davis been able to win the primary, he faced a daunting reality. White voters in Alabama don't have much of a history of voting for blacks. Even Obama, the master coalition builder, did not do well there. He won less than 40 percent of the vote and only 10 percent of the white vote. Davis would have had to do substantially better. So it's understandable that, with polls showing him easily winning the Democratic primary, he focused early on establishing his bona fides with white moderates and conservatives. What no one foresaw was how disgusted many blacks and liberal whites would become as he did that. He did not just alienate his base, said Wendy Smooth, assistant professor of women's studies at Ohio State University, "he mobilized them against him." His was not a "typical deracialized campaign."

Davis's loss showed that black politicians "can no longer take for granted they will receive the African American vote," observed Alabama state representative Roderick Scott. Davis also demonstrated how difficult it is to pull off an Obama-like victory in the Deep South.

In a sense, Obama had it easier. Voters elsewhere were somewhat less polarized than in the South. "Some people have thought that because of Obama's success, whatever penalty black candidates have faced [has] somehow evaporated. . . . Ironically, Obama's success may undercut the ability of blacks to do that," observed Vincent Hutchings, a political scientist at the University of Michigan. Because of Obama's success, Davis's run was a bit less historic and therefore less exciting. "After the novelty effect wears off, it's difficult to appeal to two constituencies that have diametrically opposed interests," said Hutchings.

When I interviewed the Reverend Jesse Jackson several months before the primary, he predicted that Davis would fail. In trying to "gain favor with the Alabama white majority," said Jackson, "he had to vote against the health care bill." Davis's district, he said, was home to "arguably the poorest, sickest citizens in that state. For a black congressman from the Black Belt with people who have abounding poverty and preexisting [medical] conditions" to go against the health care bill, said Jackson, was simply seen as betrayal of his base. "We cannot trade off the authenticity of our agenda," insisted Jackson.

So much went wrong with the Davis campaign that it's impossible to draw one simple lesson from it. But it clearly showed that race can even trip up a black politician who strives mightily to run a "deracialized" campaign. The so-called end of black politics, whatever that may mean, clearly does not mean the end of race in politics.

Four years earlier, Harold Ford Jr. was much more successful in appealing to an interracial constituency in the South, but he too, in the end, failed to win. The takeaway from Ford's race, however, is much more hopeful. He entered the last week of the race in a statistical dead heat with Republican Bob Corker. And he lost by only 2 percent of the votes.

Ford learned politics from his congressman father, taping his first political ad for his dad when he was four years old. By the time he ran for the Senate, he was only thirty-six but had already served five terms in the House. In his 2010 memoir, *More Davids Than Goliaths,* Ford acknowledges that he always assumed the issue of race would be central—at least in the beginning:

> It was on the minds of everyone who thought about me, the Senate, and Tennessee. Many of my earliest and fiercest supporters did not think Tennesseans would elect a black senator, and my opponents were counting on them not to. I refused to accept the premise that race would stop me from winning. My belief was that it would become almost irrelevant given Tennesseans' intense frustration with their lives and government's inaction on an agenda to make things better.

He decided that one way to defuse the issue of race was to get voters to see him for the man that he was. And the best way to get started on that, he concluded in a burst of inspiration, was to show up at a restaurant-bar called the Lil' Rebel and ask patrons for their votes. Festooned with Confederate flags, including a huge one painted on its wall, it was a bar he regularly passed on the way to the interstate. He chose it because it seemed likely to be filled with just the sort of voters he needed to win over.

Ford tells the story in his memoir. The crowded bar smelled of cheeseburgers and fries and was decorated not only with Confederate flags but with pinup girl calendars, the season's NASCAR schedule, and beer signs. When he walked in, people stared. And when he introduced himself, they said nothing at first. But then a pretty woman at the bar smiled and said, "Sweetheart, we've been waiting on you to stop by." She gave him a hug and told him that a certain customer was always talking him up and would be very disappointed to have missed his visit. Another patron added, "He talks about how smart you are, and how you should be judged on your merits and no one else's, and how good a senator you'd be. Man, he's going to be mad he's not here."

Ford was "shocked" at the warm reception and was delighted when the bartender let him hang one of his campaign stickers over the refrigerator door. The patrons also allowed him to plaster his bumper stickers on their cars.

I heard the story from Ford during the campaign—as did virtually everyone else he came into contact with during that time—because for Ford his triumphant visit to the Lil' Rebel showed how even the most die-heard southern whites could be won over by a black man with a compelling message.

Despite Ford's efforts, however, race never vanished as an issue. Indeed, during the closing weeks of the campaign, the Republican National Committee aired an ad calculated, in the eyes of many, to appeal to whites' worst racial preoccupations concerning white women and black men.

The thirty-second ad features a blond actress wearing a blissful expression and very little else. (The camera never pans low enough to reveal any clothes.) "I met Harold at the Playboy party," she squeals in a flirty, bubbly voice. The ad then features brief appearances from unidentified people who accuse Ford of taking money from porn producers, supporting payment of taxes after death, and being antigun. At the end, the blonde again appears onscreen. She winks and gestures as she says, "Harold—call me." The tagline reads, "Harold Ford. He's just not right."

In subsequent interviews, the blond actress, Johanna Goldsmith from Austin, Texas, acknowledged that she did not know Ford. She said that she had improvised the wink in imitation of Marilyn Monroe and other blond bombshells from the past.

"I think at the end of that campaign, two or three weeks out, they couldn't believe that I was within striking distance . . . and they started running radio ads that had strong racial overtones," Ford told me over lunch. As for the television ad: "Why didn't they use a black woman in the ad? They knew what they were trying to do. But I knew when I entered the race I was black and I knew that these issues would be relevant to some people and there were other factors in my race as well."

One big factor, he said, was George Bush's popularity, which never dropped below 50 percent in his state. In states where Democrats won, he said, Bush's numbers went down. But in Tennessee, he stayed at 51 or 52 percent, "which was about what my opponent got in the race." So he can't blame race alone for his defeats, "but there's no doubt my opponent knew what he was doing and . . . there was an intentional effort on their part to invoke race in an ugly and nasty way."

The ad was powerful and possibly decisive, Ford acknowledged. "It was a brilliant ad because, if I called them racist, I would've lost by fifteen points. . . . It was more disgusting than anything else, that they would stoop to that level. If the race had gone on two more days, we probably would have won, but the race didn't go on two more days, so we lost."

Anticipating the direction in which things might go, Ford had a response ad planned before the "call me" ad aired. It was built around the idea of a generational handoff.

> I wrote it a year out, with me, my current governor [Phil Bredesen], and my former governor [Ned McWherter] sitting in a bar on stools. . . . My current governor was going to say, "I need a partner in Washington to understand you've got to balance the budget and not take all our tax money to Washington and spend it the wrong way." And my former governor . . . was going to say, "I've known this boy all his life, and he's his own man. He's going to stand up for Tennessee and stand up for what we believe in." And I was going to say, "I'm Harold Ford, I approve this message." And I wanted the old governor to hit me on my knee and say, "Boy, I already told them you're all right." I wanted him to give them the permission slip. "So regardless of the stuff you're seeing, I know him." And he [McWherter] didn't want to do that. I didn't have a backup. The last two weeks [our] only backup was to get out and outwork him. And

we just worked and worked and worked. And I outperformed him in the debates, but I just couldn't overcome it.

Ford came close enough, however, that it is clear that had he gotten one or two breaks, he easily could have won. That may be cold comfort for a losing candidate, but it is a clear sign that even the South is not what it once was.

When I asked Ford's opinion of Davis's loss, he tried his best to be diplomatic:

I don't want to pile on my friend. But I ran a race like this, and I . . . didn't run from [the race issue]. . . . Each time I ran for office, I got accused of being out of touch with black voters. . . . When I tried to run for Senate . . . I got accused, by the Republicans, of being kind of an upper-crust guy or fancy. It's interesting [that] black politicians are painted [in unflattering ways] because they get a good education and come from middle-class families. . . . So I had to get out [and] remind people how I grew up. I grew up in the church. . . . This portrait they tried to create of me, it's not me. So, not to keep bringing it back to me, but that's the only experience that I know. You can't run from who you are. I'm not convinced that Artur did that. But he clearly could've done some things, as he's stated, differently than what he did. And you certainly can't take any voters for granted.

Even for a black candidate running against a white, race is not enough to ensure the support of fellow blacks, observed the Reverend Al Sharpton: "You can't run on black empowerment. . . . You have to come with something that really motivates."

The context for Sharpton's comment was not the Artur Davis campaign but the sea of trouble then swirling around New York governor David Paterson. The governor was alleged in early 2010 to have gone out of his way—and perhaps abused his authority in the process—to protect an aide who, some said, had a habit of manhandling the women with whom he was involved. In another age, black notables would have automatically rallied around Paterson. They would have dismissed the allegations as nothing more than propaganda from a racist establishment intent on bringing a powerful black man to his knees. That did not happen for several reasons, one being that even those who once considered themselves Paterson's intimates were not sure what to make of the situation. But there was also something else at play. The symbolism of having a trailblazer like Paterson in office is not quite as compelling as it once was. As political scientist Vincent Hutchings suggests, the very visible increase in the numbers of blacks and other people of color holding political power—including, most notably, Barack Obama—has alleviated some of the insecurity that minority communities have always felt in America.

At the same time, there is still a sense among blacks that there are important issues that particularly affect black communities—and a need for candidates who can speak to those issues. Sharpton believes that was why he made such a strong showing in black districts when he ran for president in 2004—even though another black candidate, Carol Moseley Braun, was in the contest.

Moseley Braun, he noted, "lived in Washington, D.C., as a senator, and I got three times her vote. I got twice her vote in South Carolina, [even though] Braun, on paper, was a better candidate. [She was] a former ambassador [to New Zealand], the first woman in the U.S. Senate, all of that. . . . Blacks still felt like they needed somebody out there representing their interests."

Moseley Braun, who did not run a campaign principally focused on blacks, also has strong memories and impressions as a result of the campaign. One of the strongest was her epiphany that an attractive black candidate could possibly go all the way.

> I was probably the least surprised person in the country when Barack got elected because out on the campaign trail . . . I was delighted to find how many people were open to my message, to listening to me, to engaging me around the issues. . . . Many people would bring their young daughters to debates and political events so they could see that a woman could run for president,

> who was also black. . . . And the fact that I was a nontraditional candidate didn't matter to them. They wanted the contents. The box wasn't as important as what was inside of it. So I was encouraged by that and encouraged for this country by that. So when Barack four years later was able to put together all the different pieces of the calculus that go into winning a presidential election, I knew already that the country was ready for it.

This rising crop of black politicians have had that same insight, of course, which is one of the reasons they keep reaching for prizes their parents would never have attempted to grab. But even though they are aware that we are in a new and different era, and clearly were inspired by Obama's triumph, they have not yet found a surefire template for putting together, at the state level, the kind of multiracial coalition that put Obama into office. That will be a matter of trial and error, and it is also likely to vary by state.

Cory Booker wonders whether black candidates will be granted the flexibility they need to be competitive. "I worry that people will hold a different standard for an African American politician than they will for a white politician," he confided. "I'm a Bill Clinton fan, so please take this as somebody that actually has a lot of respect for him and actually has benefited from his advice since I've been mayor," said Booker, who added, "Here's a guy that became president of the United States, and most certainly, as he was trying to appeal to different audiences, did a lot of shifting."

Booker swears that he will end the custom of "dynastic mayors in Newark." He will not grow old in office. He will either run for another office or do something entirely different. "But I know one thing is I don't want to compromise my views."

As a consequence of that determination, he has taken many controversial stands. He also has changed his mind in public, opening himself up to charges of flip-flopping. He started out believing in the sanctity of traditional public schools. "When I came into office in '98, I thought that anything but a traditional public school model was blasphemy. And it really took me getting data, from mostly parents for a year, to start changing my opinion on those things." He ended up supporting charter schools. And he has been told that "our views on education and other things will damage our ability to win any primary, Democratic primary, if I ever try to run for another office."

He hopes, he said, that "we have a little bit more tolerance for people that can admit that they were wrong . . . and based upon facts that their views have changed a little bit."

As the mayor talked, I listened in silence, thinking of how extraordinary the moment was: Cory Booker, one of the most talented and highly touted politicians of his generation, was sharing his struggle to be true to his own sense of self—to intellectual flexibility and public integrity—as he weighed the possible effect that might have on his political career.

What struck me as well was that Booker was not just sharing his thoughts on a possible political dilemma; he was actively searching for a new way to be a politician. And he was wondering out loud, in ways that went well beyond race, whether his generation could jettison the conventional political thinking of the past.

In discussing the impact of Obama's election, Harold Ford told me at one point, "The great thing about Obama's presidency, and there will be a lot of them, is it actually makes our black parents truth tellers." Those who told their children, "You can grow up to be president" are no longer liars: "You now have a group of white kids in America and black kids and brown kids who have only known a black president."

He was clearly bolstered by that thought, as he was by his conviction that there were no glass ceilings over his head. "I mean, everybody faces a wall because only a handful get to the very, very top. But it's all about how you approach it. And . . . I know that there are places I want to get to, but I don't believe I can't get there if I apply myself." His loss in Tennessee, he acknowledged, had turned his life around. But maybe that wasn't a bad thing. He had wanted to live in New York City. And now

> my life has taken a different turn. I got married. I have had a totally different set of professional work experiences over the last few years. I learned things I might not have had the opportunity to learn in the U.S. Senate. And I still have some runway in front of me in terms of opportunity. . . . Am I ignorant of realities? By no means. But I also believe that I can figure out how to get around some of those obstacles.

In Africa, Obama told me:

> I do think I'm part of a generation that doesn't see a ceiling above me. I feel confident that if you put me in a room with anybody, black, white, Hispanic, Republican, Democrat, give me half an hour and I will walk out with the votes of most of the folks [in the room]. In that sense, I don't feel constrained by race, geography, or background in terms of making a connection with people.

That's not arrogance. It's the voice of a new black generation—the typical voice of a Gen 3 Believer (and I put Obama in that cohort, even though technically he is a Gen 2, because his life experiences more closely resemble those of the Gen 3s) who is accustomed (and I use this phrase in the most benign sense) to having his way—most relevantly with whites, but also with people in general. The Gen 3s are accustomed to being treated with respect and dignity, to being perceived as individual human beings. That was not at all true for Gen 1s, and significantly less true for Gen 2s.

In his memoir, Ford writes of the inspiration he received from a preacher—Bishop Nathaniel Bond—in Jackson, Tennessee, who told him, "There are more Davids than Goliaths, and more answers than problems." It was those words that gave him the inspiration to walk into the Lil' Rebel convinced that he could get the votes of its patrons.

Among the strivers of Ford's generation are many would-be Davids out to conquer giants suckled on prejudice. And they are fully convinced that they can win—if not today, perhaps tomorrow. On that, we can only wait and see. For while there may or may not be more answers than problems, there are certainly more questions than answers when it comes to the future for Gen 3s. But without doubt they will continue testing the limits their parents knew they could never exceed.

In *Dreams from My Father,* Obama also tells a story of inspirational words from a preacher. The preacher in this case is the Reverend Jeffrey Wright, with whom Obama later had a famous parting of the ways. But when he wrote *Dreams,* he was still enamored with the holy man and took the theme of one of his sermons as the title for his own *The Audacity of Hope*.

In that sermon, Wright talked about having hope in the face of apparent hopelessness. He told the biblical story of the barren Hannah, who prayed to the Lord, weeping, for a son, whom she swore to commit to the service of the Lord. And the Lord gave her Samuel, the future prophet. Wright spoke also of his own days as a teenager gone astray. He watched, bewildered, as his mother and father broke into song, praising Jesus. Only later did Wright realize that they "were thanking Him in advance for all that they dared to hope for in me."

Obama records his own very emotional reaction:

> And in that single note—hope!—I heard something else; at the foot of that cross, inside the thousands of churches across the city, I imagined the stories of ordinary black people merging with the stories of David and Goliath, Moses and Pharaoh, the Christians in the lion's den, Ezekiel's field of dry bones. . . . And if a part of me continued to feel that this Sunday communion sometimes simplified our condition . . . I also felt for the first time how that spirit carried within it, nascent, incomplete, the possibility of moving beyond our narrow dreams.

The big difference in this new generation—Obama, Ford, Booker, Davis, and the others—is that they believe that though prejudice is persistent, they can personally overcome it. And they believe that for one simple reason: they have done it—enough times and in enough situations that they cling to that belief as an article of faith. It is what had Ford barging into redneck bars and Obama, as a candidate for senator, heading to the most segregated hamlets in downstate Illinois, searching for votes that history might have told them they had no prayer of getting. But they believe, because they have seen, if not yet a "fundamental shift," signs that one may be coming. And what they believe most importantly is that America—and in this sense, white America—has changed, and that there are enough people in America—and a growing number of them—who are capable of accepting blacks as human beings.

The most recent sign of that shift came not from any of the widely touted black Democratic hopefuls but from two black Republicans, Allen West of Florida and Tim Scott of South Carolina, who were elected to Congress by voters in predominantly white districts in the 2010 midterm elections. West and Scott "were the first black Republicans elected to the House since J. C. Watts retired in 2003," noted an article on the website The Root. Still, the election of two black Republicans, observed talk-show host Tavis Smiley, among others, is hardly proof of a "breakthrough." At most, it is a sign that a majority of white voters in certain districts, in certain circumstances, no longer disqualify candidates on the basis of race. But then, that is much more than could have been said of such southern strongholds as South Carolina even a few years ago.

The *New York Times,* in other words, got it backwards. The relevant question is not really about the end of black politics—which is just another way of asking whether previously parochial black politicians are finally ready to give up the politics of racial unity and racial grievance—but about the possible end of white politics, about the extent to which whites are capable of viewing politics, and politicians, through a lens that filters out consideration of race.

Chapter Ten

The Future of Civil Rights

This is not your parents' America. It is an America unlike anything we have previously seen—with a black president, a female secretary of state, and a Latina on the U.S. Supreme Court. It is an America in which a Cuban exile can become chairman and CEO of Kellogg (and then be named U.S. secretary of commerce), a black lawyer can become head of American Express, and a black politician can end up running the Republican National Committee (at least for a while). It is a land in which Denzel Washington and Jennifer Lopez are Hollywood royalty and Oprah is the benevolent queen. In this America, even die-hard conservatives condemn racism. And all but boors believe that discrimination is a mortal sin. Isn't it time for the civil rights brigade to graciously declare victory and triumphantly march off the field?

The NAACP doesn't think so—even though it is the creation of another century and of an altogether different age. It was born, in large measure, out of the riots that erupted in Springfield, Illinois, in 1908. Over two terrifying days in August, whites torched the black community and murdered at least two of its residents. They were outraged because two black prisoners suspected of raping white women had not been turned over to the angry mob.

Progressives saw the eruption of racist violence in Abraham

Lincoln's adopted home as a tragic summons to action. So on February 12, 1909—the centennial of Lincoln's birth and the year after the Springfield riot—many of the leading liberal voices of the day issued a "call for the Lincoln Emancipation Conference." That call read, in part:

> If Mr. Lincoln could revisit this country he . . . would learn that on January 1st, 1909, Georgia had rounded out a new oligarchy by disfranchising the negro after the manner of all the other Southern states. He would learn that the Supreme Court of the United States, designed to be a bulwark of American liberties, had failed to meet several opportunities to pass squarely upon this disfranchisement of millions by laws avowedly discriminatory and openly enforced in such manner that white men may vote and black men be without a vote in their government; he would discover, there, that taxation without representation is the lot of millions of wealth-producing American citizens, in whose hands rests the economic progress and welfare of an entire section of the country. He would learn that the Supreme Court . . . has laid down the principle that if an individual State chooses it may "make it a crime for white and colored persons to frequent the same market place at the same time, or appear in an assemblage of citizens convened to consider questions of a public or political nature in which all citizens, without regard to race, are equally interested."

The statement went on to condemn violence against Negroes; to argue that in "forging chains" for Negroes, white southerners were also "forging chains for themselves"; and to call upon "all the believers in democracy to join in a national conference for the discussion of present evils, the voicing of protests, and the renewal of the struggle for civil and political liberty."

Out of that call, whose sixty signatories included Jane Addams, John Dewey, and W. E. B. DuBois, sprang the NAACP.

To reflect on that history is to recall just how different this present era is from the one that created the NAACP. In that era, lynching was routine, discrimination was accepted, and rigid segregation was seen as part of God's natural order. For many years, despite the NAACP's existence, things did not change very much. Blacks continued to be subject to all manner of humiliations. White primaries were common, particularly in the South; the armed services remained segregated; and blacks, no matter how well prepared, ambitious, or talented, were expected to grin for crumbs, dance for pennies, and ride in the back of the bus. In such a blatantly bigoted and unjust America (and of course, even then most Americans did not consider themselves racist—blacks, like apes, were just an inferior breed), civil rights groups were not hard-pressed to justify their existence.

To Americans living today, those times are as remote as the days of the corset and the crinoline hoop skirt. What role does the NAACP—or any other such organization rooted in the sins of yesteryear—play in this new, more enlightened era?

For the past two decades, the NAACP has struggled to demonstrate its vitality and relevance. After the board dismissed CEO Ben Chavis for improperly using the group's funds to settle a sexual harassment suit, the wounded association barely limped through the early 1990s. In 1996, Kweisi Mfume left his job as a Maryland congressman to become president and CEO of the NAACP. He restored its dignity and nursed it back to financial health, but it remained a shadow of what it was in its glory days.

Bruce Gordon, a retired Verizon executive, was named president and CEO in June 2005; his mission was to reinvigorate the association and move it into the modern age. But the NAACP quickly wore him down. He resigned in 2007 after only nineteen months on the job and blasted its sixty-four-member board for getting in his way. Many of the members, he suggested, were more interested in micromanagement than results. "And as you probably might have picked up in some of the news stories, there is at least one board member who made the observation that I believed that my job was to make the NAACP more effective. She believed that I was wrong about that, and that instead, my job was to do what the board told me to do. I don't think that I came on board for that reason whatsoever," he confided to PBS's Tavis Smiley the day after submitting his resignation.

Benjamin Todd Jealous was named president and CEO in May 2008. He took office that September, with the strong backing of NAACP chairman Julian Bond. Jealous was not just a new face but a radical break with the past. Shortly after Jealous came aboard, Bond interviewed him for the University of Virginia's black leadership archives. Bond's first comment underscored the difference in the breadth and depth of their direct experience in the fight for racial justice. "We generally begin with a question about the *Brown* decision," observed Bond, "and you were born two decades after the *Brown* decision."

Bond was the creation of an earlier and much uglier version of America when it came to matters of race. A Gen 1 Fighter, he was fourteen in 1954 when the Supreme Court handed down *Brown v. Board of Education,* the seminal school desegregation decision that forced a reluctant South to begin to abolish its "separate but equal" school systems—a process that was met with every conceivable type of resistance. He was fifteen in 1955 when fourteen-year-old Emmett Till whistled at a white woman while visiting Leflore County, Mississippi, and for that crime was murdered and dumped in the Tallahatchie River—a seventy-five-pound cotton-gin fan draped around his lifeless neck. In 1957, when Bond entered Morehouse College, a group of black schoolchildren dubbed "the Little Rock Nine" were under assault by foul-mouthed mobs for trying to attend Central High School in Little Rock, Arkansas. Governor Orval Faubus ordered the National Guard to keep the children out, and President Dwight Eisenhower reluctantly sent the 101st Airborne to escort them in. In 1960, more than a decade before Jealous was born, Bond cofounded the Student Nonviolent Coordinating Committee.

Tall, confident, biracial, and Ivy League educated, Jealous is a former community organizer and Rhodes Scholar who sees himself as the face of America's future. And like Obama's, his is a story that could only have been written in America.

Jealous became, at age thirty-five, the youngest president in the NAACP's history. His appointment was the first step in the generational handoff completed in February 2010 when Roslyn Brock, a forty-four-year-old health care executive, replaced Julian Bond as chairman of the board. She became the youngest (and second female) chair in the association's history. The symbolism of the handoff was obvious, but Jealous underscored the point after the meeting at the New York Hilton where Brock was elected. "This historic election, at the beginning of our second century, marks a generational shift in the civil and human rights movement," said Jealous.

During a long conversation in his hotel suite following Brock's election, Jealous reflected on the place his generation occupies in this new world: "We were children of the dream. We were told Jim Crow was dead . . . and all the big victories have been won. 'Your job is just to go forth and prosper, because the rules are fair.' . . . And that worked pretty well for many of us," Jealous said as we sipped wine and nibbled on snacks from the hotel minibar.

It certainly seems to have worked well for Jealous, who, like Newark mayor and fellow Rhodes Scholar Cory Booker, has garnered the kind of glittery, high class credentials that make headhunters salivate. Jealous acknowledged as much. "You know, I've accumulated so many gold stars—prep school, Ivy League, Rhodes Scholar. I have a name that on a résumé is not recognizably black. I've never been concerned that whatever door I wanted to open, I couldn't open just as easily as the next guy."

That Jealous is now heading America's premier civil rights organization instead of shooting for a robber baron lifestyle at a Fortune 500 company has a lot to do with the example set by his parents. Both were activists. Ann Todd desegregated Western High School for Girls in her hometown of Baltimore; as a college student, she spent summers integrating lunch counters in southern Virginia. Fred Jealous, scion of an old-line New England family, took part in sit-ins with the Congress of Racial Equality. He was "the only white guy in jail with a bunch of black activists," said

Jealous. After college, both went overseas—Ann to the Philippines with the Peace Corps and Fred to Turkey with a Mennonite volunteer group.

Both went to graduate school at Antioch University during the 1960s. They met while participating in a university program teaching high school in West Baltimore. One evening, stranded by a winter storm, Fred trudged through the snow to Ann's house. Ann's astonished father "looked out the window, and there was this white boy shoveling his walk," said Ben Jealous.

The couple surreptitiously started dating. To avoid the appearance of being out together, they would arrive separately at a Baltimore theater, walk down different aisles, meet in the middle, and depart alone. Tossing racial convention and concerns aside, Fred soon proposed marriage—three times in a two-week period. The third time, Ann accepted. The ceremony took place in the District of Columbia in 1966, the year before the Supreme Court struck down so-called antimiscegenation laws, which prevented them from getting married in Ann's home state of Maryland.

Though Fred's family prided itself on its progressive activism, its broad-mindedness did not encompass him marrying a black woman. "My father was disowned," said Ben Jealous, "essentially banished from New England, where his family had been since the 1630s. . . . His mother stuck with him, his brothers stuck with him [his father was deceased], but his grandfather and his uncle disowned him. He was dead to them."

Jealous traces his sense of public responsibility to traditions on both sides of his family. His father's family fought in the American Revolution, opposed slavery, and supported women's suffrage. They had "a real sense of belonging to this country and being invested in the American experiment." On his mother's side were former slaves who had been statesmen during Reconstruction and others who had been involved in starting black colleges and banks. There was "a real sense of humility and commitment, a sense of purpose. 'Go out and get the best education you possibly can. Put it to good use.'" For Ben that meant leaving Monterey, California, where he had been raised, and heading to Columbia University in New York City. The draw was Jack Greenberg, the renowned civil rights attorney who was part of the NAACP team that had successfully argued *Brown v. Board of Education*.

Aware that Jealous was thinking of becoming a civil rights lawyer, a family friend and sitting judge told him to connect with Greenberg, who was then Columbia's undergraduate dean. Greenberg became a mentor, arranging summer work for Jealous at the NAACP Legal Defense and Educational Fund. But the relationship grew strained when Jealous got involved with students protesting Columbia's plans to turn the Audubon Ballroom into a biomedical research facility. The students wanted the building to remain a memorial to Malcolm X, who was assassinated there in 1965. They occupied Hamilton Hall in December 1992, with Jealous among them.

Following a strained and "bizarre conversation between an aspiring protégé and an old master," recalled Jealous, "Jack kicked me out of college." Though he was suspended for only a few months, Jealous stayed away for two years. He went to Mississippi, first working as an organizer for the NAACP and later for a black newspaper in Jackson. Working as a journalist convinced him that a legal career was not for him. Litigation "meant you were going to be working one case for a generation," but "in a two-year period of being a journalist in Mississippi, I saved an inmate's life, got a black farmer exonerated, and had a couple of other smaller successes. . . . That was a pace I could work with."

He returned to Columbia more "focused." Carlton Long, a black political scientist and Rhodes Scholar then at Columbia, suggested that Jealous apply for the Rhodes scholarship. The first line in his application essay was, "I come from a long line of healer-warriors." Jealous won the scholarship and, after leaving Columbia in 1995, studied criminology and comparative social research at the University of Oxford.

He returned thinking of becoming an Episcopal priest but instead took a job running the predominantly black National

Newspaper Publishers Association. NNPA newspapers had millions of readers, compared to "eighty-five folks we have at church on Sunday," a priest friend pointed out. For Jealous, who was hungry to make an impact, the observation sold him on the NNPA. Later, he went to Amnesty International (he was "eager to get back in the fight" because Attorney General John Ashcroft was "tearing apart the Constitution"), where he launched a domestic human rights program. The Rosenberg Foundation, a San Francisco–based foundation focusing on working families and minorities, found him there and offered him its presidency. He remained at the Rosenberg Foundation until he was recruited by the NAACP.

The NAACP's call came at a critical point for him psychologically. Though he had a prestigious job with a great salary, he was increasingly uneasy. After his daughter was born in 2006, "I had anxieties that I just didn't expect to have when I left California in 1990." Watching what was going on in the streets, he had seen black kids getting caught up in crime, being stereotyped as delinquents, and getting carted off to prison all out of proportion to their numbers. He worried about what the future held for his daughter, about how she would be treated in school, and "whether she would get shot just hanging out with other black kids on the weekend. And I saw an urgent need for the generation that was raising black children in this country to be leading the organization, because our fight is fundamentally about the future."

He also had ingested a growing body of research showing how difficult it is for black men, whatever the reality of their individual lives, to avoid being typecast as criminals. A 2004 analysis by researchers Harry Holzer, Steven Raphael, and Michael Stoll concluded, "[If] California employers do not check criminal backgrounds . . . they are likely to discriminate in hiring against those they suspect of being ex-offenders, namely black men." He was also aware of the study by Princeton sociologists Devah Pager and Bruce Western that concluded, "Blacks remain at the very end of the hiring queue, even in relation to (white) applicants who have just been released from prison."

For Jealous, the juxtaposition of those academic studies was damning:

> So one study says it's harder for a black man with no criminal record to find a job than a white man with a criminal record. The other study says most employers assume all black men are crooks. You put the two together and what that suggests is that the white man who says he has a criminal record is seen as the honest crook and the black man who has none because he really doesn't is seen as the lying crook.

The glaring racial disparities in and around the criminal justice system filled him with fury, but also with resolve to change things. A major part of the new mission for the NAACP—and one that it has not especially been known for embracing in the past—is fighting for reform in virtually every aspect of criminal justice. For Jealous, that means taking a closer look at policing, pushing employers to reduce discrimination against the formerly incarcerated, and fighting for those wrongly convicted. (His was one of the voices demanding that Troy Davis, a death row inmate in Georgia, be allowed to present evidence that might prove his innocence.) At the same time, he believes that the issues the NAACP has always taken on—employment, education, discrimination—require a more vigorous, street-level approach: "Our job is to make and maintain the mandate for great change in this country." That means becoming a grassroots organization that mobilizes people—and not just black people. The new NAACP, if Jealous gets his way, will be part of a progressive coalition fighting for the very heart of America. He sees a nation divided into three groups—one made up of "hard-core, dedicated bigots," a second "truly dedicated to a multiracial democracy," and a third in the middle that could "go either way." The political right, he believes, is fighting for those in the middle, and the left has to fight as well. "We have to decide that we're as hungry as the right is and go after [them]."

His NAACP will be broader in virtually every way:

> As we go into our second century, [the NAACP] is very conscious of its roots as a multiracial movement for human rights that prioritized its objectives based on the experience of black people but won victories that benefited everybody. Our first campaign was against lynching; the second most frequently lynched group were Catholics, which is to say they were almost as happy as we were when the lynching ended. History books have largely forgotten that.

Jealous sees the association rededicating itself to that broader mission as a way of returning to its roots but also, more importantly, as a way of making the NAACP relevant to the twenty-first century. And one step in making that happen will be reimagining the NAACP as not just a civil rights group but a human rights organization: "Civil rights in this country are typically negative rights: the rights to be free from censorship, discrimination." Jealous thinks that it is necessary to also fight for positive rights—"the right to a good school, to a good job, to good health care, to the opportunity to buy and own a home"—which takes him back to the need to remake the NAACP as a grassroots force. "To achieve civil rights, what you need are good lawyers and judges who are willing to hear and tell the truth. Human rights is about extending and amending the human contract. That's not a legal task; that's an organizing task."

Jealous is not alone in believing that civil rights organizations must expand their mission. In 2009 the Leadership Conference on Civil Rights became the Leadership Conference on Civil *and Human* Rights. The Washington-based coalition counts more than two hundred groups among its members, ranging from the National Council of La Raza to B'nai B'rith International. And like Jealous, the conference felt a need to embrace "positive rights."

The name change coincided with the Leadership Conference's semicentennial, a natural occasion for rethinking. It coincided as well with the ascension of Barack Obama, whose presidency represented a leap forward for minorities even as it provoked attacks on them and their rights—and of course, on Obama himself.

Wade Henderson, president of the Leadership Conference, thinks that the spike in hate crimes "triggered by the election" reflects "deep-seated racial animosity," as do many of the attacks on Obama by partisans of the political right: "The Obama as joker, the Obama as Nazi. That kind of license is not characteristic, even of people who have been antigovernment critics, when a leader has been white."

Shortly after Obama's election, the Leadership Conference came up with a set of legislative objectives for his first year. "The Lilly Ledbetter Fair Pay Act, the hate crimes bill, the state children's health insurance program, and the stimulus package with aid to inner-city communities—all four became law," said Henderson, who attributed that success largely to the goodwill of the Obama administration. "In whose administration have we ever experienced a four-for-four record of accomplishment on our top issues? *None.*"

But that sense that Obama understands and generally supports their agenda also fuels frustration with his unwillingness to directly confront issues of racial inequality. "This president is hypersensitive to the perception that he is somehow using his position in an inappropriate way to benefit the black community," observed Henderson. "But I think there is a certain expectation that any president will recognize that when there is a legitimate problem, that targeted assistance is justified."

Al Sharpton, the former boy preacher and activist who founded and heads the National Action Network, accepts Obama's restraint on race as simple political pragmatism. He recalled being introduced to Obama in July 2004 by Harvard professor Charles Ogletree during the Democratic National Convention. Both were speaking at the convention—Obama on Tuesday and Sharpton that Wednesday. As Sharpton recalled:

> Obama says, "I'm going to be much more middle-of-the-road than you . . . but I respect what you do." And so I said, "Let me

> just say this to you. You got to get elected. You do what you gotta do for that, because I'm going to take care of the brothers tomorrow night." And we started laughing. And that sort of became our relationship. We kind of understood each other had different roles.

Obama, then running for U.S. senator from Illinois, delivered a now legendary speech on the "audacity of hope" that was also a celebration of America and of his uniquely American journey. Sharpton focused more on America's unfulfilled promise—in essence, on its failings—and on the need, as he put it, to "make America beautiful for everybody."

For Sharpton, Obama's refusal to carry a civil rights flag simply reflected the differences in those roles:

> Barack Obama is not an extension in my judgment of Dr. King. He's an extension of [former Massachusetts senator] Ed Brooke and [former Virginia governor] Doug Wilder. [He represents] that train of thought in our community of people that negotiate the system and make it work for them, and [he] never pretended to be anything else—and therefore shouldn't be expected to be anything else. [Former New York] Mayor [David] Dinkins here was the same mode as Obama. So working with him even as president was no different than me, as an activist, working with Mayor Dinkins.

Older black activists, said Sharpton, never had to deal with blacks with largely white political constituencies: "There were no black mayors they had to work with, so they never had to negotiate between the two. I did."

When he was a young man, recalled Sharpton, who is now in his midfifties, he and several other ambitious young black men would regularly gather at a soul food restaurant in Harlem.

> We used to sit around Sylvia's every month . . . [dreaming] about what we wanted to be. One of them was [future New York governor] David Paterson, and we said, "He's going to be our Dave

> Dinkins." Dave [Paterson] was about six months older than me. [Future congressman] Greg Meeks was my age. He wanted to be a congressman. He was in the [state] assembly. I said, "I want to be a big civil rights guy like Jesse [Jackson], 'cause I grew up with the movement." . . . And we met about six months ago and said, "Well, we just about got where we wanted to get." That kind of meeting wouldn't have been feasible twenty years ago, when Jesse [Jackson] and them were coming along, but it was feasible in our time.

Several months before Sharpton and I sat down for our formal interview, he, Ben Jealous, and National Urban League president Marc Morial met with Obama in the White House to talk about black unemployment. The meeting came about somewhat unexpectedly. The three had been considering the convening of a press conference to criticize the nation's inaction on black unemployment when they realized that their criticisms could be construed as an attack on Obama. So they wrote the White House and asked for a meeting before issuing any statement.

To Sharpton's astonishment, senior presidential adviser Valerie Jarrett called two days after getting the letter and asked when they wanted to meet. "So then the tension becomes how you meet with him on black unemployment without making him look like he's trying to do a race-based bill," which would have been its political death, figured Sharpton.

The meeting took place on a blustery February day when Washington was shut down by a blizzard. When they stepped out of the White House and met the press, snow swirling around them, the three civil rights leaders quickly distanced themselves from a race-based approach to job creation. Yes, they said, unemployment was much higher among blacks than among whites, but they were advocating geographically focused, not racially targeted, solutions. "This is about place, not about race," said Jealous.

"We didn't meet on a race agenda," Sharpton said several weeks later.

> We met on everybody's jobs. But we were concerned about our jobs in particular. [President Obama] could live with that politically, and we could live with it politically 'cause we are now in a position to move forward a jobs bills that would help blacks. . . . That's the delicate balance. My job is to keep the issue out there and make something happen. I'm not a psychoanalyst. I'm not trying to make the president lie down on the couch and find out where his heart is. I'm trying to say, "How do we get this done? And if your framework is here, then how do we fit it in the framework? 'Cause I'm trying to make sure Harlem and the West Side of Chicago got the jobs."

Jesse Jackson doesn't see much new in the dance around race. Long before there was a black president, he said, civil rights leaders had to be careful of white sensitivities.

> There's never been a black agenda that was defined as such. Dr. King's last campaign was a poor people's campaign. He pulled together blacks and Jews and whites and Native Americans. Affirmative action was more female than [black]. The war on poverty wasn't a war for blacks on poverty. It was driven at least as much by the picture of Robert Kennedy holding the white baby in West Virginia as any other image of that period.

When I asked Jackson whether making the argument to redress inequality was harder when the nation was led by a black president, he responded, "Not if you make a speech in Appalachia. Not if you make that speech outside of a coal mine where workers are white. . . . The black agenda's never been an exclusive agenda. It's always been a redemptive agenda. . . . We've always had to couch our quest in a national interest agenda."

Jackson is fundamentally right. Whether it was abolishing slavery, integrating the armed forces, or ending Jim Crow in the South, the nation's great civil rights crusades were never just about helping blacks; they were all fundamentally about making America a better place. Still, Obama presents issues for civil rights advocates that are quite different from those presented by previous presidents. Lyndon Baines Johnson became a stalwart fighter for civil rights, but he was never suspected, as Obama has been in certain circles, of being a black racist or the product of a radical anti-American madrassa or a citizen of another country. And whereas Toni Morrison famously, and rather oddly, wrote of "murmurs" that Bill Clinton, his "white skin notwithstanding . . . is our first black president" ("blacker than any actual black person who could ever be elected in our children's lifetime"), the election of a white southerner with a "born poor, working-class, saxophone-playing, McDonald's-and-junk-food-loving boy" persona was not greeted as the passing of some colossal racial milestone.

Obama's very existence is seen as evidence by some that all racial barriers have fallen. That certainly was the not at all subtle subtext of Sarah Palin's "Obama's election means we're postracial" Facebook posting in response to the NAACP's charge of racism within the Tea Party. She invoked the memory of Ronald Reagan. ("He condemned any sort of racism, as all good and decent people do today. He also called it a 'point of pride for all Americans' that as a nation, we have successfully struggled to overcome this evil.") And she ended her message with a declaration: "It is time to end the divisive politics." Racism, in other words, was something from the distant past, utterly repugnant to the America of today—as evidenced by the election of Barack Obama. And those who complained of racism were engaging in a destructive political ploy, cynically rupturing the serenity of our new postracial society.

Obama's success not only makes allegations of racism less credible—and thereby emboldens critics to spout rhetoric that sounds a lot like old-fashioned bigotry—but it also, at least to some Americans, signifies the dawning of a new, and worrisome, racial reality.

Despite what some people herald as a new postracial America, Cesar Perales, head of Latino Justice PRLDEF, believes that society is becoming more racially charged. "Certainly if you . . . look at the Latino community, they are feeling much more victimized by what is going on. . . . More people than ever are calling to complain about discrimination. And we have seen hate crimes going up. And I think that is certainly a manifestation of an anger on the part of working-class white folks."

Lillian Rodríguez López, president of the Hispanic Federation, thinks that, in some ways, Latinos are experiencing a version of what blacks went through a few decades back.

> People bring the same values and attitudes and unfortunately the same . . . bigotry to the next generation of people who they believe threaten their way of life. In the fifties and the sixties, it was really seen as color. . . . Now it's a language issue to a certain degree as well as a color issue. . . . If you look like you're white and you don't open your mouth, you're not going to [be] subject to the same kind of discrimination.

"Some years ago someone was telling me, 'Oh, MALDEF [the Mexican American Legal Defense and Educational Fund] has become irrelevant,'" recalled Antonia Hernández, president of the California Community Foundation and former head of MALDEF. "Well, look at Arizona. It is more relevant today than ever."

Arizona, of course, enacted legislation in 2010 (challenged by the U.S. Justice Department) that required police "when practicable" to detain and arrest anyone they thought might be an illegal immigrant. Arizona legislators were also considering a bill to deny citizenship to babies born to women illegally in the United States—despite the apparent conflict with the Fourteenth Amendment's guarantee of citizenship to those born in the United States. In May 2010, shortly after the Arizona immigration law passed, the *Arizona Republic* reported the shooting of a Latino man, Juan Varela, by his white neighbor. Investigators told the newspaper that the neighbor "repeated a racial slur several times and told Varela to 'go back to Mexico' or he would die."

Murder is an insane response to any social problem. And no one would suggest that such incidents have become routine in Arizona or anywhere else in the United States—although the January

2011 shooting in Tucson that left six people dead and fourteen wounded, including Congresswoman Gabrielle Giffords, caused many to wonder whether extremist rhetoric was stoking the fires of violent insanity.

Whatever motivated the shooter behind that tragedy, it is clear that temperance has lost its appeal in many quarters. America instead has entered one of those periods when anxiety is high and extremism is rising.

"We are in the midst of one of the most significant right-wing populist rebellions in United States history," observed Chip Berlet of Political Research Associates, a nonprofit that researches the political right, in a 2010 essay published in *Religion Dispatches,* an online magazine. "Right-wing populist movements appear periodically throughout U.S. history during times when the participants feel they are being 'displaced' and losing political, social, or economic power. [Racial] anxiety and anti-immigrant xenophobia is a major text or subtext of these movements," he concluded.

Intelligence Report, a publication of the Southern Law Center, commented that, in 2009,

> hate groups stayed at record levels—almost 1,000—despite the total collapse of the second largest neo-Nazi group in America. Furious anti-immigrant vigilante groups soared by nearly 80%, adding some 136 new groups during 2009. . . . The anger seething across the American political landscape—over racial changes in the population, soaring public debt and the terrible economy, the bailouts of bankers and other elites, and an array of initiatives by the relatively liberal Obama Administration that are seen as "socialist" or even "fascist"—goes beyond the radical right. The "tea parties" and similar groups that have sprung up in recent months cannot fairly be considered extremist groups, but they are shot through with rich veins of radical ideas, conspiracy theories and racism.

What it all adds up to is an America that is psychologically and politically divided in the most bizarre way. One America is celebrating the rise of a black president and the beginning of the end of racism, while the other drowns in paranoia and racial fears. In one America, anger is mellowing even as in the other it explodes. In one America, the future seems brighter than ever, while in the other it is cloaked in gloom.

The complex and contradictory ways of viewing this present moment are both a reflection and a result of the uncertainty that has come to define our age. And for civil rights groups, as for others fighting for a better and fairer America, the way ahead is not, in all respects, clear.

In November 2006, then–NAACP chairman Julian Bond gave a lecture at Cornell University, titled "The Future of Civil Rights," in which he argued that, "in some important ways, nonwhite Americans face problems more difficult to attack now than in all the years that went before." When I asked him four years later, via e-mail, to explain what he meant, Bond noted what he called a "paradox." The very fact that so much has been accomplished—that some blacks have risen to such prominence—makes it "more difficult to argue for civil rights remedies" and "makes further progress more difficult."

The e-mail exchange with Bond was on my mind when I sat down several weeks later with Alan Jenkins, founder of the Opportunity Agenda, a New York–based nonprofit that promotes equal opportunity. Jenkins—like Ben Jealous, Corey Booker, and Barack Obama—is yet another post–civil rights wars baby. And like them, he is a product of the audacious dreams that era engendered and also of the Ivy League.

He was born in 1963 (making him a Gen 2 Dreamer) on Long Island, New York. His mother's parents immigrated from the Bahamas; his father's parents hailed from Detroit. Both parents were public school teachers (his mother eventually earned a doctorate from Columbia University), his father in Great Neck, where Jenkins attended public schools ("I was the integration"), and his mother in neighboring Manhasset. Jenkins went to Harvard for both college (class of 1985) and law school with the idea of becoming a civil rights attorney. His taste for social justice had been whetted in high school by his involvement in events connected to the Atlanta child murders as well as by a coach, "an avowed racist and eugenicist," who told students that whites were "more intelligent than blacks."

After law school, Jenkins clerked for Federal District Judge Robert Carter, who had been the lead attorney arguing the NAACP's case in *Brown v. Board of Education*. While working for Carter, Jenkins received word that he had been selected to clerk for Supreme Court Justice Harry Blackmun. He experienced "euphoria and then just terror. Like, how in the world! Am I ready for this?" At the high court, one of his projects was the *Board of Education of Oklahoma City v. Dowell* desegregation case: "I remember just the incredible sense of responsibility." After his clerkship, he headed to the NAACP Legal and Educational Fund, where one of his assignments was working on *Hopwood v. Texas*. After being rejected by the University of Texas law school, four white students had sued the university, claiming that its affirmative action program violated their civil rights; Jenkins represented the black students. From there, Jenkins went to the solicitor general's office during the Clinton administration and then to the Ford Foundation, where he rose to director of the social justice unit. In 2004, after seven years at Ford, he left to form the Opportunity Agenda. It was a chance to get back in the trenches of civil rights activism, while bringing to bear what he had learned through the years.

Over the course of a lengthy conversation, I asked Jenkins whether he felt that it was easier or harder now than in the civil rights glory days to be a civil rights advocate. Without hesitating, he replied:

> I think it's easier. . . . Judge Carter, whom I clerked for, writes when he was a civil rights attorney . . . he had to deal with hostile courts. The Klan was trying to kill him, his clients were afraid to work with him. He couldn't stay anywhere. No place. No hotels would take him. When he went to his first Supreme

Court argument as a student—it was one of the early school desegregation cases in which Charles Hamilton Houston [the now legendary black civil rights litigator] argued—Justice [James Clark] McReynolds swiveled his chair [and] turned his back to Charles Hamilton Houston. . . . So there's no question that my job is easier. . . .

We often, in hindsight, act as if there was absolute public clarity about segregation in the fifties, that there was this bright line and everyone knew what was right or wrong. But that's not the way it was. There were defenders of segregation. And there were people who thought that it was wrong [but] felt that it shouldn't be challenged or shouldn't be challenged so quickly. . . .

The story that's told now is [told the way it is] in part because the North felt that it was able to wave its finger at the South, and you don't have that same kind of dynamic now. But I feel that I have the same level of clarity in my mind about what's right and wrong and what needs to change that I suspect Judge Carter had fifty years ago, and I think I have a much greater ability to achieve it. . . .

Part of what is different from his struggle is that I do feel the importance of bringing everyone along with us. It made perfect sense in 1950 or '54 or even '63 for him to be focusing on African Americans' struggle, but in ways that had significant societal benefits. But I think we're in an era where it's important to think about how we can all move forward together.

Personally, I'm concerned about the plight of African Americans, but I'm also concerned about the plight of immigrants. I want to see women, not just my daughters but all women, be able to fully participate in our economic and political, social life. . . . The challenge I've taken on is really, "How can I be simultaneously thinking about all the people in our society?" But you know, I also think that's one of the reasons why we're likely to succeed.

Jenkins, like Jealous, is arguing, in essence, for civil rights groups to adopt a much broader agenda. And in an era when arguing narrowly for inclusion of blacks has become something of a non-starter, that is probably the only way to go. Broadening a mission, however, is not necessarily synonymous with broadening one's appeal. The challenge facing civil rights groups, both traditional ones and relatively new ones, will be convincing the public that the battle for civil rights is anything but a relic in this age when inequality seems not to provoke a great deal of outrage and old-fashioned racism grows weaker by the day.

Chapter Eleven

Prejudice, Equality, and Our Capacity for Change

Imagine if, on the verge of the American Civil War, the South had suddenly shifted course. What if instead of trying to secede from the Union, the states that formed the Confederacy had declared their faith in the promise of the United States? What if instead of rising up in anger, people of goodwill had decided that the common good required working together to make that promise a reality?

This is, of course, a fantasy. It's impossible to say what future would have unfolded in America since, in the end, fate only allows one course. It's plausible, however, that this country could have avoided the bloodiest war (in terms of U.S. casualties) in its history and come eventually to a saner, and perhaps easier, reckoning regarding slavery and race. Whatever one thinks of the human potential for folly, it's tempting to imagine that calm consideration could have led us to a better place than rage did.

I am not suggesting that these times are comparable to the period leading up to the Civil War. But I am suggesting that we are in a very interesting moment—when black rage has been largely set aside, when a people who previously had a hard time believing in their country's capacity to acknowledge their potential are rethinking assumptions held for generations. I am also suggesting that this moment may be something of a gift—a period that the nation, ideally, could devote to calm reflection as it reaffirms its belief in the notion that all are created equal and tries to figure out a way to make that motto true.

It is as impossible to predict the future as it is to change the past, so it's not entirely clear where the current turn of events will take us. I do suspect that there will be a time, however, when people of goodwill and intellect will regret that we did not seize this moment—that instead we allowed public discourse to be dominated by those angry over where America seems to be headed and determined to take it back to where they believe it used to be.

This book has never been intended to be a road map out of that conundrum. It has always had a narrower focus: to explore the breaking out of a curious brand of optimism in a most unexpected time and place. That phenomenon, I have argued, seems to stem from three things. One is a sort of generational evolution in which each successive American generation harbors fewer racial hang-ups and preconceptions than the one that preceded it. Another is a transformation of American values: the idea of racial equality—at least in the abstract—has become an almost universally shared ideal. And the third is an event singular in American history—the election of a man whose race alone would have made it impossible, in another era, for him to dream, however audacious he might be, of becoming president of the United States. That man's election, whatever one thinks of his performance on the job, has changed in some substantial way how many Americans view their country.

The more deeply I reflected on these issues, the more I saw the wisdom behind psychologist Claude Steele's casual comment: "You are formed in an era, and it gives you the lenses through which you see things. And things can change before you drop those lenses."

Repeatedly in working on this book, I have seen the basic truth of Steele's observation borne out, particularly as I have absorbed and reflected on the interviews with people of various generations—and I will be forever grateful to the more than six hundred individuals who agreed to be surveyed and/or interviewed on my behalf—and on the impact they had on certain interviewers.

I am thinking of one interviewer in particular. Paula* is a trained scholar in her sixties whom I asked to focus on older whites—Gen I Hostiles and the older Gen 2 Neutrals. As with all interviewers, I gave Paula a list of questions but told her that she should feel free to abandon the script at any point and let the conversation flow naturally. Paula, like virtually all of the interviewers of older whites, is white. Her color and her age, I assumed, would help interviewees feel comfortable enough to be candid. The problem for Paula, it turned out, was not a lack of candor but the things that candor brought out.

Among her interview subjects was Sam,* a retired biotech investor of seventy-six with a Harvard MBA. Sam's father worked for gangsters involved in the gambling and liquor trades and often took Sam with him when he was working. During that period, Sam made his first black friend, a man everyone called "Nigger Gene," an employee of his father's who was a source of endless delight. Sam recalled an evening when his father's buddies offered Gene a swig of 180 proof alcohol just to watch him spit it out. Instead, "Nigger Gene" swallowed the liquor and, to Sam's amusement, smiled and proclaimed, "You got some mighty fine liquor, Mr. G."

For the most part, said Sam, he had little contact with blacks other than "Nigger Gene" and the black cleaning lady who came to his home once a month: "She and my mom were bosom buddies." But because blacks "can't read and are functionally illiterate," with the exception of some "high-class" sorts, there generally was no reason to spend time with them.

Jews were a different matter. During his high school years, "we dated Jewish girls who were popular. They had swimming pools. Like Elaine Greenberg.* [She had a] pool and a fridge full of beer near the pool house. We made sure that she always had a date."

Certain friends of his frequented a black brothel, where they would go upstairs to have sex. The girls, he reported, "were very simple, mostly dumb," and required about five dollars for their services: "It was not slavery since the girls were happy to make easy money." A buddy of his asked one girl how many trips she made upstairs on a typical busy night. "Maybe twelve," she replied. "Isn't that hard?" he asked. Yes, she said, "that's a lot of stairs to climb." That story, like most of Sam's stories, filled him with mirth. Sam recalled a black bar, next to the brothel, where there was always laughter and music, a memory that moved Sam to remark, "My dad used to say, 'I'd like to be black, but just on Saturday night.'"

After high school, Sam joined the Navy. His service entitled him to "tuition and free khaki pants." So he enrolled in Northwestern University, where he recalled encountering some blacks, but none with whom he hung out: "We would sit in the Grill with them. But they didn't get invited to join fraternities at all." After college, Sam decided that business school made sense. So he applied to Harvard Business School and got in.

His business eventually led him to set up shop in San Francisco, whose liberal ways he found charming, but he tried to avoid Oakland. There was "too much black crime." He never hired blacks because "none applied." Plus, they didn't have "qualifications." As for the lack of blacks in his country club, "it's not a race thing; it's just that there are not many black people you would find who are interesting and who you want to be friends with."

Sam prided himself on having overcome the prejudice of his childhood: "A lot of people believed, like me when I was little, that black people are dirty and uneducated. No one told me that, but that's what I concluded." But he soon realized that what he had been told was not true—at least not true of the blacks he liked, including "Nigger Gene" and his mother's cleaning lady.

After that interview, Paula pronounced herself "unsettled." She was stunned, she said, not just by Sam's lack of self-reflection but by the discovery that others she had talked to suffered from the same malady. "I had chosen people with whom I could comfortably talk about race—not that we had ever explicitly discussed it—and who had in their lives gone a major distance." They had traveled, she said, from essentially all-white areas to places where they came into regular contact with a wide variety of people, including African Americans: "I assumed that they would have reflected a lot on that change in their lives. Apparently they had not."

She was also struck by their "lack of friends from other backgrounds. . . . They all deal with people very different from their backgrounds in their daily lives, but I don't think they count one African American as a friend. And this wasn't something they felt they had to explain or give excuses for." Instead, they had tidy explanations. For one it was about the difference in culture, for another it was that there were no African Americans in town, and for Sam it was that blacks simply weren't smart or "interesting." The interviewing experience, said Paula, had left her questioning people's capacity for change, including her own: "My question to myself through this whole experience has been, 'How much distance have *I* traveled?'"

Sherrie Nattrass, a devout Mormon and life coach, age fifty, similarly found her interviewing to be eye-opening. Of her interview subjects, Sherrie said,

> You could see that they felt a great deal of pride, of self-satisfaction, that they were warm and welcoming of all people, regardless of skin color. And I would experience what I considered an authentic sense of lack of prejudice. When I was on the topic of how black people should be treated, they articulated support for equal rights and said that the civil rights movement was a very good thing.

Sherrie's interviewees were proud that their parents had taught them to not be prejudiced.

> But when I would talk of relationships, or ask if they would ever date a black person, I would watch the body language. For the majority, there was disgust at the thought. . . . I don't know how to reconcile that. . . . When they would say, "I love black people," that seemed authentic. And yet, when it came to being intimately related or married to a black person, something changed.

She noticed that virtually everyone she interviewed cited delinquency and sometimes laziness as African American racial traits. That troubled her, as she was sure that they would not have ascribed to all whites the deficiencies of a few. And she was simply perplexed by the man who told her, "You notice when a black person comes into a room, where you don't if it's a white person."

The interviews, she said, had left her questioning whether "the programming of prejudice is so deeply imbedded that we are not able to reject the opinions handed down to us." When "the seed of the idea is planted by someone you respect and look up to, how damaging that can be as it is passed on from generation to generation," she added.

Her daughter, Sherrie confided, was dating a black man "and loves him more than she has ever loved anyone. For her generation, I don't think those deeply held core programs are holding. . . . It probably does take generations to overcome them. . . . And here I was, thinking I knew how people thought, and I realize I wasn't aware."

I found it fascinating that the assignment had caused both Paula and Sherrie to question some deeply held beliefs about their fellow Americans—and caused them to wonder, as well, about the human capacity for change.

I believe, as I suspect most people do, that the potential for change among human beings is virtually limitless. But I also believe—and my work on this book has strengthened this belief—that it takes a truly exceptional person to transcend his or her social environment and that we are shaped (and limited) by our backgrounds and by the thinking of our generation more than we know or are comfortable admitting, even to ourselves.

Nonetheless, it is clear to me, as it is to most thinking people, that Americans have traveled a huge distance when it comes to issues of discrimination and race. The paradox of our time may be that, despite that progress, equality of opportunity for all seems as elusive a goal as it has ever been.

For every Tanasha Bennett (the young Army officer from Harlem) who escapes a depressed community and becomes a success, there are a dozen left behind. It is not, I suspect, that we don't know how to provide a detour away from dead-end streets in perilous neighborhoods; it's that we so often choose not to. Nor is it that we don't know how to make life better for the millions who are buffeted by a brutal economy and barely holding on; it's that we simply have other priorities.

In September 2010, the Center for Responsible Lending issued a report derived from home mortgage disclosure statistics highlighting what it called a "national tragedy." Blacks and Latinos, reported CRL, were losing their homes to foreclosure at much higher rates than whites and also had significantly less access to credit. "Among recent borrowers, we estimate that nearly 8% of both African Americans and Latinos have lost their homes to foreclosures, compared to 4.5% of whites. . . . The disproportionate impact of abusive lending, tight lending, and foreclosures is taking its toll, as the homeownership gap between non-Hispanic white borrowers and borrowers of color has widened."

That same month, a study by the Pew Charitable Trust confirmed what the clients of the Fortune Society have figured out on their own—that a prison record can wreak havoc on one's ability to earn a living: "Incarceration reduces former inmates' earnings by 40 percent and limits their future economic mobility. . . . This is a growing challenge now that 1 in every 28 children in America has a parent behind bars, up from 1 in 125 just 25 years ago," reported Pew. And for African Americans, the numbers were downright dispiriting: "One in 87 working-aged white men is in prison or jail compared with 1 in 36 Hispanic men and 1 in 12 African American men. Today, more African American men aged 20 to 34 without a high school diploma or GED are behind bars (37 percent) than are employed (26 percent)."

A third report issued in September 2010, this one by the Kirwan Institute for the Study of Race and Ethnicity at Ohio State University, brought yet more sobering news: "Over the past year (since August 2009), Black unemployment has risen by 8.5 percent while Latino and White unemployment have fallen by 6.3 and 3.2 percent respectively."

I could cite a hundred more studies or reports, and they essentially would all make the same point—that our society is splitting apart and that those who are poor and relatively uneducated are becoming progressively worse off compared to those who are well to do and well educated, and that for blacks and Latinos who have not made it into the privileged class, life is particularly rough these days. However upbeat many blacks are right now—and the polls, as I have noted, say they are pretty upbeat—at some point, absent real change, reality is likely to force a reassessment.

"I believe that Obama is not a fulfillment of King's vision, but rather is a consequence of King's struggle, and that distinction between fulfillment and consequence looms very large," Professor Eddie Glaude observed during a long conversation one sunny afternoon in his Princeton office. The point he was making was not that different from the point that Al Sharpton had made to me a few months earlier: "Dr. King's dream was not [about] shifting some blacks at the top. It was about changing the whole social economic landscape of America, which means you have to measure from the bottom up, not the top down. . . . He was organizing a poor people's march when he died . . . because it was always about the bottom being lifted."

Howard Dodson Jr., the retired director of the New York Public Library's Schomburg Center for Research in Black Culture, made much the same point: "These issues cannot be looked at exclusively on the basis of individuals and individual achievement. . . . We have always had as part of our agenda these quests to break through these ceilings, but they were means to an end, not ends in and of themselves."

"We can have a black president at the same time we have [a] historic gap between rich and poor," pointed out Michelle Alexander, a law professor at Ohio State University and author of *The New Jim Crow: Mass Incarceration in the Age of Colorblindness*.

> We have these paradoxes that exist and yet have a black face, you know, at the helm. . . . I think it helps to illustrate the ways in which the rhetoric around colorblindness has allowed us to be comfortable with certain types of black people in positions of power. . . . In many ways, that form of black exceptionalism facilitates policies and practices that continue to punish those [who] are considered undeserving and actually helps to maintain systems of gross racial inequality. . . . [Despite Barack Obama's presidency] things may not change as much as you might expect them to because it's the structure of the system itself that guarantees persistent racial inequality.

One of the more clear-headed thinkers I know in the field of social policy is john powell, director of Ohio State University's Kirwan Institute. He believes fervently that the time is ripe for a new social vision, that the old language of opportunity and inequality, so much of which is narrowly focused on race, needs to become significantly broader. A new movement for social justice, as he sees it, would recognize the broad nature of America's unfinished business and bring various groups together in the embrace of what he calls "targeted universalism."

I asked him to explain targeted universalism. "I'll give you one example," he responded.

> Some people invited me to talk about health care. [And] I started out by saying, "How many of you know a relative, friend, family member, who doesn't have insurance?" About half the people raise their hands. "How many people do you know who have lost their insurance because they have a serious illness?" Within two questions or three questions, you get everybody. . . . And I said, "We should do something about this. This problem that affects your community, affects your family, actually affects the black and Latino community even more so." At that point, nobody walks away. So now the black and Latino community is in the conversation, but it's in the conversation in a way that they can empathize with. What we often do—and this is why

> we shouldn't start with just disparities—is that we say, "There's this huge gap between blacks and whites, and we need to fix it." Well, if I'm talking to a white audience and that's the start of my conversation, they're not in the conversation. I'm not saying I'm acknowledging your pain or your condition at all. All I'm saying is that you should be concerned about the unfairness to the black and Latino community. They're not going there.

> The Tea Party is small, he said at another point,

> but the Tea Party is reaching a much larger portion of America because they're speaking to America's anxiety. And I'm saying the liberals are not speaking to the anxiety. We come back factually. And the unconscious is not a factual process. It's much more emotional. We need to acknowledge, "Yeah, you know, there are scary things out there. The world is changing." But people can organize around their fear and their worst aspects, or they can organize around their hopes and their best aspects. And obviously we want the latter. And most of us, all of us, have the capacity to do both.

It is far beyond the scope of this book to explore the feasibility of powell's approach, which ultimately would lead not only to a new vocabulary and a new way of talking about inequality but to a renewed determination by more people to fight it. I will say only that I hope that he is right. And what better time to commit to that new and yet unfinished agenda than this present moment—when black anger has ebbed, racism has receded, and the problems facing us all are relatively clear? Otherwise, one fine day we are likely to awaken and discover that we have indeed arrived at that point where, as King prophesied, "the sons of former slaves and the sons of former slave owners will be able to sit down together at the table of brotherhood." The only problem will be that the rich blacks, Latinos, Asians, and whites will be at one table, and the poor of all races at another.

Acknowledgments

THE HELP OF MANY PEOPLE WAS CRITICAL TO THE PRODUCtion of this book. First among them are the alumni of A Better Chance and the members of the Harvard Business School African-American Alumni Association. Had they not filled out my rather lengthy survey instrument, I would have had no data to report. And had not so many consented to follow-up interviews, there would be no context for that data.

I am also very much indebted to HBSAAA president Kenneth A. Powell and to his colleagues Selena Cuffe and Jack Butler. They had enough confidence in me to embrace my project and to facilitate my work at every stage along the way. I am grateful for their help and their faith.

I am equally indebted to Sandra E. Timmons, president of A Better Chance. Sandra and Sunil Oommen, ABC's director of development, provided much more than access to their alumni network. They provided wise counsel, good cheer, and vital feedback. I am very much in their debt.

John Morton, Scott Winship, and Samantha Lasky of the Economic Policy Group of the Pew Charitable Trust did me the enormous favors of critiquing my questionnaire and sharing their ideas. Their impressive body of research provided an excellent foundation as I studied issues they have already done so much to illuminate.

Kate Black reviewed the survey, provided countless suggestions, and skillfully led the team that conducted follow-up interviews with Harvard Business School alumni. She was more than ably assisted by Stan Alcorn.

Jason C. Dean, my longtime assistant, capably led the team that interviewed ABC alumni. He was assisted by Erin Skarda and Ashlei N. Stevens.

Among those who pitched in to do supplementary interviews were Diane McWhorter, a highly decorated journalist who gave up valuable time from her own book labors to help with mine; Sue Gronewold, who brought the wide-ranging perspective of a professional historian to the task; and Sherrie Nattrass, whose insights and interviewing skills yielded some of the most revealing profiles in this book.

Alex Kopecky and Nick Earhart diligently transcribed numerous interviews.

Dawn Davis, my editor, saw the value in this book when it was nothing more than an idea. Her skilled editing and insightful feedback made it much better than it otherwise would have been.

Will Lippincott, my agent, contributed ideas, advice, and enthusiasm at every stage of this project. Without him, this book would not exist.

Peter Kougasian read behind me during the crucial final editing stage.

An array of friends and colleagues provided counsel, encouragement, and insights as I thought through the issues explored in these pages. Among them are Stephen Bright, Christina Clusiau, Kathleen Day, John Dotson, Corey Ealons, Nigel Farinha, John Irwin, Hanako Kawabata, Martin Macwan, Keith Magee, Alisa Miller, Steve Montiel, Judy Newton, Noel, John Relman, John Rogers, Danny Simmons, James Stineson, Susan Sturm, Arthur Wallenstein, Verdine White, and Alford Young.

My wife, Lee Llambelis, served—as she always has—as chief critic, sounding board, and cheerleader. She was an unswerving source of counsel and support. Finally, I thank my daughter Elisa, whose job, which she did extremely well, was to remind me that there is much more to life than writing a book—even if sometimes that meant prying me away from my all-consuming computer.

I, of course, accept full responsibility for any defects this volume may contain.

Black Harvard MBAs Share Their Rules for Success

THE UNITED STATES IS SUCH A DIFFERENT PLACE THAN IT was in the 1950s, when Ulric Haynes, then an eager, young Yale Law School graduate, set out to start his career. Few among us, I imagine, could have summoned the energy to go through one interview after another—more than seventy in all—in hopes of finding that one firm that would not slam the door in our face. And few of us, I suspect, could have accepted, without bitterness, the realization that hard work, brains, talent, credentials, and ambition counted for nothing in the eyes of prospective employers for those who happened to be members of the wrong race.

Haynes, as I have recounted (originally in *The Rage of a Privileged Class),* went on to overcome his early setbacks and to enjoy a series of distinguished careers in the diplomatic corps, in the foundation world, in business, and in academia. What he required in order to succeed was a break. His came from William Averill Harriman, then governor of New York. Success, in his case, also required that he leave the country—both to get over the ordeal of repeated rejection in his homeland and to find an environment nurturing of a talented black achiever.

These days, of course, ambitious, well-educated blacks are not likely to experience anything like Haynes's ordeal. For those deemed to have the right stuff, career opportunities are virtually unlimited. But what exactly does it mean to have the right stuff?

How, in other words, can ambitious, highly motivated people of color coming up today best ensure their success in a world that is more racially inclusive than it has even been but where, as Harold Ford Jr. pointed out, "only a handful get to the very, very top"?

There is, of course, no single or easy answer to that question. But I reasoned that whatever else Harvard MBAs may have spent their time thinking about, they have most assuredly pondered the question of success and how to achieve it. So to those who agreed to follow-up interviews after completing my survey, I put the following question: "Obviously there is no magic formula for economic success in this country, but could you sum up what you consider to be the most important factors contributing to individual success in America?" This appendix, in the form of ten concise rules, is a distillation of what they had to say.

RULE 1: *You can only go as far as your networks will take you.*

Anyone who goes to Harvard Business School automatically becomes part of a global network. That, after all, is a major reason why students are so willing to pay so much to attend. Indeed, virtually every survey respondent said, in one way or another, "Without a network, you are nothing." Or as one put it: "I was taught that all you have to do is perform and success will follow. But to get to the exclusive [top] level requires as much relationship building as performance."

"The whole process of forming relationships is the way that 80 percent of people who have their jobs got their jobs," said another. "Although we place a lot of value on education, I can tell you there's a whole world that revolves just around those relationships."

"The networks and opportunities that get presented to you right out of Harvard Business School are somewhat unique. Doors get opened to you just because of the degree," said one respondent. Others made the point, however, that building a strong network does not require an Ivy League degree. Indeed, well before many even got to college, they had realized the importance of surrounding themselves with the right people and with building relationships—in their community, in their schools, and elsewhere—with those who had their best interests at heart. "I've had so many people in my life that have opened so many doors," said one.

Building a network is not optional if you are serious about success—it's part of your job: "It takes networking to get ahead in corporate America. If you are not part of that *in* circle . . . then you will never get ahead—no matter how smart you are or hard you try." What that means, among other things, is "learning to find commonality with others, even if you don't think it's there."

Many also said that they especially valued their professional minority networks—both those related to their school and those totally separate from it. "The reality is that networks make or break your career, regardless of ethnicity. If you happen to already have connections in your place of employment, that is very helpful. If you don't and you are black, it is helpful that a network exists that you can join on day one just because you are black."

"Having successfully spent sixteen years on Wall Street," said another, "I can attribute a large part of my success to the mainly informal racial social-professional networks I have been a part of."

"The two positions I have had post-HBS have been a direct result of networking with my black HBS peers," said yet another. "I am currently pursuing a new opportunity, which again, came to me through a black HBS classmate. These minority professional networks also allow me the opportunity to 'be myself' and focus solely on meeting like-minded individuals who seem focused on advancing each other's careers."

RULE 2: *Turn customers, clients, and friends into assets.*

This rule is very much related to the first rule in that it acknowledges that relationships are just as important, in terms of building a business, as the work itself. Doing a good job is generally a prerequisite for success, but so is getting satisfied clients to spread the word. If they like what you do, let them know they should tell others.

"The biggest reason for the success of my accounting business versus my other self-employment opportunities is that I am now receiving significantly more leads and ultimately new clients based on referrals from current clients, strategic partners, and friends and relatives," confided one respondent. "No matter how talented you are, no one person can generate enough leads on his or her own to really grow the business."

Turning customers into fans "requires the ability to interact in many different areas and to interact with many types of people," said another respondent, who labeled those traits a "skill set" worth developing.

RULE 3: *Be bold—but also be competent.*

America always admires those who are willing to think big and to take on big challenges—and that is as true for people of color as for everyone else. As one corporate consultant put it, "In this country, people like decisiveness. People like a ton of self-confidence. Humility is very out of fashion. The ability to display confidence gracefully is very determinative of success."

But simply being confident is not enough, said a marketing executive, because "people will challenge you," and you'd better be good at defending and executing your ideas.

RULE 4: *Embrace self-discipline and perseverance as virtues.*

His determination not to be defeated was not only what allowed Ulric Haynes to persevere through Yale Law School but also what kept him knocking on doors, once he graduated, until he found one that would open. Those abilities—to be both disciplined and persistent—were traits that several respondents brought up. As one put it:

> You have to be able to hunker down and do what you need to do. Learn as much as you can. Take constructive feedback. . . . [Still,] things are going to happen and get in your way. Being able to work through those failures [is one] of the better experiences you will have. Most successful people I know of can talk about some pretty significant failures, and once they got through, they were that much more successful.

Along with that perseverance, said another, "you need an unrelenting focus on creating opportunity for yourself—as opposed to relying on a company or someone else to do it for you."

RULE 5: *Work, to the extent possible, in areas where results are quantifiable.*

"Where do you see the people who are black and are millionaires?" asked one corporate consultant rhetorically.

> Overwhelmingly, they work in sports and entertainment. Those are very quantifiable fields. You hit the ball or you didn't. You sold the record or you didn't. Your success is there as a number that people can track. . . . So one of the things I think helps with success is to have a quantifiable role, somewhere where the metrics are objective and observable.

RULE 6: *Take some time to figure out what you are good at.*

To successfully sell anything, including yourself, you have to able to convince people that you have something of value to offer. As one respondent put it, "Capitalism is about free choice, and you must provide a service at such a level that others are willing to both choose you and pay for it at a price that is profitable." That requires understanding not only why you think your skills or products are useful but why others should think that as well: "Time and time again, I've seen people who have the book smarts, but if you don't understand the context to be able to use that information, you aren't going to be successful." It's worth keeping in mind, however, that the ability to evaluate oneself critically "isn't necessarily something you're born with. It could be developed over time."

Others skills, of course, can also be developed. So if you don't know what you are good at, "then in the meantime get educated in something that interests you." In fact, get well educated, regardless. As one respondent put it, "Your mother's advice is true. Get as much education as you can stand because no one can take that away from you." Hard work counts, but credentials count as well—particularly for people of color. And a fancy degree can often trump prejudice.

RULE 7: *Cultivate people who are more powerful and important than yourself.*

When Basil Paterson complained that "too few of us have an uncle or a father or a mother or an aunt who can put them someplace," he was talking about the power of mentorship. And a number of my Harvard correspondents agreed. It's important, said one, to "surround yourself with great mentors, your own personal board of directors, to help guide and influence your decision-making and to provide valuable insights and perspective as well as advocacy at the right moments."

"I found older white men to be my best mentors and sponsors. I am not sure if it is genuine interest, curiosity, desire to leave a legacy, or guilt that makes them take me under their wing. Regardless of the reason, I have benefited from their interest in my career," said a female health care executive.

If you can't get any big shots to notice you, said another, or even if you can, "get a posse of people you can rely on. Peer mentors are what work for African Americans. There are no senior mentors. We have to depend on each other."

Rule 8: *Expose yourself to the wider world.*

A businesswoman living in Germany observed, "Most black people live in segregated, underserved communities where access to the American Dream is as remote for them as it is for me living here." One thing a number of respondents mentioned was the importance of exploring the world beyond the familiar—and of doing so as early in your life as possible.

"For me," said one, becoming successful "was all about exposure. Opportunities to explore new cultures, careers, and perspectives to ultimately figure out what I like and who I am."

Another put it this way: "Children should be given exposure to a better quality of life because, unless they see it, they don't know what it looks like. If we never see blacks, women, and other minorities in all walks of life, all levels of achievement, then we can't model it."

She was talking not only about exposure to the world through foreign travel but about exposure to the range of ways in which people achieve their goals. So if you are in school, by all means find some way to travel, if only by spending an academic year abroad. But what is even more important is to expose yourself to people, subjects, and professions beyond those you feel you already know.

Rule 9: *Believe!*

The one thing above all others that distinguishes Gen 3s from Gen 1s and Gen 2s is that they believe they can crash through so-called glass ceilings. They believe they can conquer the corporate structure and make it work for them.

> I don't feel, for lack of a better term, "shackled" to preconceived notions of what my success should be. For me, it's all about effort. . . . When I have conversations with [some] African Americans, sometimes they think I'm silly to believe that X can be accomplished. I remember there was a lot of [surprise] when Obama was elected, but it made sense to me.

Another, reflecting on her own experience, commented, "There is no other country in the world besides America where a little black girl from a Third World country—the daughter of a teacher and a taxi driver—could arrive and in less than a decade reach the top percentile in terms of education and income. Racial issues aside, America is a blessed, magical place."

"I don't think any black Harvard Business School MBA would admit to a glass ceiling. If that is how you see the world, you have defeated yourself," observed one correspondent.

RULE 10: ***Never talk about race (or gender) if you can avoid it, other than to declare that race (or gender) does not matter.***

This point was made by so many people—and not simply in response to my questions about success—that it simply has to be included. To engage in any serious and critical discussion of race, they cautioned, is to risk being marginalized—and therefore to risk your career. "You cannot create bonds of trust if you dare to discuss social inequalities in business or social settings with whites in the power structure. . . . So any hint of social activism must be purged from your very being in order to form the bonds that are required to build trust," said one. "Does race play a factor?" he asked rhetorically.

> Yes. Less because of the *blackness* itself [and] more because of how being black may make it more difficult to form the trusting bonds that are required for people in positions of power to take personal risk and place a bet on a "black horse." The ability

to assimilate comfortably into the power structure is a key factor for success.

I have this very clear memory of being at my five-year reunion from HBS and one of my white "friends" proclaimed that I was a real racist. Of course, we were at a bar in Boston and he was drunk when he said it. But I believe that what he said may have represented the underlying feelings that other classmates may harbor because I was so outspoken about racial inequalities. For me to have fought my way from Compton to Harvard Business School, then pretend that "anyone can do it," is not my style. But I may have paid a price for my candor. . . . One has to learn how to not be perceived as a threat. One has to learn how to hold one's tongue—true for all, but more so for us.

The southern utility executive I wrote about earlier arrived at essentially the same conclusion, as concerns both race and gender. "Speaking about these experiences isn't only not wanted or appreciated, it is [punished]," she said. One thrives by hiding such opinions, by engaging in a "masquerade."

The larger point, unsettling and unpleasant as it may be, is that honesty about one's innermost thoughts is not generally a good strategy for advancement. For to share certain views honestly—and perceptions about race seem to top the list—is to risk being seen as a divisive presence who probably doesn't belong on the team. One day that may well change. But that day, in the opinion of many of my respondents, is not on the horizon.

Index

About the Author

Ellis Cose, a longtime columnist and contributing editor for *Newsweek* magazine (1993 through 2010) and former chairman of the editorial board and editorial page editor of the New York *Daily News,* began his journalism career as a weekly columnist for the *Chicago Sun-Times.* Cose has been a contributor and press critic for *Time* magazine, president and chief executive officer of the Institute for Journalism Education, and chief writer on management and workplace issues for *USA Today.* He has appeared on *The Today Show, Nightline, Dateline,* ABC's *World News, Good Morning America,* the PBS *Time to Choose* election special, *Charlie Rose,* CNN's *Talk Back Live,* and a variety of other nationally televised and local programs. He has received fellowships or individual grants from the Ford Foundation, the Andrew Mellon Foundation, and the Rockefeller Foundation, among others, and has received numerous journalism awards, including four National Association of Black Journalists first-place awards. Cose is the author of *Bone to Pick: On Forgiveness, Reconciliation, Reparation, and Revenge, The Envy of the World,* the bestselling *The Rage of a Privileged Class,* and several other books.